Q&A
Questions & Answers

Financial Accounting- Elementary Techniques

Q&A
Questions & Answers

Financial Accounting- Elementary Techniques

Second Edition

Linda Defriez

Financial Training

First published in Great Britain by Financial Training Publications Limited, Avenue House, 131 Holland Park Avenue, London W11 4UT

© Financial Training Publications Limited, 1986
Second Edition, 1986

ISBN: 1 85185 0120

All rights reserved. No part of this book may be reproduced or transmitted in any form or by any means, electronic or mechanical, including photocopying, recording, or any information storage or retrieval system, without prior permission from the publisher.

Typeset by LKM Typesetting Ltd, Paddock Wood, Nr Tonbridge
Printed by The Garden City Press Ltd, Letchworth, Herts

Contents

Introduction		vii
Acknowledgements		viii
1	The accounting equation	1
2	Ledger accounting and trial balance	17
3	Year-end adjustments	39
4	Books of prime entry	83
5	Control accounts	92
6	Bank reconciliations	109
7	Suspense accounts, adjustments to profits and entended trial balances	118
8	Incomplete records	141
9	Receipts and payments accounts	176
10	Company accounts	204
11	Manufacturing accounts	223
12	Interpretation of accounts	243
13	Source and application of funds statements	261
14	Partnership accounts	274
15	Departmental accounts	310
16	Written questions	325
	Index	349

Introduction

This book, Financial Accounting — Elementary Techniques, includes questions and answers which will give a thorough grounding in bookkeeping and elementary accounting techniques. It is therefore intended for, and particularly suited to, candidates preparing for the following accounting examinations:

ACCA Level 1
ICAEW Graduate Conversion Course and Foundation examinations
ICMA Stage 1
AAT Preliminary and Intermediate Stages
ICSA Part 2

There are, of course, minor differences in the syllabuses, which may cause one or two of the chapters to be inappropriate for certain examination candidates. However, the vast bulk of questions in this book are thoroughly suitable for students preparing for the examinations referred to above.

The book contains 132 questions and is divided into 16 chapters, each chapter dealing with one aspect of bookkeeping or elementary accounting. Within each chapter, the simpler questions are followed by those of a complex nature, and the chapters are arranged so that the student can master the basic techniques before progressing onto the more difficult topics.

Each chapter is prefaced by an explanation of the type of question and subject area covered, and students will find that each chapter will demand knowledge from the preceding chapters, but not from subsequent chapters.

Although most of the questions are from past examinations, it has been necessary to include some, at the beginning of the earlier chapters, which have been specifically devised in order to cover the groundwork areas which are so vital to an understanding of accounting. Each question has been allocated a specific number of marks as an indication both of its relative importance for examination purposes and also of the time in which you should be capable of answering it under examination conditions. It is important that you acquire progressively more speed at tackling the questions as you work through this book. It is particularly true of bookkeeping and accounting examinations that the examiners expect a student to do a great deal of work in a relatively short time.

The answers in this book illustrate the clear approach that you should aim to develop. Points of particular difficulty are treated very thoroughly in separate workings which explain precisely how a particular figure is made up. As with all examinations, the neatness and clarity of your answer is most important, and you should aim to imitate the clear, logical approach of the answers in this book.

The second edition of this book incorporates a number of recent examination questions from the various professional bodies, so that students will gain familiarity with the type of question currently encountered in elementary financial accounting papers.

Acknowledgements

The author and publishers wish to thank the following professional bodies for their kind permission to include selected past examination questions in this publication:

The Chartered Association of Certified Accountants
The Institute of Chartered Accountants in England and Wales
The Institute of Cost and Management Accountants
The Association of Accounting Technicians

1 The accounting equation

The questions in this section illustrate the most basic but also the most important rule of book-keeping and accounts: the accounting equation, i.e., that the PROPRIETOR'S INTEREST equals the NET ASSETS of a business.

The questions are designed to ensure that students understand the accounting equation and can produce simple trading and profit and loss accounts and balance sheets. Students are not expected to be able to account for year-end adjustments, such as accruals and prepayments, but should appreciate the effect that they have on the profit and loss account and balance sheet.

QUESTIONS

1 MOORE

Moore is an ex-regular soldier who retired from the army on 1 October 19X0 and started up a car-hire firm with a gratuity of £2,500 and no other assets or liabilities.

On 30 September 19X3 he borrowed £20,000 from his brother-in-law so that he could expand his business. Just before the receipt of the money from his brother-in-law, Moore owned a fleet of cars valued at £35,000 and stocks of spares of £470. His customers owed him £1,860 and his bank balance was £2,190. Deposits received in advance from prospective hirers amounted to £250 and he owed £2,100 to various suppliers.

On 30 September 19X5 the Inland Revenue became aware of the existence of the business and required to be informed of the profits or losses from the date of Moore's discharge from the army.

At 30 September 19X5, the fleet of cars was valued at £55,000 and stocks at £2,100 while debtors stood at £5,630. There was a bank overdraft of £1,190, deposits of £350 and creditors of £6,300.

Moore has kept no books of account but estimates that his drawings from the business were £80 per week from 1 October 19X0 to 30 September 19X3 and £250 per week from 1 October 19X3 to 30 September 19X5.

You are required to:

(a) calculate the apparent profit up to 30 September 19X3;

(b) calculate the profit or loss from 1 October 19X3 to 30 September 19X5; and

(c) state whether it would have made any difference if Moore claimed to have won £10,000 at a race-track during 19X4 and used it in the business.

12 marks

2 WOODWARD

Woodward commenced business with £1,000 cash on 1 February 19X1. From his records, on 28 February 19X1, he extracted the following information: Cash balance £20; Bank balance in hand £100; Creditors £400; Debtors £50; Drawings £80; Premises £800; Equipment £300 (cost); Stock in trade £60.

He considered that depreciation of £10 should be charged on the equipment.

You are required to:

(a) calculate the net profit or loss for February 19X1;

(b) prepare a balance sheet as at 28 February 19X1; and

(c) calculate the estimated profit and prepare an estimated balance sheet at 31 March 19X1, based on the following considerations:

(i) stock in trade at 31 March 19X1 would have increased by 25%;

(ii) trade creditors would be £360;

(iii) the ratio of debtors to creditors was unchanged;

(iv) depreciation on equipment to be £10 per month;

(v) receipts and payments by cheque, £800 and £850 respectively, including £95 for drawings;

(vi) all other assets remain unchanged.

14 marks

3 ABRAHAM

Abraham started business on 1 January 19X2 with a legacy of £2,000 from his aunt. On 31 December 19X2 he tells you he has two chariots worth £600 each (cost £700), four horses worth £300 each, ploughing equipment worth £200 (cost £250), and a store of wheat valued at £500. He owes creditors £450 and is owed £870 by customers. He also has £200 hidden in his tent. (The tent had been his only asset before he received the legacy.)

You are required to prepare Abraham's accounting equation as at 31 December 19X2 on the alternative assumptions:

(a) Abraham had not drawn anything for his own use from the business.
(b) Abraham had drawn £500 for his own use during the year.

12 marks

4 ARNOLD

Arnold started trading on 1 January 19X8. For Christmas in 19X7 he had been given by his uncle £6,500 worth of stocks with which to start the business. The following is a summary of his transactions for 19X8:

	£
Cash sales	25,300
Cash received on account of credit sales	31,250
Amount due from debtors at 31 December 19X8	1,700
Cash paid to suppliers	30,900
Amount due to creditors at 31 December 19X8	3,120
Assistant's salary	2,100
Arnold's personal drawings	4,350
Cleaner's wages	416
Rent for 13 months (including Jan. 19X9)	1,300

	£
Rates for 9 months (excludes Oct, Nov & Dec. 19X8)	810
Electricity for the year	270
Telephone for 9 months (excludes Oct, Nov & Dec. 19X8)	150
Postage and packing	85
Advertising and other promotion expenses	390

At 31 December 19X8 closing stock is valued at £7,600; Arnold owed his accountant £105 for work done in the year and had promised Christmas bonuses of £50 for his assistant and £10 for the cleaner, which were not paid until January 19X9.

Produce trading and profit and loss accounts from the above information for the year ended 31 December 19X8.

12 marks

5 DAVID YORK

David York set up in business on 1 April 19X0 when he contracted to become a concessionaire for Puffin Shower Units Ltd. Under the agreement he is to receive a 30% trade discount on all shower units which he purchases, and a cash discount of 5% on payments made within one month of purchase. The manufacturer's list price for Puffin Shower Units was £150, but David York has maintained a selling price of £180 each. All sales are for cash. The manufacturers raised their list price to £160 per unit on 1 January 19X1.

David York ran the business on his own until 1 October 19X0 when he engaged Valerie Johnson as a sales person responsible for all sales. Valerie receives a salary of £420 per month, and a commission of £15 on each unit sold. This commission is payable at the end of the month following the end of the quarter in which the sales are made.

When he started the business David York possessed only a second-hand van worth £2,800 and with an expected working life of four years, and £3,880 in cash. He leased a small shop with storage facilities at the rear, and paid rent of £2,400 on 1 April 19X0 to cover the period to 30 September 19X1. David was careful to pass all receipts and payments through the bank account.

Significant information for the year ended 31 March 19X1 is:

Showers bought and sold per quarter		**Paid to Puffin**
April to June 19X0	Bought 85 Sold 65	7,500
July to September	Bought 95 Sold 100	9,450
October to December	Bought 115 Sold 125	11,550
January to March 19X1	Bought 100 Sold 85	10,080

Cash discount received from Puffin was £913.

Administrative expenses were £2,480, and selling expenses net of commission £3,560 for the year. David York drew £150 per week from the business bank account to meet his family expenses.

You are required to produce trading and profit and loss accounts for year ended 31 March 19X1 and a balance sheet as at that date for David York's business.

16 marks

6 JOHN SMITH

The following balances remained in John Smith's ledger after his trading and profit and loss account for the year ended 30 September 19X1 had been prepared:

	£
A. Abe (customer)	1,600
B. Bloggs (customer)	300
C. Cain (supplier)	500
D. Daniel (customer)	700
E. Edwards (supplier)	1,100
Freehold land and buildings, cost	40,000
Freehold land depreciation provision	10,000
Cash in hand	100
Rates prepaid	100
John Smith – Capital	50,000
Plant and machinery, cost	20,000
Plant and machinery depreciation provision	5,000
Stock at cost	10,000
Rent owing	300
Furniture and fittings, cost	8,000
Furniture and fittings depreciation provision	3,000
Bank balance	1,200
John Smith – Drawings	12,000
Net profit for year	24,100

You are required to prepare John Smith's balance sheet at 30 September 19X1 in a form suitable for presentation.

12 marks

7 A. S. UMPTION

Arthur Stanley Umption is an acquaintance who acquired a small shop on 1 January, and has asked you to act as his accountant. In the first instance he needs to know the profit he has made during the first quarter's trading. From the cheque stubs, bank statement and other vouchers available you discover the following information:

1 January – The lease, fixtures and fittings of the shop were bought for £5,000 leaving a balance in Mr Umption's bank account of £3,000 at the end of that day. Rent on the shop is payable quarterly in arrears, on the quarter day at a rate of £1,000 per annum. Mr Umption introduced stocks into the business, which he had bought on credit for £2,000 during December; he also put his old van at the disposal of the business. When questioned as to the value of the van he says he thinks it was worth £200 on 1 January.

During the Period – Cash sales total £9,000, and sales on credit terms £11,000. Goods have been purchased for cash in the sum of £4,000 and on trade credit for £11,000. A shop assistant has been paid £20 per week out of the till.

31 March — A stock take showed the closing stock at cost as £1,000. According to a file of unpaid bills, £6,000 was owed to suppliers, as well as an electricity bill for £500 dated 28 February.

The bank statement shows a credit balance of £4,000, and Mr Umption informs you that, according to his tally, customers owe him £6,000.

There are no expenses other than those arising from the transactions above.

You are required to:

(a) prepare a trading and profit and loss account for the business for the quarter ending 31 March, and a balance sheet as at that date; *12 marks*

(b) state briefly three assumptions you have made in the computation of the profit figure. *6 marks*

18 marks

ANSWERS

1 MOORE

(a) Profit to 30 September 19X3

Net assets at 30 September 19X3

	£	£
Cars		35,000
Spares		470
Debtors		1,860
Bank balance		2,190
Deposits in advance	250	
Creditors	2,110	
		(2,306)
		37,160

Increase in net assets to 30 September 19X3
= £37,160 − £2,500 = £34,660

Drawings = £80 × 3 × 52 = £12,480
Profit = Increase in net assets + drawings
= £34,660 + £12,480 = £47,140

(b) Profit from 1 October 19X3 to 30 September 19X5

Net assets at 30 September 19X5

	£	£
Cars		55,000
Stocks		2,100
Debtors		5,630
Overdraft	1,190	
Deposits	350	
Creditors	6,300	
Loan	20,000	
		(27,840)
		34,890

Decrease in net assets = £34,890 − £37,160
= (£2,270)
Drawings = £250 × 2 × 52 = £26,000
Profit = Decrease in net assets + Drawings
= (£2,270) + £26,000
= £23,730

(c) Profit if £10,000 capital has been introduced

Profit for last two years = Decrease in net assets + Drawings − Capital introduced
= (£2,270) + £26,000 − £10,000
= £13,730

Profit for the first 3 years (1 October 19X0 – 30 September 19X3) is unchanged.

2 WOODWARD

(a) **Profit or loss for February 19X1**

Net assets at 1 February 19X1 = £1,000
Net assets at 28 February 19X1

	£
Cash	20
Bank	100
Creditors	(400)
Debtors	50
Premises	800
Equipment	290
Stock	60
	920

Decrease in net assets = 920 – 1,000
= (£80)
Profit = Decrease in net assets + Drawings
= (£80) + £80
= NIL

(b) **Balance sheet at 28 February 19X1**

	Cost £	Depreciation £	£
Fixed assets			
Premises	800	–	800
Equipment	300	10	290
	1,100	10	1,090
Current assets			
Stock		60	
Debtors		50	
Bank balance		100	
Cash in hand		20	
		230	
Current liabilities			
Creditors		400	
			(170)
			920
Proprietor's interest			
Capital at 1 February 19X1			1,000
Profit for the month			–
			1,000
Less: Drawings			80
			920

(c) **Estimated profit and balance sheet at 31 March 19X1**

Net assets at 31 March 19X1

	£	£
Stock		75
Creditors		(360)
Debtors (1/8th creditors)		45
Equipment		280
Premises		800
Cash in hand		20
Bank – at 28 Feb	100	
receipts	800	
	900	
payments	(850)	
		50
Net assets		910

Decrease in net assets = 910 – 920
= (£10)
Profit = Decrease in net assets + Drawings
= (£10) + £95
= £85

Balance sheet at 31 March 19X1

	Cost	Depreciation	
	£	£	£
Fixed assets			
Premises	800	–	800
Equipment	300	20	280
	1,100	20	1,080
Current assets			
Stock		75	
Debtors		45	
Bank balance		50	
Cash		20	
		190	
Current liabilities			
Creditors		360	
			(170)
			910
Proprietor's interest			
Balance at 28 February 19X1			920
Profit for the month			85
			1,005
Less: Drawings			(95)
			910

3 ABRAHAM

Net assets at 31 December 19X2

	(a) £	(b) £
Assets		
2 Chariots	1,200	1,200
4 Horses	1,200	1,200
Ploughing equipment	200	200
Wheat store	500	500
Debtors (owed by customers)	870	870
Cash in tent	200	200
	4,170	4,170
Less: Liabilities		
Creditors	450	450
Net assets	3,720	3,720
Amount due to Abraham	3,720	3,720

The amount due to Abraham is known as the proprietor's interest and can be analysed as follows:

	(a) £	(b) £
Proprietor's Interest		
Capital at 1 January 19X2	2,000	2,000
Profit for the year	1,720	2,220
	3,720	4,220
Less: Drawings	–	500
	3,720	3,720

Clearly if Abraham had taken £500 for his own use during the year in (b), he must have made £500 more profit to be left with the same net assets at the end of the year.

4 ARNOLD

Trading and profit and loss accounts for the year ended 31 December 19X8

	£	£
Sales		58,250
Opening stock	6,500	
Purchases	34,020	
	40,520	
Closing stock	7,600	
Cost of goods sold		32,920
Carried forward		25,330

	£	£
Brought forward		25,330
Less: Expenses		
Assistant's salary	2,150	
Cleaner's wages	426	
Rent	1,200	
Rates	1,080	
Electricity	270	
Telephone	200	
Postage and packing	85	
Advertising and promotion	390	
Accountancy	105	
		5,906
Net profit for year		19,424

Tutorial note: The profit and loss account is charged with those expenses which relate to 19X8. Hence rent is $^{12}/_{13} \times £1,300$. Rates are $^{12}/_{9} \times £810$ and the telephone charge is $^{12}/_{9} \times £150$. It is assumed that these expenses accrue at the same rate over the last three months of the year as for the first nine months.

5 DAVID YORK

Trading and profit and loss account for the year ended 31 March 19X1

	£	£
Sales (W2)		67,500
Cost of sales		
Purchases (W1)	42,175	
Closing stock (W1)	2,240	
		39,935
Gross profit		27,565
Miscellaneous income – Cash discount		913
		28,478
Expenses: Rent (W3)	1,600	
Salary (W7)	2,520	
Commission (W8)	3,150	
Administrative costs	2,480	
Selling costs	3,560	
Depreciation of van (W5)	700	
		14,010
Net profit		14,468

Balance sheet at 31 March 19X1

	Cost £	Depreciation £	£
Fixed assets: van	2,800	700	2,100
Current assets: Stock (W1)		2,240	
Prepayment (W3)		800	
Bank (W10)		12,165	
		15,205	
Less: Current liabilities			
Creditors (W9)	2,682		
Commission (W8)	1,275		
		3,957	
			11,248
			13,348
Opening capital (W4)			6,680
Net profit		14,468	
Less: Drawings		7,800	
			6,668
			13,348

Workings

1. Cost of sales £
   Showers bought April to Dec. 1980   295 × (70% × £150)   30,975
   Showers bought Jan to March 1981   100 × (70% × £160)   11,200

   Total =   395   42,175
   Showers sold   375
   Closing stock (FIFO)   20 × (70% × £160)   2,240

   Cost of sales   39,935

2. Sales revenue   375 × £180   67,500

3. Rent prepaid   £2,400 × $\frac{1}{3}$ 800

4. Opening capital   £2,800 van +
                       £3,880 cash   6,680

5. Depreciation   £2,800 ÷ 4   700

6. Drawings   £150 × 52 weeks   7,800

			£
7.	Salary Valerie Johnson	6 × £420	2,520
8.	Commission Valerie Johnson	£15 × 210	3,150
	Commission paid Valerie Johnson	£15 × 125	1,875
	Commission as creditor Valerie Johnson	£15 × 85	1,275

9. Owed to Puffin
   Showers purchased   42,175
   Cash paid   38,580

                                                                     3,595
   Less: Cash discount received   913

                                                                     2,682

10. Bank account: Opening balance   £   3,880
                   Receipts   67,500

                                                                    71,380
                   Payments:
                   Puffin   38,580
                   Salary (£420 × 6)   2,520
                   Commission   1,875
                   Administrative expenses   2,480
                   Selling expenses   3,560
                   Drawings   7,800
                   Rent   2,400
                                                      ------   59,215

                   Closing balance   12,165

6 JOHN SMITH

Balance sheet at 30 September 19X1

Fixed assets	Cost	Aggregate depreciation	
	£	£	£
Freehold land and buildings	40,000	10,000	30,000
Plant and machinery	20,000	5,000	15,000
Furniture and fittings	8,000	3,000	5,000
	68,000	18,000	50,000

	£	£	£
Current assets			
Stock at cost		10,000	
Debtors		2,600	
Prepayments		100	
Bank		1,200	
Cash		100	
		14,000	
Less: Current liabilities			
Creditors	1,600		
Accruals	300		
		1,900	12,100
			62,100
Proprietor's interest:			
Capital, 1 October 1980			50,000
Add: Net profit for year		24,100	
Less: Drawings		12,000	
			12,100
			62,100

Workings

		£
1.	Debtors	
	A. Abe	1,600
	B. Bloggs	300
	D. Daniel	700
		2,600
2.	Creditors	
	C. Cain	500
	E. Edwards	1,100
		1,600

7 A. S. UMPTION

(a)　　**Trading and profit and loss account for the quarter ended 31 March**

	£	£
Sales		20,000
Less: Cost of goods sold		
Opening stock	2,000	
Purchases	15,000	
	17,000	
Less: Closing stock	1,000	
		16,000
Gross profit, carried forward		4,000

	£	£
Gross profit, brought forward		4,000
Less: Expenses		
Rent	250	
Electricity (W1)	750	
Wages	260	
		1,260
Net profit		2,740

Balance sheet at 31 March

	£	£	£
Fixed assets			
Lease and fittings			5,000
Van			200
			5,200
Current assets			
Stock		1,000	
Debtors		6,000	
Cash		4,000	
		11,000	
Current liabilities			
Creditors	6,000		
Accrual	750	6,750	
			4,250
			9,450
Capital at 1 January			8,200
Net profit for the quarter			2,740
			10,940
Less: Drawings			1,490
			9,450

(b) Three assumptions made in the computation of the profit figure could cover the following matters:

    (i)   that there is no need to provide for any bad or doubtful debts;
    (ii)   that no depreciation is charged;
    (iii) that electricity is accrued at a constant rate;
    (iv) that the cash deficit is drawings;
    (v)   that the business is a going concern.

Workings

			£
1.	Electricity		
	Bill for January and February		200
	Estimated accrual for March		100
			300

2. Capital
   Fixtures and fittings — 5,000
   Bank account — 3,000
   Van — 200
   8,200

3. Drawings
   This is the balancing figure.

2 Ledger accounting and trial balance

The questions in this section involve the recording of day-to-day transactions in the ledger accounts and the preparation of a trial balance. As in the first section, students should be able to prepare a trading and profit and loss account and balance sheet, including such adjustments as accruals and prepayments, but are not expected to record these in the ledger accounts.

QUESTIONS

1 SMILEY

Smiley started up a small business on 1 August 19X2. During the month of August, the following transactions took place:

- 1 August   Introduced £3,000 of his own cash as capital and borrowed £2,000 from Guillam. The funds were all put into a business bank account.
- 1 August   Signed a three-year lease for office premises with an annual rental of £1,200. Paid five months rent to the end of 19X2.
- 2 August   Employed an assistant, Fawn, at an agreed salary of £100 per month to be paid at the end of each month.
- 3 August   Bought goods for cash of £550 from Mendel.
- 4 August   Bought goods on credit from Esterhase and Haydon for £420 and £600 respectively.
- 8 August   Bought office equipment for £250 cash.
- 10 August Made cash sales to Westerby of £1,200.
- 12 August Made sales on credit to Lacon for £850.
- 15 August Bought a car from Enderby for an agreed price of £4,000. Paid him £1,000 as a deposit.
- 18 August Made drawings for personal expenses of £400.
- 20 August Made cash sales to Prideaux for £200.
- 22 August Paid Fawn his salary for the month of August.
- 22 August Received £450 on account from Lacon.
- 23 August Paid £450 to Esterhase and £450 to Haydon.
- 26 August Paid motor expenses of £75.
- 31 August Paid sundry expenses of £120.

You are required to:

(a) show by means of T accounts how the above transactions would be recorded in the books of Smiley; and

(b) balance off the accounts and extract a trial balance as at 31 August 19X2.

20 marks

2 ANGUS

Angus started up a business as a butcher on 1 September 19X2. The following is a summary of the transactions which Angus entered into during September 19X2:

(a) Borrowed £5,000 from his father and paid the money into a business bank account.

(b) Made cash purchases totalling £3,000.

(c) Made cash sales totalling £4,000.

(d) Bought a delivery bicycle for £70 cash.

(e) Paid rent for one month £120.

(f) Made credit purchases totalling £2,000 and by the end of the month had paid all but £500 of this amount.

(g) Made credit sales totalling £3,800 and at the end of the month debtors still owed him £1,700 of this amount.

(h) Received a legacy of £1,000 and paid this into the business bank account.

(i) Paid for electricity for one month £90.

(j) Drew £120 for his personal expenses.

You are required to prepare:

(a) a trial balane as at 30 June 19X4;

(b) balance the accounts and prepare a trial balance at the end of September;

(c) close off the accounts to the trading and profit and loss account and then to the capital account, where necessary.

Ignore closing stock, depreciation and accruals.

16 marks

3 MACLEAN

The following balances are included in the books of Maclean at 31 December 19X2:

	£
Capital on 1 January 19X2	15,743
Freehold factory at cost	120,000
Motor vehicles at cost	42,000
Provision for depreciation on motor vehicles at 1 January 19X2	19,350
Stocks at 1 January 19X2	12,500
Debtors	5,200
Provision for doubtful debts at 1 January 19X2	290
Cash in hand	75
Bank overdraft	27,462
Creditors	26,300
Sales	106,000
Purchases	55,000
Rent and rates	11,800
Discounts allowed	2,200
Insurance	950
Sales returns	3,500
Purchases returns	2,100
Loan from bank	80,000
Sundry expenses	15,320
Drawings	8,700

You are required to prepare a trial balance as at 31 December 19X2.

8 marks

4 CAMPBELL

The following balances are included in the books of Campbell at 30 June 19X4:

	£
Sales	15,620
Purchases	10,400
Stock at 1 July 19X3	4,140
Motor vehicles	16,400
Provision for depreciation at 1 July 19X3	7,900
Debtors	12,300
Creditors	15,600
Cash at bank	3,215
Motor expenses	620
Rent and rates	1,160
Insurance	185
Electricity	120
Postage and telephone	250
Drawings	4,100
Sundry expenses	270
Capital at 1 July 19X3	?

You are required to prepare:

(a) a trial balance as at 30 June 19X4;
(b) a trading and profit and loss account for the year then ended;
(c) a balance sheet as at 30 June 19X4, based on the following considerations:

   (i) Stocks at 30 June 19X4 were £7,350.

   (ii) Depreciation of £1,200 is to be charged.

   (iii) Expenses accrued at 30 June 19X4 were electricity £45, telephone £65 and sundry expenses £24.

   (iv) Expenses prepaid at 30 June 19X4 were rent and rates £240, insurance £40.

20 marks

5 ADAM

Adam commenced trading on 1 January 19X6. Below is a list of balances extracted at 30 June 19X6:

	£
Capital introduced 1 January 19X6	1,000
Cash at bank	300
Purchases	3,225
Sales	7,500
Drawings	3,000
6 months rent and rates	200

	£
Casual wages	1,100
Electricity	150
Professional fees	105
Tools and equipment	300
Office furniture and fittings	160
Debtors	130
Creditors	170

You are required to produce:

(a) a trial balance as at 30 June 19X6;

(b) a trading and profit and loss account for the six months ended 30 June 19X6; and

(c) a balance sheet as at 30 June 19X6.

Ignore accruals, prepayments, stock and depreciation.

12 marks

6 ARTHUR LEGGE

Arthur Legge commenced business as a retail butcher on 1 January 19X9. All expenses were paid by cheque and any cash received was banked daily. The following is a summary of the transactions which took place during the first year of trading:

(a) Cash sales amounted to £15,000.

(b) Credit sales totalled £8,000, and of this £1,500 was outstanding at the end of the year.

(c) On 1 January 19X9 Arthur paid £4,000 into the business bank account.

(d) A delivery van was purchased on 1 January 19X9 at a cost of £3,900. It was agreed that this should not be depreciated.

(e) During the period suppliers had been paid £7,200 for meat and invoices totalling £600 remained unpaid at 31 December 19X9.

(f) Sundry expenses (all paid during the period and relating to it) amounted to £2,200, and during the year Arthur drew £2,000 from the business.

(g) The annual rent of the shop was £1,200 and Arthur paid this amount on 1 March 19X9.

(h) Arthur paid his assistant £1,900 during the year.

You are required to:

(a) write up the ledger accounts and cash book of Arthur to 31 December 19X9;

(b) extract a trial balance as at 31 December 19X9; and

(c) assuming Arthur had closing stock of £850, prepare a trading and profit and loss account for the year ended 31 December 19X9 and a balance sheet as at that date.

22 marks

7 WHITE CARS LTD

The draft final accounts for the year ended 30 Deptember 19X0 of White Cars Ltd, a trading company, show a gross profit of £36,000 and a net profit of £15,160.

Since preparing these accounts, White Cars Ltd has received the following statement for September 19X0 from Excel Supplies Ltd, a major supplier:

Excel Supplies Limited
Statement of Account – September 19X0
Customer's Name – White Cars Limited

19X0		Dr. £	Cr. £
1 Sept.	Balance b/fwd.	2,700	
12 Sept.	Cheque received		2,400
22 Sept.	Goods supplied	4,000	
24 Sept.	Goods supplied	870	
29 Sept.	Goods returned		210
30 Sept.	Goods supplied	610	
30 Sept.	Balance c/fwd.		5,570
		£8,180	£8,180

According to the accounting records of White Cars Ltd, £14,700 was owing to Excel Supplies Ltd on 1 September 19X0.

Subsequent investigations by the accountant of White Cars Ltd reveal the following:

(a) Goods received, on a sale or return basis, from Excel Supplies Ltd in August 19X0 at a 'pro forma' invoice cost of £12,000, have been regarded as 'purchases' in the books of White Cars Ltd.

Furthermore, a quantity of these goods returned to Excel Supplies Ltd on 17 September 19X0 have been regarded by White Cars Ltd in their accounting records as a credit sale at a selling price of £520, being 'cost' plus 30%.

White Cars Ltd did not sell any of the goods received in August 19X0 on a sale or return basis until November 19X0.

(b) Materials costing £3,000 for shelving in the sales office of White Cars Ltd were bought from Excel Supplies Ltd in July 19X0. Although not included in the stock in trade at 30 September 19X0 the only accounting record in the books of White Cars Ltd for this shelving material concerns its acquisition which was debited in the purchases account and credited in the account of Excel Supplies Ltd.

(c) White Cars Ltd has been debited inadvertently by Excel Supplies Ltd for goods costing £870 supplied to Whitehorse Ships Ltd on 24 September 19X0.
Note: White Cars Ltd has no connections with Whitehorse Ships Ltd.

(d) Goods costing £610 sent by Excel Supplies Ltd on 30 September 19X0 to White Cars Ltd were not received by the latter until 3 October 19X0.

(e) Goods costing £240 returned by White Cars Ltd on 26 September 19X0 were not received by Excel Supplies Ltd until 7 October 19X0.

(f) A payment of £2,400 to Excel Supplies Ltd on 10 September 19X0 for a car engine tuning machine was debited to 'car expenses' in the books of White Cars Ltd.
Note: In August 19X0, when the car engine tuning machine was delivered to White Cars Ltd, the correct entries had been made in the company's appropriate fixed asset account and also in Excel Supplies Ltd's account.

(g) The goods debited to White Cars Ltd by Excel Supplies Ltd on 22 September 19X0 at a cost of £4,000 included goods costing £500 purchased by T. Green, a former executive of White Cars Ltd.
Note: Excel Supplies Ltd was advised over a year ago of the policy of White Cars Ltd that employees are not permitted to purchase goods for their own use through White Cars Ltd; further, in July 19X0, Excel Supplies Ltd was advised that T. Green had left White Cars Ltd.

It is the policy of White Cars Ltd to provide depreciation on fixed assets at the rate of 10% of the cost of assets held at the end of each financial year.

In the valuation of stock in trade at 30 September 19X0 by White Cars Ltd, goods held on a sale or return basis were included as stock in trade.

You are required to prepare:

(a) the account of Excel Supplies Ltd for September 19X0 as it should appear in the books of White Cars Ltd; *6 marks*

(b) a computation of the corrected gross profit and net profit for the year ended 30 September 19X0 of White Cars Ltd; *8 marks*

(c) the account of White Cars Ltd for September 19X0 as it should appear in the books of Excel Supplies Ltd. *3 marks*

17 marks

ANSWERS

1 SMILEY

(a)

Cash book

	£		£
August 19X2		August 19X2	
1 Capital	3,000	1 Rent	500
1 Guillam – loan	2,000	3 Purchases	550
10 Sales	1,200	8 Office equipment	250
20 Sales	200	15 Enderby	1,000
22 Lacon	450	18 Drawings	400
		22 Salaries	100
		23 Esterhase	420
		23 Haydon	450
		26 Motor expenses	75
		31 Sundry expenses	120
		31 Balance c/d	2,985
	6,850		6,850
September 19X2			
1 Balance b/d	2,985		

Capital

	£		£
August 19X2		August 19X2	
31 Balance c/d	3,000	1 Cash	3,000
		September 19X2	
		1 Balance b/d	3,000

Guillam – Loan

	£		£
August 19X2		August 19X2	
31 Balance c/d	2,000	1 Cash	2,000
		September 19X2	
		1 Balance b/d	2,000

Rent

	£		£
August 19X2		August 19X2	
1 Cash	500	31 Balance c/d	500
September 19X2			
1 Balance b/d	500		

Purchases

	£		£
August 19X2		August 19X2	
3 Cash	550		
4 Esterhase	420		
4 Haydon	600	31 Balance c/d	1,570
	1,570		1,570
September 19X2			
1 Balance b/d	1,570		

Esterhase

	£		£
August 19X2		August 19X2	
23 Cash	420	4 Purchases	420

Haydon

	£		£
August 19X2		August 19X2	
23 Cash	450	4 Purchases	600
31 Balance c/d	150		
	600		600
		September 19X2	
		1 Balance b/d	150

Office equipment

	£		£
August 19X2		August 19X2	
8 Cash	250	31 Balance c/d	250
September 19X2			
1 Balance b/d	250		

Sales

	£		£
August 19X2		August 19X2	
		10 Cash	1,200
		12 Lacon	850
31 Balance c/d	2,250	20 Cash	200
	2,250		2,250
		September 19X2	
		1 Balance b/d	2,250

Lacon

	£		£
August 19X2		August 19X2	
12 Sales	850	22 Cash	450
		31 Balance c/d	400
	850		850
September 19X2			
1 Balance b/d	400		

Motor car

	£		£
August 19X2		August 19X2	
15 Enderby	4,000	31 Balance c/d	4,000
September 19X2			
1 Balance b/d	4,000		

Enderby

	£		£
August 19X2		August 19X2	
15 Cash	1,000	15 Motor car	4,000
31 Balance c/d	3,000		
	4,000		4,000
		September 19X2	
		1 Balance b/d	3,000

Drawings

	£		£
August 19X2		August 19X2	
18 Cash	400	31 Balance c/d	400
September 19X2			
1 Balance b/d	400		

Salaries

	£		£
August 19X2		August 19X2	
22 Cash	100	31 Balance c/d	100
September 19X2			
1 Balance b/d	100		

Motor expenses

	£		£
August 19X2		August 19X2	
26 Cash	75	31 Balance c/d	75
	===		===
September 19X2			
1 Balance b/d	75		

Sundry expenses

	£		£
August 19X2		August 19X2	
31 Cash	120	31 Balance c/d	120
	===		===
September 19X2			
1 Balance b/d	120		

(b) **Trial balance at 31 August 19X2**

	Dr £	Cr £
Cash	2,985	
Capital		3,000
Guillam – loan		2,000
Rent	500	
Purchases	1,570	
Haydon		150
Office equipment	250	
Sales		2,250
Lacon	400	
Motor car	4,000	
Enderby		3,000
Drawings	400	
Salaries	100	
Motor expenses	75	
Sundry expenses	120	
	10,400	10,400

2 ANGUS

(a)

Cash

			£				£
Loan – father	(a)		5,000	Purchases	(b)		3,000
Sales	(b)		4,000	Bicycle	(d)		70
Cash	(g)		2,100	Rent	(e)		120
Capital	(h)		1,000	Creditors	(f)		1,500
				Electricity	(i)		90
				Drawings	(j)		120
				Balance c/d			7,200
			12,100				12,100
Balance b/d			7,200				

Loan – father

	£				£
Balance c/d	5,000	Cash	(a)		5,000
		Balance b/d			5,000

Sales

	£				£
Balance c/d	7,800	Cash	(c)		4,000
		Debtors	(g)		3,800
	7,800				7,800
Trading account*	7,800	Balance b/d			7,800

Purchases

		£		£
Cash	(b)	3,000		
Creditors	(f)	2,000	Balance c/d	5,000
		5,000		5,000
Balance b/d		5,000	Trading account*	5,000

Bicycle

		£		£
Cash	(d)	70	Balance c/d	70
		70		
Balance b/d				

28

Rent

		£			£
Cash	(e)	120	Balance c/d		120
Balance b/d		120	Profit and loss account*		120

Creditors

		£			£
Cash	(f)	1,500	Purchases	(f)	2,000
Balance c/d		500			
		2,000			2,000
			Balance b/d		500

Debtors

		£			£
Sales	(g)	3,800	Cash	(g)	2,100
			Balance c/d		1,700
		3,800			3,800
Balance b/d		1,700			

Capital

	£			£
Balance c/d	1,000	Cash	(h)	1,000
Drawings*	120	Balance b/d		1,000
Balance c/d*	3,470	Profit and loss account*		2,590
	3,590			3,590
		Balance b/d*		3,470

Electricity

		£		£
Cash	(i)	90	Balance c/d	90
Balance b/d		90	Profit and loss account*	90

Drawings

		£		£
Cash	(j)	120	Balance c/d	120
		===		===
Balance b/d		120	Capital	120
		===		===

(b) **Trial balance at 30 September 19X2**

	Dr £	Cr £
Cash	7,200	
Loan – father		5,000
Sales		7,800
Purchases	5,000	
Bicycle	70	
Rent	120	
Creditors		500
Debtors	1,700	
Capital		1,000
Electricity	90	
Drawings	120	
	14,300	14,300

After the trial balance, the profit and loss account will be prepared and the entries marked with an asterisk will be made in the ledger accounts.

(c) **Trading and profit and loss account**

	£		£
Purchases	5,000	Sales	7,800
Gross profit c/d	2,800		
	7,800		7,800
	===		===
Rent	120	Gross profit b/d	2,800
Electricity	90		
Net profit – to capital account	2,590		
	2,800		2,800
	===		===

3 MACLEAN

Trial balance at 31 December 19X2

	Dr £	Cr £
Capital on 1 January 19X2		15,743
Freehold factory at cost	120,000	
Motor vehicles at cost	42,000	
Provision for depreciation on motor vehicles at 1 January 19X2		19,350
Stocks at 1 January 19X2	12,500	
Debtors	5,200	
Provision for doubtful debts at 1 January 19X2		290
Cash in hand	75	
Bank overdraft		27,462
Creditors		26,300
Sales		106,000
Purchases	55,000	
Rent and rates	11,800	
Discounts allowed	2,200	
Insurance	950	
Sales returns	3,500	
Purchase returns		2,100
Loan from bank		80,000
Sundry expenses	15,320	
Drawings	8,700	
	277,245	277,245

4 CAMPBELL

(a) Trial balance at 30 June 19X4

	Dr £	Cr £
Sales		15,620
Purchases	10,400	
Stock at 1 July 19X3	4,140	
Motor vehicles	16,400	
Provision for depreciation at 1 July 19X3		7,900
Debtors	12,300	
Creditors		15,600
Cash at bank	3,215	
Drawings	4,100	
Motor expenses	620	
Rent and rates	1,160	
Insurance	185	
Electricity	120	
Postage and telephone	250	
Sundry expenses	270	
Capital at 1 July 19X3		14,040
	53,160	53,160

(b) **Trading and profit and loss account for year ended 30 June 19X4**

	£	£
Sales		15,620
Less: Cost of goods sold		
Opening stock	4,140	
Purchases	10,400	
	14,540	
Less: Closing stock	7,350	
		7,190
Gross profit		8,430
Less: Motor expenses	620	
Rent and rates	920	
Insurance	145	
Electricity	165	
Postage and telephone	315	
Sundry expenses	294	
Depreciation	1,200	
		3,659
Net profit		4,771

(c) **Balance sheet at 30 June 19X4**

	£ Cost	£ Depreciation	£
Fixed assets			
Motor vehicles	16,400	9,100	7,300
Current assets			
Stocks		7,350	
Debtors		12,350	
Prepayments		280	
Cash at bank		3,215	
		23,145	
Current liabilities			
Creditors	15,600		
Accrued expenses	134		
		15,734	
			7,411
			14,711

	£
Representing:	
Proprietors' interest	
Capital at 1 July 19X3	14,040
Profit for the year	4,771
	18,811
Less: Drawings	4,100
	14,711

5 ADAM

(a) **Trial balance as at 30 June 19X6**

		Dr £	Cr £
Capital at 1 January 19X6	B		1,000
Cash at bank	B	300	
Purchases	P	3,225	
Sales	P		7,500
Drawings	B	3,000	
6 months rent and rates	P	200	
Casual wages	P	1,100	
Electricity	P	150	
Professional fees	P	105	
Tools and equipment	B	300	
Office furniture and fittings	B	160	
Debtors	B	130	
Creditors	B		170
		8,670	8,670

Tutorial note: Everything in the trial balance goes either into the profit and loss account (P) or into the balance sheet (B).

(b) **Trading and profit and loss account for the six months ending 30 June 19X6**

	£	£
Sales		7,500
Less: Purchases		3,225
Gross profit		4,275
Less: Expenses		
Rent and rates	200	
Casual wages	1,100	
Electricity	150	
Professional fees	105	
		1,555
Net profit for six months		2,720

(c) **Balance sheet as at 30 June 19X6**

	£	£
Fixed assets		
Tools and equipment		300
Furniture and fittings		160
carried forward		460

	£	£
brought forward		460
Current assets		
Debtors	130	
Cash at bank	300	
	430	
Current liabilities		
Creditors	170	
Net current assets		260
		720

	£
Proprietor's interest	
Capital at 1 January	1,000
Profit for period	2,720
	3,720
Less: Drawings for period	3,000
	720

Tutorial note: Adam has withdrawn more money from the business than it has made during the year. If he continues to do that the business will become insolvent.

6 ARTHUR LEGGE

(a)
Cash book (Bank)

	£		£
Sales — cash	15,000	Delivery van	3,900
— credit	6,500	Suppliers	7,200
Capital	4,000	Sundry expenses	2,200
		Drawings	2,000
		Rent	1,200
		Assistant's wages	1,900
		31 December 19X9 Balance c/d	1,100
	25,500		25,500
Balance b/d	7,100		

Sales account

	£		£
31 December 19X9 Balance c/d	23,000	Cash sales	15,000
		Debtors	8,000
	23,000		23,000
		31 December 19X9 Balance b/d	23,000

Debtors' account

	£		£
Sales	8,000	Cash	6,500
		31 December 19X9	
		Balance c/d	1,500
	8,000		8,000
31 December 19X9 Balance b/d	1,500		

Capital account

			£
		1 January 19X9 Cash	4,000

Delivery van

	£		
1 January 19X9 Cash	3,900		

Suppliers (Creditors)

	£		£
Cash	7,200	Purchases	7,800
31 December 19X9 Balance c/d	600		
	7,800		7,800
		31 December 19X9	
		Balance b/d	600

Purchases

	£		£
Suppliers	7,800		

Sundry expenses

	£		£
Cash	2,200		

Drawings

	£		£
Cash	2,000		

Rent

	£		£
Cash	1,200		

Assistant's wages

	£		£
Cash	1,900		

(b) **Trial balance as at 31 December 19X9**

		£	£
Cash book	B	7,100	
Sales account	P		23,000
Debtors	B	1,500	
Capital account	B		4,000
Delivery van	B	3,900	
Suppliers	B		600
Purchases	P	7,800	
Sundry expenses	P	2,200	
Drawings	B	2,000	
Rent	P	1,200	
Assistant's wages	P	1,900	
		27,600	27,600

Tutorial note: P = Profit and loss account item; B = Balance sheet item. The trial balance is extracted before final adjustments are made to ensure that the double entry has so far been correctly dealt with.

(c) **Trading and profit and loss account for the year ended 31 December 19X9**

	£	£
Sales		23,000
Less: Cost of goods sold		
Purchases	7,800	
Closing stock on 31 December 19X9	850	
		6,950
Gross profit		16,050
Less: Expenses		
Sundry	2,200	
Rent	1,200	
Assistant's wages	1,900	
		5,300
Net profit		10,750

Balance sheet as at 31 December 19X9

	£	£
Fixed assets		
Delivery van		3,900
Current assets		
Stocks	850	
Debtors	1,500	
Cash at bank	7,100	
	9,450	
Current liabilities		
Creditors	600	
Net current assets		8,850
		12,750

	£
Financed by:	
Proprietor's interest	
Capital at 1 January	4,000
Profit for the year	10,750
	14,750
Less: Drawings	2,000
	12,750

Tutorial note: All figures are as per the trial balance with the exception of stock. Students will note that it appears as a credit in the profit and loss account and as an asset (debit balance) in the balance sheet.

7 WHITE CARS LTD

(a) **Excel Supplies Ltd**

	£		£
Sept.		Sept.	
10 Cash	2,400	1 Balance b/d (W1)	2,700
26 Returns	240	22 Purchases	3,500
29 Returns (Note)	210		
30 Balance c/d	3,350		
	6,200		6,200
		Oct.	
		1 Balance b/d	3,350

Note: These are shown in Excel Supplies Ltd's statement and appear not to be in dispute.

37

(b)

		Gross profit £	Net profit £
Per draft accounts		36,000	15,160
Less:			
Profit taken on goods returned	(a)	120	120
Depreciation on shelving	(b)	—	300
		120	420
		35,880	14,740
Add:			
Shelving treated as purchases	(c)	3,000	3,000
Payment treated as expenses	(f)	—	2,400
		3,000	5,400
		38,880	20,140

(c) **White Cars Ltd**

Sept.		£	Sept.		£
1	Balance b/d	2,700	10	Cash	2,400
22	Sales	3,500	29	Returns	210
30	Sales	610	30	Balance c/d	4,200
		6,810			6,810
Oct.					
1	Balance b/d	4,200			

Workings

		£
1.	Balance per question	14,700
	Less: Goods on sale or return	12,000
	Corrected balance	2,700

3 Year-end adjustments

The questions in this chapter explore, in greater detail, such year-end adjustments as accruals and prepayments, depreciation, bad and doubtful debts and stocks. Students should be able to record these items in the ledger accounts as well as understanding their effect on the trading and profit and loss account and balance sheet.

There are many acceptable methods for the recording of these adjustments and students will probably have seen more than one method used in practice. The solutions aim to keep to **one** method for each item; for example, bad and doubtful debts are dealt with in **two** accounts. If students are accustomed to using the **one** account method for bad and doubtful debts, they are advised to continue to use that method: they should ensure that their answer agrees with the suggested solution, in that the effect on the profit and loss account and balance sheet is correct.

As can be seen from the number of questions involved, these topics are fairly popular with examiners at this level: depreciation is possibly the greatest favourite.

QUESTIONS

1 FURZE

The balances on Furze's insurance account at 31 March 19X2 were a prepayment of £250 and an accrual of £100. During the year ended 31 March 19X3 the following insurance premiums were paid:

Policy	£	Period covered		
A	460	1 January 19X2	–	31 December 19X2
B	270	1 April 19X2	–	31 March 19X3
C	240	1 June 19X2	–	31 May 19X3
D	220	1 October 19X2	–	30 September 19X3
E	150	1 December 19X2	–	30 November 19X3
A	500	1 January 19X3	–	31 December 19X3
F	180	1 January 19X3	–	31 December 19X3

You are required to:

(a) write up Furze's insurance account for the year ended 31 March 19X3 assuming that there are no insurances unpaid at the year-end; and

(b) do a calculation to show how the profit and loss charge is made up.

10 marks

2 HEATHER

Heather rents three shops and maintains **one** account for rent and rates for all three premises. The rents are fixed for each year and increases take effect as from 1 January.

At 31 December 19X3, he had paid all of the rent up-to-date but there was a prepayment in relation to rates of £1,100.

During the year ended 31 December 19X4 he made the following payments:

Date	Shop	£		
10 January	A	540	Rent for January 19X4	– June 19X4
10 April	A	800	Rates for April 19X4	– March 19X5
3 July	A	540	Rent for July 19X4	– December 19X4
29 December	A	600	Rent for January 19X5	– June 19X5
3 February	B	1,200	Rent for January 19X4	– December 19X4
28 March	B	1,060	Rates for April 19X4	– March 19X5
6 January	C	350	Rent for January 19X4	– March 19X4
24 March	C	1,600	Rates for April 19X4	– March 19X5
15 May	C	350	Rent for April 19X4	– June 19X4
10 September	C	350	Rent for July 19X4	– September 19X4

You are required to write up the rent and rates account for 19X4, showing the total profit and loss account charge.

10 marks

3 RBD & CO

The ledger of RBD & Co included the following account balances:

	At 1 June 19X4	At 31 May 19X5
	£	£
Rents receivable: prepayments	463	517
Rent and rates payable:		
prepayments	1,246	1,509
accruals	315	382
Creditors	5,258	4,720
Provision for discounts on creditors	106	94

During the year ended 31 May 19X5, the following transactions had arisen:

	£
Rents received by cheque	4,058
Rent paid by cheque	7,491
Rates paid by cheque	2,805
Creditors paid by cheque	75,181
Discounts received from creditors	1,043
Purchases on credit	to be derived

You are required to post and balance the appropriate accounts for the year ended 31 May 19X5, deriving the transfer entries to profit and loss account, where applicable.

13 marks

4 GORSE

Gorse rents premises at a rental of £1,000 per annum.

He sublets part of the premises to Hill at £300 per annum and another part to Pine at £200 per annum.

On 1 January 19X4 Gorse had paid his own rent up-to-date; Hill's rent was 3 months in arrears and Pine had paid his rent to 31 March 19X4.

During the year 19X4:

(a) Gorse paid his rent at the end of each quarter except the amount due at 31 December 19X4 which was outstanding;

(b) Gorse received the following amounts from Hill: 31 January £150; 1 April £75; 5 July £75; 4 December £150; and

(c) Gorse received the following amount from Pine, 10 October £100.

You are required to show the accounts for rent payable and rent receivable in Gorse's ledger for the year ended 31 December 19X4 on the basis that no personal accounts are kept for Hill and Pine.

8 marks

5 BILBERRY

You are required, using the information given below, to compile Bilberry's stationery and telephone account for the year ended 31 January 19X4, showing clearly the charge to profit and loss account.

The value of Bilberry's stock of stationery on 31 January 19X3 was £241. At that date the prepaid telephone rental amounted to £20; there was an accrued liability of £137 for telephone calls during December 19X2 and January 19X3, and accrued liability of £25 for stationery.

During the year ended 31 January 19X4 the following transactions occurred:

19X3		£	£
February 20	Purchase of stationery		103
March 19	Payment of telephone bill		262
	(being rent for quarter ended 31 May 19X3	60	
	calls for December 19X2	79	
	January 19X3	58	
	February 19X3	65)	
June 28	Payment of telephone bill		281
	(being rent for quarter ended 31 Aug. 19X3	60	
	and calls for March to May 19X3	221)	
August 12	Purchase of stationery		156
September 15	Payment of telephone bill		305
	(being rent for quarter ended 30 Nov. 19X3	75	
	and calls for June to August 19X3	230)	
November 13	Purchase of stationery		74
December 20	Payment of telephone bill		282
	(being rent for quarter ended 29 Feb. 19X4	75	
	and calls for September to November 19X3	207)	

At 31 January 19X4 the stock of stationery was valued at £199 and there was an accrued liability for stationery of £13. On 23 March 19X4 a telephone account of £298 was paid, consisting of:

	£
rent for the quarter ended 31 May 19X4	75
calls for December 19X3	86
January 19X4	63
February 19X4	74

12 marks

6 GOSPORT

Gosport purchased four lorries during 19X2 at a cost of £4,000 each. He expects to use the lorries for a period of five years, after which time they will be traded in for new vehicles. He is now considering whether to charge depreciation annually at 40%, by the reducing balance method, or at 18½% by the straight line method. He would charge a full year's depreciation in the year of purchase. He prepares his accounts to 31 December in each year.

You are required to:

(a) produce schedules showing the depreciation charged in each of the years 19X2 to 19X6 under the two methods;

(b) show the value of the assets in the accounts at 31 December in each of the five years under the two methods; and

(c) show the ledger accounts recording the assets and their depreciation for the first two years only, assuming that he decides on the reducing balance method.

12 marks

7 FOREST

Forest is a small textile manufacturer who started in business on 1 January 19X1. It is the practice to depreciate all fixed assets using the straight line method; a full year's depreciation is charged in the year of purchase and none in the year of sale. The business had purchased fixed assets for cash as follows:

Year of purchase	Purchased	Total cost £	Depreciation rate %
19X1	4 new knitting machines	2,400	10
19X2	1 new dyeing machine	1,500	10
19X5	2 new knitting machines	1,800	10
19X6	Motor car	2,100	20
19X7	Motor van	1,500	20

In 19X8 Forest gave a cheque for £5,000 to the supplier of four new knitting machines, to replace those purchased in 19X1, and he was allowed £600 in part exchange on the old knitting machines. The car, which was purchased in 19X6, was replaced by a new vehicle which cost £4,800, and £1,500 was allowed in part exchange on the old vehicle. A shrink wrapping machine was purchased during the year at a cost of £1,500 and like the other similar fixed assets it is to be depreciated at 10% on cost.

You are required to write up the accounts for fixed assets, the provision for depreciation, and the fixed asset disposal account for:

(a) plant and machinery; and
(b) motor vehicles

for the year ended 31 December 19X8.

12 marks

8 MITCHELL

At 1 August 19X6 the balance sheet of the company showed:

	£
Motor vehicles at cost	77,600
Accumulated depreciation	43,520
	34,080

Depreciation is calculated at 25% per annum on the reducing balance method with a full year's depreciation in the year of purchase and none in the year of sale. The following transactions take place during the year to 31 July 19X7:

(a) A Jaguar car which cost £8,160 in August 19X3 was exchanged for a Cortina (list price £6,640) and an allowance of £2,400 was given for the Jaguar.

(b) A Renault motor car which cost £5,600 in March 19X5 was exchanged in May 19X7 for a Mini (list price £4,400) for a cash payment of £400.

(c) A Ford Escort van which cost £4,800 in September 19X2 was sold to a scrap merchant for £240 in December 19X6, and replaced by a Bedford van (list price £6,000).

You are required to write up the vehicles, provision for depreciation and disposal accounts for the year ended 31 July 19X7.

12 marks

9 ROVER

Rover owns a small factory situated on a trading estate. He uses the reducing balance method of depreciation for plant, with a 20% write off each year, and maintains a plant account to record all entries concerning the plant.

An extract from the balance sheet as at 30 September 19X6 is as follows:

Fixed assets	Cost £	Depreciation £	Net £
Land and buildings	520,000	–	520,000
Plant	410,100	159,180	250,920
	930,100	159,180	770,920

Plant purchased on 12 October 19X2 for £46,800 was sold for £16,212 on 4 December 19X6. New plant costing £81,400, was purchased on 15 May 19X7. Depreciation is charged in full in the year of purchase, but no depreciation is charged in full in the year of purchase, but no depreciation is charged in the year of sale.

You are required to:

(a) write up the plant account, provision for depreciation, depreciation expense and disposal accounts for the year ended 30 September 19X7; and

(b) draft a balance sheet extract for fixed assets as at that date.

10 marks

10 J. FOSTER

J. Foster Ltd, a company with a turnover of £30,000 per year acquired a machine on 1 January 19X5, for £8,000. It was company policy to depreciate machinery on a straight line basis at 20% per year. During 19X7, a modification was made to the machine to improve its technical reliability at a cost of £800 which it was considered would extend the useful life of the machine by two years. At the same time, an important component of the machine was replaced at a cost of £500, because of excessive wear and tear. Routine maintenance during the year cost £250.

You are required to:

(a) Show the asset account, the provision for depreciation account, and the charge to profit and loss account in respect of the machine for the year ended 31 December 19X7. *8 marks*

(b) Once an asset such as a machine is installed, what factors should be considered when deciding whether to capitalise or treat as expense subsequent expenditure relating to that asset? *6 marks*

14 marks

11 HUCKNALL HAULIERS LTD

Hucknall Hauliers Ltd commenced business on 1 January, 19X3. They purchased one vehicle each year paying £2,000, £3,000 and £4,000 respectively from 19X3 to 19X5. After much argument and deliberation they decided to use the reducing balance method of depreciation, employing a rate of 24%. All assets are to be depreciated in the year of their purchase, but not in the year of their sale. In December 19X5 they sold their oldest vehicle for £1,000.

You are required to:

(a) record the above transactions in the appropriate accounts and show the balance sheet entry for vehicles as at 31 December 19X5; *8 marks*

(b) suggest arguments used for and against the reducing balance method during the initial discussions at the firm. *6 marks*

14 marks

Note: Calculations to the nearest £1.

12 DISPOSALS LTD

Shown below is an extract from the balance sheet of Disposals Ltd as at 31 March 19X5:

	£
Lorries, at cost	67,500
Less: Provision for depreciation	30,900
Net book value at 31 March 19X5	36,600

During the year to 31 March 19X5 the following transactions took place, the lorries being identified by their registration numbers:

(a) Two lorries were sold. DV 100 had originally cost £7,000 in January 19X2 and was sold for £2,000 on 30 June 19X5, whilst EV 200 had cost £15,000 in January 19X3 and was sold for £5,000 on 31 January 19X6.

(b) Three new lorries were purchased: IV 600 on 1 July 19X5 at a cost of £15,000 and IV 800 on 1 February 19X6 at a cost of £25,000. However, IV 600 proved to be too small, and was replaced with IV 700 on 1 December 19X5. This would have cost £30,000, but £20,000 was accepted by the supplier in part exchange for IV 600.

The company uses the straight line method of depreciation at a rate of 20% per annum on original cost. A full year's depreciation is charged in the year of acquisition, but no depreciation is charged in the year of disposal.

You are required to:

(a) write up the lorries account, the provision for depreciation account, and the lorry disposal account for the year to 31 March 19X6; *12 marks*

(b) show how the balances would appear on the balance sheet as at that date.
2 marks
14 marks

13 KIPLING

On 31 December 19X5 the balance on Kipling's motor vehicles account was £75,400 and there was a provision for depreciation of £36,300.

When finalising the accounts for the year it was found that:

(a) A motor vehicle (cost £4,000) had been bought on hire purchase. The terms of the agreement included a deposit of £500 and this was paid on 10 December 19X5. The only entries which have been made were to credit the cash book and debit the motor vehicles account in respect of the deposit.

(b) A vehicle which was purchased in June 19X2 for £3,200 was scrapped. There were no proceeds and no entries have been made in relation to the disposal.

(c) A vehicle which was purchased in March 19X3 for £4,000 was sold in August 19X5 for £2,500. The only entry made in respect of the disposal was to debit cash and credit the motor vehicles account with the proceeds.

(d) No depreciation has yet been charged for the year of 19X5. The company charges depreciation at 25% per annum on the cost of motor vehicles held at the year end.

You are required to write up the motor vehicles account, provision for depreciation account, depreciation expense account and disposals account for the year ended 31 December 19X5.

13 marks

14 GREENACRES LTD

Greenacres Ltd, a well-established company, specialising in the distribution of agricultural buildings, equipment and fertilisers, commenced a machinery repair service on 1 January 19X7.

From the beginning of the new venture, the repair service used a prefabricated building which the company bought originally with the intention of selling it.

In fact, the building was included in trading stock at cost at 31 December 19X6, at £10,000 and was then displayed for retail sale at £13,000.

In preparing the building for use as a workshop on 1 January 19X7, the following expenditure was incurred:

	£
Foundations and erection costs	1,000
Interior and exterior painting	600
Heating and lighting systems	3,000

On 1 January 19X8, further work was undertaken on the repair service building's heating system at a total cost of £1,400, half of which related to repairs and the rest concerned the installation of additional thermostatic controls.

On 30 June 19X8, the following work was completed on the workshop building:

	£
Installation of partition walls	1,600
Renewal of wooden window frames	1,000

Early in 19X9, following the closure of the machinery repair service, the workshop building, including the heating and lighting systems, was sold for £8,000. It is company policy to provide depreciation annually on prefabricated buildings at the rate of 10% of cost at the end of each financial year (31 December).

You are required to produce:

(a) The following ledger accounts as they would appear in the books of Greenacres Ltd for each of the financial years ended 31 December 19X7, 19X8 and 19X9:

    (i) repair service workshop building;
    (ii) repair service workshop building provision for depreciation.

Note: The balances on accounts should be brought down at the end of each financial year.

(b) The repair service workshop building disposal account.

17 marks

15 SOULT

On 31 December 19X5 the balance on Soult's provision for doubtful debts account was £3,200, being 5% of debtors at that date.

During the years ended 31 December 19X6 and 31 December 19X7, bad debts amounting to £2,000 and £2,500 respectively were written off. At the end of these two years, the debtors were £83,000 and £76,000 respectively, after writing off the bad debts.

Soult wishes to maintain a general provision for doubtful debts of 5% of debtors outstanding at the year-end.

You are required to write up the bad debts expense account and the provision for doubtful debts account for the years ended 31 December 19X6 and 31 December 19X7.

10 marks

16 NEY

Ney set up a business on 1 September 19X2. The following figures relate to the years ended 31 August 19X3 and 31 August 19X4.

	19X3 £	19X4 £
Credit sales	120,000	150,000
Cash received from debtors	95,000	130,000
Bad debts written off	500	1,500
Cash received in respect of a bad debt written off during the year ended 31 August 19X3		100

Ney feels that a reasonable provision for doubtful debts would be 5% of debtors outstanding at the year-end.

You are required to prepare Ney's sales ledger control account (total debtors), provision for doubtful debts account and the bad debts expense account for the years ended 31 August 19X3 and 31 August 19X4.

10 marks

17 GROUCHY

On 31 December 19X4, the balance on Grouchy's sales ledger control account was £8,238 and there was a provision for doubtful debts of £478. This latter balance represented £165 against the debt of Murat and £73 against the debt of Brune, the balance being a general provision of £240 (3%) against the remaining debtors.

On 31 December 19X5 the balance on the sales ledger control account was £9,619. No adjustments have yet been made to the provision for doubtful debts. During 19X5, the following events occurred:

(a) £45 was received from Berthier in respect of a debt written off in 19X4. When the cash was received, it was credited to the sales ledger control account.

(b) Murat was declared bankrupt and it has been decided to write off the debt of £165 which had previously been provided against.

(c) The debt of £143 owed by Moncey is in doubt and Grouchy has decided to make a provision against the debt.

(d) There is an outstanding balance from Jourdan of £56. It has been discovered that Jourdan died, penniless, during the year.

(e) Brune has paid the debt of £73 which had been provided against. The only entries made were to debit cash and credit the sales ledger control account.

Grouchy wishes to maintain a general provision of 3% against debts not specifically provided against.

You are required to show the necessary entries in the sales ledger control account, provision for doubtful debts account and bad debts expense account.

15 marks

18 ARNOLD

After examination of the sales ledger at 31 May 19X5, it was decided to make specific provision for the following doubtful debts:

	£
Bennett	21
Clayhanger	50
Darius	175
Edwin	52

Arnold also decided to make a general provision of 5% on other debtors at 31 May 19X5. The debtors at 31 May 19X5 amounted to £4,898 after writing off bad debts during the year of £73 and before making any provisions. There was no provision for doubtful debts at 31 May 19X4.

During the year ended 31 May 19X6 Arnold received the £21 from Bennett, together with £100 of the £175 owed by Darius. Arnold had to write off a debt of £56 from Clara and received £10 from Enoch relating to a debt written off in the year ended 31 May 19X5.

Credit sales during the year ended 31 May 19X6 were £42,100, and the cash received from debtors was £41,379 including the amounts from Bennett, Darius and Enoch.

At 31 May 19X6, Arnold decided to write off the debts from Clayhanger and Edwin of £50 and £52 respectively and to write off the balance outstanding from Darius of £75. It was also felt necessary to make a specific provision of £36 against the debt from James and to make a general provision of 5% against those debtors not specifically provided against.

You are required to prepare the bad debts expense and provision for doubtful debts accounts for the years ended 31 May 19X5 and 31 May 19X6.

15 marks

19 DOCKS LTD

Docks Ltd, a window replacement company, offers fairly generous credit terms to its high risk customers. Provision is made for bad debts at a varying percentage based on the level of outstanding trade debtors, and an assessment of general economic circumstances, resulting in the following data for the last three accounting periods:

Year to 31 March:	19X0 £	19X1 £	19X2 £
Trade debtors at the year end (before allowing for any bad debts)	186,680	141,200	206,200
Estimated bad debts (companies in liquidation)	1,680	1,200	6,200
Provision for bad debts	10%	12.5%	15%

The provision for bad debts at the beginning of the year ended 31 March 19X0 was £13,000.

You are required to:

(a) prepare the provision for doubtful debts and bad debts expense accounts for each of the three years to 31 March 19X0, 19X1 and 19X2 respectively, showing how the balances would appear on the balance sheets as at these dates; and
12 marks

(b) assuming that a debt of £1,000 written off as bad in 19X0 was subsequently recovered in cash in 19X1, state briefly how this would have affected the profit for the year to 31 March 19X0, and also how it would be treated in the accounts for the year to 31 March 19X1.
3 marks
15 marks

20 RICKWOOD

Rickwood started a business retailing video machines on 1 January 19X0. The sales for the first year were £560,000, the purchases were £480,000 and the cost of the closing stocks at 31 December 19X0 was £75,000.

In the following year to 31 December 19X1 the sales were £700,000, the purchases £580,000 and the closing stocks at 31 December 19X1 were £120,000.

You are required to:

(a) show the stock, purchases and sales accounts for both years; and

(b) prepare the trading account for the years ended 31 December 19X0 and 31 December 19X1.
8 marks

21 A BUSINESSMAN

A businessman started trading with a capital in cash of £6,000 which he placed in the business bank account at the outset.

His transactions, none of which were on credit, were as follows (in date sequence) for the first accounting period. All takings were banked immediately and all suppliers were paid by cheque. He traded in only one line of merchandise.

Purchases		Sales	
Quantity	Price per unit	Quantity	Price per unit
No.	£	No.	£
1,200	1.00		
1,000	1.05		
		800	1.70
600	1.10		
		600	1.90
900	1.20		
		1,100	2.00
800	1.25		
		1,300	2.00
700	1.30		
		400	2.05

In addition he incurred expenses amounting to £1,740, of which he still owed £570 at the end of the period.

You are required to prepare separately using both the FIFO (first in first out) and the LIFO (last in first out) methods of stock valuation:

(a) a statement of cost of sales for the period; and
(b) a balance sheet at the end of the period.

Note: Workings are an integral part of the answer and must be shown.

18 marks

22 FISHER

Fisher sells, *inter alia*, two items of stock – X and Y. During one trading period, the sales and purchases of those two commodities were:

Commodity	Purchases	Sales on credit
X	10 Units at £4 each	
	15 Units at £1.50 each	30 Units at £6 each
	20 Units at £5 each	
Y	15 Units at £2 each	
	10 Units at £3 each	20 Units at £4 each

At the end of the trading period, it was known that the purchase price of further stocks of X would be at £6 per unit, and of Y at £2.50 per unit. The sales of Y were discovered to have been made to a customer where there was a high risk of default, and no payment has been received during the period.

You are required to:

(a) Draw up a table showing, the gross and net profit on X and Y, and the value of the closing stock of each commodity. *6 marks*

(b) Explain clearly the basis for your answer to (a), stating what accounting principles you have applied. *8 marks*

14 marks

23 RINGERS LTD

The annual stocktaking of Ringers Ltd did not take place on the company's year-end on 30 April 19X0 owing to staff illness.

However, stock was taken at the close of business on 8 May 19X0 and the resultant valuation of £23,850 was used in the preparation of the company's draft accounts for the year ended 30 April 19X0 which showed a gross profit of £158,000, a net profit of £31,640 and net current assets at 30 April 19X0 of £24,600.

Subsequent investigations indicated that during the period from 30 April to 8 May 19X0 sales were £2,900, sales returns £340, purchases £4,200 and purchases returns £500.

In addition it was discovered that:

(a) A quantity of stock bought 10 years previously and included in the stock valuation at 8 May 19X0 at cost of £700 was, in fact, worthless. Instructions have now been given for the destruction of this stock.

(b) Two of the stock sheets prepared on 8 May 19X0 had been overcast by £100 and £40 respectively.

(c) The stock valuation of 8 May 19X0 included the company's office stationery stock of £1,400.

Note: It can be assumed that the stationery stock did not change between 30 April and 8 May 19X0.

(d) The valuation at 8 May 19X0 had not included goods, which had cost Ringers Ltd £400, sent on a sale or return basis to John Winters Ltd in February 19X0. Half of these goods, in value, were bought by John Winters Ltd on 29 April 19X0, but the sale has not been recorded in the company's draft accounts for the year ended 30 April 19X0.

Note: Ringers Ltd achieves a uniform rate of gross profit of 20% on all sales revenue.

You are required to produce:

(a) A computation of the Ringers Ltd's corrected stock valuation at 30 April 19X0.

(b) A computation of Ringers Ltd's corrected gross profit and net profit for the year ended 30 April 19X0, and the corrected net current assets at 30 April 19X0. *17 marks*

24 PRICE

Price's trial balance as at 30 September 19X1 included the following items:

	Debit £	**Credit** £
Rent	2,000	
Rates	900	
Plant and machinery, at cost	6,000	
Depreciation provision		1,500
Stock, 1 October 19X0	3,600	
Insurance	200	
Debtors	8,000	
Provision for bad debts		350

Your enquiries elicit the following information:

(a) the policy is to maintain the provision for bad debts at 5% of debtors;

(b) the insurance represents a premium of £200 covering the year to 31 December 19X1;

(c) stock on hand at 30 September 19X1 was valued at £4,000;

(d) the plant and machinery is being written off over its estimated useful life of eight years using the straight line method of depreciation;

(e) on 30 September 19X1 rates were prepaid by £150;

(f) the annual rent is £2,400 but the amount due for August and September was outstanding at 30 September 19X1.

You are required to:

(a) open accounts (you need not show the dates) for each of the items requiring adjustment;

(b) show in the accounts

   (i) the amount of the adjustment

   (ii) the amount, if any, which would be transferred to trading or profit and loss account;

(c) balance the accounts and carry down the balances for the commencement of the following year.

15 marks

ANSWERS

1 FURZE

Insurance

	£		£
Balance b/d	250	Balance b/d	100
Cash (A)	460		
Cash (B)	270		
Cash (C)	240	Profit and loss charge	1,410
Cash (D)	220		
Cash (E)	150		
Cash (A)	500		
Cash (F)	180	Balance c/d	760
	2,270		2,270
Balance b/d	760		

Workings

(a) **Prepayment at 31 March 19X3**

Policy	Months prepaid	Prepayments	£
A	9	$\frac{9}{12} \times £500$	= 375
B	—		—
C	2	$\frac{2}{12} \times £240$	= 40
D	6	$\frac{6}{12} \times £220$	= 110
E	8	$\frac{8}{12} \times £150$	= 100
F	9	$\frac{9}{12} \times £180$	= 135
			760

(b) **Profit and loss charge**

This can be calculated as the balancing figure in the T account or as follows:

Policy	Charge	£
A	$(£460 - £100) + (\frac{3}{12} \times £500) =$	485
B		270
C	$\frac{10}{12} \times £240$	200
D	$\frac{6}{12} \times £220$	110
E	$\frac{4}{12} \times £150$	50
F	$\frac{3}{12} \times £180$	45
		1,160
Add: Prepayment at 31 March 19X2 (policies C, D, E, F)		250
		1,140

The charge for policy A could also be calculated as

$(\frac{9}{12} \times £460) + (\frac{3}{12} \times £500) + 15$
$= 345 + 125 + 15$
$= £485$

(The £15 relates to the under-provision for policy A made at 31 March 19X2.)

2 HEATHER

Rent and rates

19X4		£	19X4		£
1 Jan	Balance b/d	1,100			
6 Jan	Cash (C)	350			
10 Jan	Cash (A)	540			
3 Feb	Cash (B)	1,200			
24 Mar	Cash (C)	1,600			
28 Mar	Cash (B)	1,060			
10 April	Cash (A)	800			
15 May	Cash (C)	350	31 Dec	Profit and loss	
3 July	Cash (A)	540		charge	7,375
10 Sept	Cash (C)	350			
29 Dec	Cash (A)	600			
31 Dec	Balance c/d	350	31 Dec	Balance c/d	1,465
		8,840			8,840
19X5			19X5		
1 Jan	Balance b/d	1,465	1 Jan	Balance b/d (W2)	350

Workings

(a) **Prepayment at 31 December 19X4**

Shop	Expense	£
A	Rent	600
	Rates	200
B	Rent	—
	Rates	265
C	Rent	—
	Rates	400
		1,465

(b) **Accrual at 31 December 19X4**

Shop	Expense	£
C	Rent	350

3 RBD & CO

Rent receivable

		£	19X4		£
	Profit and loss account	4,004	1 May	Balance b/f	463
19X5				Bank	4,058
31 May	Balance c/f	517			
		4,521			4,521

Rent and rates payable

19X4		£	19X4		£
1 June	Balance b/f	1,246	1 June	Balance b/f	315
	Bank — rent	7,491		Profit and loss	
	— rates	2,805		account	10,100
19X5			19X5		
31 May	Balance c/f	382	31 May	Balance c/f	1,509
		11,924			11,924

Creditors

		£	19X4		£
	Bank	75,181	1 June	Balance b/f	5,258
	Discount	1,043		Purchases on credit	
19X5				— trading account	75,686
31 May	Balance c/f	4,720			
		80,944			80,944

Provision for discount

19X4		£			£
1 June	Balance b/f	106		Creditors	1,043
	Profit and loss account	1,031	19X5		
			31 May	Balance c/f	94
		1,137			1,137

4 GORSE

Rent payable

	£		£
Cash	750	Profit and loss account	1,000
Balance c/d	250		
	1,000		1,000
		Balance b/d	250

Rent receivable

	£		£
Balance b/d (3m – Hill)	75	Balance b/d (3m – Pine)	50
		Cash (6m – Hill)	150
Profit and loss account	500	Cash (3m – Hill)	75
		Cash (3m – Hill)	75
		Cash (6m – Hill)	150
		Cash (6m – Pine)	100
Balance c/d (3m – Hill)	75	Balance c/d (3m – Pine)	50
	650		650
Balance b/d (3m – Pine)	50	Balance b/d (3m – Hill)	75

5 BILBERRY

Stationery and telephone account

19X3		£	19X3		£
1 Feb	Stocks of stationery b/f	241	1 Feb	Accrual for stationery b/f	25
	Prepaid telephone rent b/f	20		Accrual for telephone b/f	137
20 Feb	Purchase of stationery	103			
19 Mar	Cash – telephone bill	262			
28 June	Cash – telephone bill	281			
12 Aug	Purchase of stationery	156			
15 Sept	Cash – telephone	305	19X4		
13 Nov	Purchase of stationery	74	31 Jan	Profit and loss account	
20 Dec	Cash – telephone	282		Stationery	363
19X4				Telephone	1,137
31 Jan	Accrual for stationery c/f	13	31 Jan	Stocks of stationery c/f	199
31 Jan	Accrual for telephone c/f	149	31 Jan	Prepaid telephone rent c/f	25
		1,886			1,886

6 GOSPORT

(a) **Depreciation schedule for one lorry:**

	Reducing balance		Straight line £
19X2	40% × 4,000	= 1,600	740
19X3	40% × (4,000 − 1,600)	= 960	740
19X4	40% × (4,000 − 1,600 − 960)	= 576	740
19X5	40% × (4,000 − 1,600 − 960 − 576)	= 346	740
19X6	40% × (4,000 − 1,600 − 960 − 576 − 346)	= 207	740

For four lorries:

	Reducing balance £	Straight line £
19X2	6,400	2,960
19X3	3,840	2,960
19X4	2,304	2,960
19X5	1,384	2,960
19X6	828	2,960
Total depreciation	14,756	14,800

(b) **Value in the accounts**

		Reducing balance			Straight line		
At 31 December		Cost £	Dep'n £	NBV £	Cost £	Depc'n £	NBV £
19X2	Lorries	16,000	6,400	9,600	16,000	2,960	13,040
19X3	Lorries	16,000	10,240	5,760	16,000	5,920	10,080
19X4	Lorries	16,000	12,544	3,456	16,000	8,880	7,120
19X5	Lorries	16,000	13,928	2,072	16,000	11,840	4,160
19X6	Lorries	16,000	14,756	1,244	16,000	14,800	1,200

(c) **Ledger accounts**

Lorries' account

19X2		£	19X2		£
Cash		16,000	31 Dec Balance c/d		16,000
		16,000			16,000
19X3			19X3		
1 Jan Balance b/d		16,000	31 Dec Balance c/d		16,000
		16,000			16,000
19X4					
1 Jan Balance b/d		16,000			

58

Provision for depreciation account

19X2 31 Dec Balance b/d	£ 6,400	19X2 31 Dec Depreciation expense	£ 6,400
	6,400		6,400
19X3 31 Dec Balance c/d	£ 10,240	19X3 1 Jan Balance b/d 31 Dec Depreciation expense	£ 6,400 3,800
	10,240		10,240
		19X4 1 Jan Balance b/d	10,240

Depreciation expense account

19X2 31 Dec Provision for dep'n	£ 6,400	19X2 31 Dec Profit and loss account	£ 6,400
	6,400		6,400
19X3 31 Dec Provision for dep'n	£ 3,840	19X3 31 Dec Profit and loss account	£ 3,840
	3,840		3,840

7 FOREST

(a) **Plant and machinery**

19X8	£	19X8	£
Balance b/d	5,700	Disposals	2,400
Disposal – allowance	600		
Cash – balance	5,000	Balance c/d	10,400
Cash	1,500		
	12,800		12,800
19X9 Balance b/d	10,400		

Plant and machinery — Provision for depreciation

19X8	£	19X8	£
Disposals (W1)	1,680	Balance b/d (W1)	3,120
Balance c/d	2,480	Depreciation expense charge for year 10% × 10,400	1,040
	4,160		4,160
		19X9	
		Balance b/d	2,480

Plant and machinery — disposals

19X8	£	19X8	£
Plant and machinery	2,400	Plant allowance	600
		Provision for depreciation	1,680
		Loss on disposal	120
	2,400		2,400

(b) **Motor vehicles**

19X8	£	19X8	£
Balance b/d	3,600	Disposal	2,100
Disposal — allowance	1,500	Balance c/d	6,300
Cash — balance	3,300		
	8,400		8,400
19X9			
Balance b/d	6,300		

Motor vehicles — provision for depreciation

19X8	£	19X8	£
Disposals (W1)	840	Balance b/d (W1)	1,140
Balance c/d	1,560	Depreciation expense — charge for year 20% × £6,300	1,260
	2,400		2,400
		19X9	
		Balance b/d	1,560

Motor vehicles – disposals

19X8	£	19X8	£
Motor vehicles	2,100	Motor vehicles – allowance	1,500
Profit on disposal	240	Provision for depreciation (W1)	840
	2,340		2,340

Workings

Depreciation at 1 January 19X8:

(a) **Plant and machinery:**

		£
Purchased 19X1	Cost £2,400	
	Depreciation 7 years @ 10% × £2,400	1,680
Purchased 19X2	Cost £1,500	
	Depreciation 6 years @ 10% × £1,500	900
Purchased 19X5	Cost £1,800	
	Depreciation 3 years @ 10% × £1,800	540
Accumulated depreciation		3,120

(b) **Motor vehicles:**

		£
Purchased 19X6	Cost £2,100	
	Depreciation 2 years @ 20% × £2,100	840
Purchased 19X7	Cost £1,500	
	Depreciation 1 year @ 20% × £1,500	300
		1,140

8 MITCHELL

Vehicles

19X6–19X7	£	19X6–19X7	£
Balance b/d	77,600	Jaguar – Disposal	8,160
Cortina – Disposals (allowance)	2,400	Renault – Disposal	5,600
– Cash (balance)	4,240	Escort – Disposal	4,800
Mini – Disposal (allowance)	4,000		
– Cash (balance)	400	Balance c/d	76,080
Bedford – Cash	6,000		
	94,640		94,640
19X7–19X8			
Balance b/d	76,080		

Provision for depreciation

19X6–19X7	£	19X6–19X7	£
Jaguar – Disposal (W1)	4,718	Balance b/d	43,520
Renault – Disposal (W1)	2,450		
Escort – Disposal (W1)	3,281		
Balance c/d	33,071		
	43,520		43,520
		19X6–19X7	
		Balance b/d	33,071
Balance c/d	43,823	Depreciation expense	
		25% (76,080 – 33,071)	10,752
	43,823		43,823
		19X7–19X8	
		Balance b/d	43,823

Disposals

19X6–19X7	£	19X6–19X7	£
Jaguar – vehicles	8,160	Jaguar – Provision for depc	4,718
Renault – vehicles	5,600	Renault – Provision for depc	2,450
Escort – vehicles	4,800	Escort – Provision for depc	3,281
		Jaguar allowance – plant	2,400
		Renault allowance – plant	4,000
		Escort – cash	240
		Loss on disposals	1,471
	18,560		18,560

Workings

Depreciation on disposals:

			£
(a)	Jaguar – Cost		8,160
	Depreciation 19X3–19X4		2,040
			6,120
	Depreciation 19X4–19X5		1,530
			4,590
	Depreciation 19X5–19X6		1,148
	NBV at 1 August 19X6		3,442
	Accumulated depreciation		4,718

			£
(b)	Renault – Cost		5,600
	Depreciation 19X4–19X5		1,400
			4,200
	Depreciation 19X5–19X6		1,050
	NBV at 1 August 19X6		3,150
	Accumulated depreciation		2,450

			£
(c)	Escort – Cost		4,800
	Depreciation 19X2–19X3		1,200
			3,600
	Depreciation 19X3–19X4		900
			2,700
	Depreciation 19X4–19X5		675
			2,025
	Depreciation 19X5–19X6		506
	NBV at 1 August 19X6		1,519
	Accumulated depreciation		3,281

9 ROVER

(a)

Plant account

	£		£
Balance b/d – 30.9.X6	410,100	Disposals	46,800
Cash	81,400	Balance c/d	444,700
	491,500		491,500
Balance b/d	444,700		

Provision for depreciation account

	£		£
Disposals (W1)	27,630	Balance b/d	159,180
Balance c/d	131,550		
	159,180		159,180

	£		£
Balance c/d	194,180	Balance b/d	131,550
		Depreciation expense – charge for year 20% (444,700 – 131,550)	62,630
	194,180		194,180
		Balance b/d	194,800

Depreciation expense account

	£		£
Provision for depreciation	62,630	Profit and loss account	62,630
	62,630		62,630

Disposal account

	£		£
Plant	46,800	Provision for depreciation (W1)	27,630
		Cash	16,212
		Loss on disposals	2,958
	46,800		46,800

(b) **Extract from the balance sheet as at 30 September 19X7:**

	Cost £	Depreciation £	Net £
Fixed assets			
Land and buildings	520,000	–	520,000
Plant	444,700	194,180	250,520
	964,700	194,180	770,520

Workings

Depreciation on plant sold:

	£
Cost (19X2 to 19X3)	46,800
Depreciation 19X2 to 19X3	9,360
	37,440
Depreciation 19X3 to 19X4	7,488
carried forward	29,952

	£
brought forward	29,952
Depreciation 19X4 to 19X5	5,990
	23,962
Depreciation 19X5 to 19X6	4,792
Net book value at 30 September 19X6	19,170

Accumulated depreciation at 30 September 19X6 is £27,630.

10 J. FOSTER

(a)   **Asset account**

Balance at 1 Jan 19X7	8,000	Balance at 31 Dec 19X7	8,800
Modification	800		
	8,800		8,800

Provision for depreciation

Balance at 31 Dec 19X7	4,320	Balance at 1 Jan 19X7	3,200
		Depreciation for 19X7 (W1)	1,120
	4,320		4,320

Profit and loss account (extract)

Depreciation	1,120
Maintenance and replacements (W2)	750

Workings:

1. The net book value of the asset is to be written off over the remaining useful life which is a **further** 5 years.

Asset (cost)	8,800
Depreciation to date	3,200
	5,600
Depreciation 1/5th	1,120

2. The £500 for renewal has been charged to profit and loss account as it would appear to have no connection with the improvements which extend the useful life.

(b) Capital expenditure is expenditure incurred in the acquisition of fixed assets, or in the subsequent alteration or improvement of such assets for the purpose of increasing their profit earning capacity. So it must be considered whether:

(i) the life of the asset is extended;
(ii) the operating costs are reduced;
(iii) the output is increased.

If any of these is the case then it is capital expenditure.

If the expenditure merely **maintains** the revenue earning capacity (i.e., repairs and renewals) then it is revenue expenditure.

11 HUCKNALL HAULIERS LTD

(a)   Lorries account

	£		£
19X3 Cash	2,000		
19X4 Cash	3,000		
19X5 Cash	4,000	19X5 Disposals	2,000
		19X5 Balance c/f.	7,000
	9,000		9,000
19X6 Balance b/d	7,000		

Provision for depreciation

	£		£
19X5 Disposals	845	19X3 Depreciation expense (P & L)	480
19X5 Balance c/d	720	19X4 Depreciation expense	1,085
	1,565		1,565
		19X5 Balance b/d	720
19X5 Balance c/d	2,227	19X5 Depreciation expense (P & L)	1,507
	2,227		2,227
		19X6 Balance b/d	2,227

Disposals account

	£		£
19X5 Vehicles	2,000	19X5 Depreciation provision	845
		19X5 Cash	1,000
		19X5 P/L A/c. Loss on Disposal	155
	2,000		2,000

Balance sheet as at 31 December 19X5

Fixed assets	Cost	Depreciation	Net
	£	£	£
Vehicles	7,000	2,227	4,773

(b) **Arguments pro**

(i) The reducing balance method gives a heavy charge in early years when repair bills are light. And a light charge later on when repair bills can be expected to be significant. Depreciation thus compensates repairs and gives a similar combined cost each year.

(ii) The real value of a vehicle falls away quickly after purchase, so that a heavy initial charge reflects the facts of the case.

(iii) The impact of obsolescence or any other reason for reducing the working life of the vehicle will be reduced if a significant part of the cost is written off in early life.

(iv) A balance against which depreciation can be charged remains if the vehicle has a longer life than that now estimated as the vehicle is never fully depreciated.

Arguments against

(i) The cost should be spread evenly over the years of the life, or should be spread according to use. This method follows neither principle.

(ii) Any attempt to even out the annual cost for depreciation and repairs may not reflect the true cost of using the vehicle each year and thus the accountant will allocate cost in such a way as to show a profit which is incorrect. As vehicles do get older they cost more and operating them is less profitable.

(iii) Difficulties of calculation, especially at the time of disposal.

Workings

Depreciation 19X3 = 24% × £2,000 = £480
Depreciation 19X4 = 24% × (£5,000 − £480) = £1,085
Depreciation 19X5 = 24% × (£7,000 − £720) = £1,507

12 DISPOSALS LTD

(a)

Lorries account

19X5		£	19X5		£
1.4	Balance b/d	67,500	30.6	Lorry Disposal– DV 100	7,000
1.7	Bank–IV 600	15,000	1.12	Lorry Disposal – IV 600	15,000
1.12	Lorry Disposal A/c IV 700	10,000	19X6		
1.12	Bank–IV 700	20,000	31.1	Lorry disposal – EV 200	15,000
19X6			31.3	Balance c/d	100,500
1.2	Bank–IV 800	25,000			
		137,500			137,500
1.4	Balance b/d	100,500			

Provision for depreciation account

19X5		£	19X5		£
30.6	Lorry Disposal–DV 100	5,600	1.4	Balance b/d	30,900
19X6			19X6		
31.1	Lorry Disposal–EV 200	6,000	31.3	Depreciation expense P & L charge for the year (20% × £100,500)	20,100
31.3	Balance c/d	39,400			
		51,000			51,000
			1.4	Balance b/d	39,400

Lorry disposal account

19X5		£	19X5		£
20.6	Lorries–DV 100	7,000	30.6	Lorry Depreciation– DV 100	5,600
1.12	Lorries–IV 600	15,000		Bank–cash received– DV 100	2,000
19X6			1.12	Lorries–IV 700, part exchange	10,000
31.1	Lorries–EV 200	15,000	19X6		
			31.1	Depreciation–EV 200	9,000
				Bank–EV 200, cash received	5,000
			31.3	Profit and loss–loss on exchange	5,400
		37,000			37,000

(b) Fixed assets   £
    Lorries, at cost   100,500
    Less: Provision for depreciation   39,400

                                                                                             61,100

Workings

Disposals	DV 100 £	EV 200 £	IV 600 £	Total £
Cost	7,000	15,000	15,000	37,000
Less: Depreciation to 31.1.X5	5,600(1)	9,000(2)	—	14,600
	1,400	6,000	15,000	22,400
Sale proceeds	2,000	5,000	10,000	17,000
Deficit/(Surplus) on disposal	(600)	1,000	5,000	5,400(3)

Notes:

(1) for four years
(2) for three years
(3) written off to the profit and loss account

13 KIPLING

Motor vehicles account

	£		£
Balance b/d	75,400	Disposals (b)	3,200
Creditors (a)	3,500	Disposals (c)	4,400
Disposals – proceeds (c)	2,500	Balance c/d	73,800
	81,400		81,400
Balance b/d	73,800		

Provision for depreciation account

	£		£
Disposals (b)	2,400	Balance b/d	36,300
Disposals (c)	2,200	Depreciation expense	18,450
Balance c/d	50,150	(d)(25% × £73,800)	
	54,750		54,750
		Balance b/d	50,150

Depreciation expense

	£		£
Provision for depreciation (d)	18,450	Profit and loss account	18,450

Disposals account

	£		£
Motor vehicles (b)	3,200	Provision for depreciation (b)	2,400
Motor vehicles (c)	4,000	Provision for depreciation (c)	2,200
		Motor vehicles (d)	2,500
		Loss on disposals – profit and loss account	500
	7,600		7,600

14 GREENACRES LTD

(a) **Repair service workshop building account**

19X7		£	19X7		£
Jan 1	Building – from stock	10,000	Dec 31	Balance c/d	14,600
Jan 1	Foundation costs etc.	1,000			
Jan 1	Painting costs	600			
Jan 1	Heating system etc.	3,000			
		14,600			14,600
19X8			19X8		
Jan 1	Balance b/d	14,600	Dec 31	Balance c/d	16,900
Jan 1	Heating system additions	700			
June 30	Partition walls	1,600			
		16,900			16,900
19X9			19X9		
Jan 1	Balance b/d	16,900	Early	Repair service workshop disposal	16,900
		16,900			16,900

Provision for depreciation account

19X7		£	19X7		£
Dec 31	Balance c/d	1,460	Dec 31	Depreciation for year	1,460
		1,460			1,460

19X8		£	19X8		£
Dec 31	Balance c/d	3,150	Jan 1	Balance b/d	1,460
			Dec 31	Depreciation for year	1,690
		3,150			3,150
19X9			19X9		
Early	Workshop disposal	3,150	Jan 1	Balance b/d	3,150
		3,150			3,150

(b) **Repair service workshop building disposal account**

19X9		£			£
Repair service workshop		16,900	Provision for depreciation		3,150
			Cash proceeds		8,000
			Profit and loss account — loss on sale		5,750
		16,900			16,900

15 SOULT

Bad debts expense

19X6	£	19X6	£
Debtors written off	2,000		
Provision for doubtful debts	950	Profit and loss account	2,950
	2,950	Balance c/d	2,950
19X7		19X7	
Debtors written off	2,500	Provision for doubtful debts	350
		Profit and loss account	2,150
	2,500		2,500

Provision for doubtful debts

19X6	£	19X6	£
		Balance b/d	3,200
Balance c/d	4,150	Bad debts expense (increase in general provision)	950
	4,150		4,150

19X7	£	19X7	£
Bad debts expense (decrease in general provision)	350	Balance b/d	4,150
Balance c/d	3,800		
	4,150		4,150
19X8		19X8	
		Balance b/d	3,800

16 NEY

Sales ledger control account (total debtors)

19X2–19X3	£	19X2–19X3	£
Credit sales	120,000	Cash received	95,000
		Bad debts written off	500
		Balance c/d	24,500
	120,000		120,000
19X3–19X4		19X3–19X4	
Balance b/d	24,500	Cash received	130,000
Credit sales	150,000	Bad debts written off	1,500
		Balance c/d	43,000
	174,500		174,500
19X4–19X5			
Balance b/d	43,000		

Provision for doubtful debts

19X2–19X3	£	19X2–19X3	£
Balance c/d	1,225	Bad debts expense	1,225
19X3–19X4		19X3–19X4	
		Balance b/d	1,225
Balance c/d	2,150	Bad debts expense (increase in provision)	925
	2,150		2,150
		19X4–19X5	
		Balance b/d	2,150

Bad debts expense

	£		£
19X2–19X3		19X2–19X3	
Debtors	500	Profit and loss account	1,725
Provision for doubtful debts	1,225		
	1,725		1,725
19X3–19X4		19X3–19X4	
Debtors	1,500	Cash (bad debts recovered)	100
Provision for doubtful debts	925	Profit and loss account	2,325
	2,425		2,425

17 GROUCHY

Sales ledger control account (total debtors)

	£		£
Balance b/d	9,619	Provision for doubtful debts (b)	165
Bad debts expense (a)	45	Bad debts expense (d)	56
		Balance c/d	9,443
	9,664		9,664
Balance b/d	9,443		

Provision for doubtful debts

	£		£
SLCA (b)	165	Balance b/d	478
Bad debts expense (e)	73	(Murat £165)	
		(Brune £73)	
		(General £240)	
		Bad debts expense (c)	143
Balance c/d	422	Bad debts expense (increase in provision)	39
	660		660
		Balance b/d	422
		(Moncey £143)	
		(General £279)	

Bad debts expense

	£		£
Provision for doubtful debts (c)	143	SLCA (a)	45
SLCA (d)	56	Provision released (e)	73
Provision (increase in general)	39	Profit and loss account	120
	238		238

General provision = 3% × £(9,443 − 143)
= £279
Increase during 19X5 = £279 − £240
= £39

18 ARNOLD

Bad debts expense

19X4–19X5	£	19X4–19X5	£
Debts written off	73		
Provision for doubtful debts			
specific	298		
general	230	Profit and loss account	601
	601		601
19X5–19X6		19X5–19X6	
Debtors written off (Clara)	56	Bad debt recovered (Enoch)	10
Provision for doubtful debts		Doubtful debt recovered	
specific provision	36	(Bennett)	21
general provision	38	Doubtful debt recovered	
Profit and loss account	1	(Darius)	100
	131		131

Provision for doubtful debts

19X4–19X5	£	19X4–19X5	£
		Bad debts expense	
		specific provisions	298
Balance c/d	528	general provision	230
	528		528

19X5–19X6	£	19X5–19X6	£
Bad debts expense		Balance b/d	528
debt recovered (Bennett)	21	Bad debts expense	
debt recovered (Darius)	100	specific provision	36
Debtors		general provision (increase)	38
provision released (Clayhanger)	50		
provision released (Darius)	75		
provision released (Edwin)	52		
Balance c/d	304		
	602		602
		19X6–19X7	
		Balance b/d	
		specific	36
		general	268

Debtors

19X5–19X6	£	19X5–19X6	£
Balance at 31 May 19X5	4,898	Cash received (working (c))	41,369
Credit sales	42,100	Bad debt written off (Clara)	56
		Provision released	
		(Clayhanger)	50
		Provision released (Darius)	75
		Provision released (Edwin)	52
		Balance c/d	5,396
	46,998		46,998
19X6–19X7			
Balance b/d	5,396		

Workings

(a) General provision at 31 May 19X5
         = 5% (£4,898 − £298)
         = £230

(b) General provision at 31 May 19X6
         = 5% (£5,396 − £36)
         (i.e., debtors less specific provisions)
         = £268

(c) This excludes the £10 received from Enoch.

19 DOCKS LTD
(a)

Provision for doubtful debts

31 March 19X0 Balance c/d	18,500	1 April 19X0 Balance b/d		13,000
		31 March 19X0 Bad debts expense (increase in provision)		5,500
	18,500			18,500
31 March 19X1 Bad debts expense (decrease in provision)	1,000	1 April 19X0 Balance b/d		18,500
31 March 19X1 Balance c/d	17,500			
	18,500			18,500
		1 April 19X1 Balance b/d		17,500
31 March 19X2 Balance c/d	30,000	31 March 19X2 Bad debts expense (increase in provision)		12,500
	30,000			30,000
		1 April 19X2 Balance b/d		30,000

Bad debts expense

31 March 19X0 Debts written off	1,680			
31 March 19X0 Provision made	5,500	31 March 19X0 Profit and loss		7,180
	7,180			7,180
31 March 19X1 Debts written off	1,200	31 March 19X1 Provision released		1,000
		31 March 19X1 Profit and loss		200
	1,200			1,200
31 March 19X2 Debts written off	6,200			
31 March 19X2 Provision made	12,500	31 March 19X2 Profit and loss		18,700
	18,700			18,700

Balance sheet extracts at 31 March

	19X0	19X1	19X2
Trade debtors	185,000	140,000	200,000
Less: Provision for bad debts	18,500	17,500	30,000
	166,500	122,500	170,000

(b) When the debt was written off in 19X0 this would have reduced the profit by £1,000: the subsequent recovery will not affect the results for 19X0.

When the debt is recovered the treatment is to debit cash and credit the bad debts expense account with the £1,000. This means that, in the year ended 31 March 19X1, there will be a net **credit** of £800 to the profit and loss account.

20 RICKWOOD

(a)

Stock account

19X0		£	19X0		£
31 Dec	Trading account	75,000		Balance c/d	75,000
19X1			19X1		
1 Jan	Balance b/d	75,000	31 Dec	Trading account	75,000
31 Dec	Trading account	120,000		Balance c/d	120,000
		195,000			195,000
19X2					
1 Jan	Balance b/d	120,000			

Purchases account

19X0		£	19X0		£
	Cash	480,000	31 Dec	Trading account	480,000
19X1					
	Cash	580,000	31 Dec	Trading account	580,000

Sales account

19X0		£	19X0		£
31 Dec	Trading account	560,000		Cash	560,000
19X1			19X1		
31 Dec	Trading account	700,000		Cash	700,000

(b) **Trading account for year ended 31 December 19X0**

	£	£
Sales		560,000
Purchases	480,000	
Less: Closing stock	75,000	
Cost of goods sold		405,000
Gross profit		155,000

Trading account for year ended 31 December 19X1

	£	£
Sales		700,000
Opening stock	75,000	
Purchases	580,000	
	655,000	
Less: Closing stock	120,000	
Cost of goods sold		535,000
Gross profit		165,000

21 A BUSINESSMAN

(a) (i) **Cost of sales — FIFO**

Purchases:

		£
1,200 × 1.00 =		1,200
1,000 × 1.05 =		1,050
600 × 1.10 =		660
900 × 1.20 =		1,080
800 × 1.25 =		1,000
700 × 1.30 =		910
5,200		5,900

Closing stock

300 × 1.25 = 375	
700 × 1.30 = 910	
1,000	1,285

Cost of sales (5,200 − 1,000 = 4,200)   4,615

(ii) **Cost of sales — LIFO**

	£	£	£
Purchases as above			5,900
Closing stock			
700 × 1.00	= 700		
300 × 1.30	= 390		
		1,090	
Cost of sales			4,810

(b) **Balance sheet**

	FIFO basis £	LIFO basis £
Stock	1,285	1,090
Balance at bank (W1)	7,050	7,050
	8,335	8,140
Creditors	570	570
	7,765	7,570
Capital introduced	6,000	6,000
Add: Profit (W2)	1,765	1,570
	7,765	7,570

Workings

1. **Bank account**

	£		£
Capital	6,000	Purchases	1,200
Sales	1,360	Purchases	1,050
Sales	1,140	Purchases	660
Sales	2,200	Purchases	1,080
Sales	2,600	Purchases	1,000
Sales	820	Purchases	910
		Expenses: (1,740 − 570)	1,170
		Balance	7,050
	14,120		14,120

79

2. **Profit and loss account**

	FIFO	LIFO
	£	£
Sales	8,120	8,120
Cost of sales	4,615	4,810
Gross profit	3,505	3,310
Expenses	1,740	1,740
Profit	1,765	1,570

22 FISHER

(a)

	X			Y		
	Units	£ per unit	£	Units	£ per unit	£
Sales	30	6	180	20	4	80
Purchases	10	4	40	15	2	30
	15	4.5	67.5	10	3	30
	20	5	100			
	45		207.5	25		60
Closing stock	15	5	75	5	3	15
Cost of goods sold	30		132.5	20		45
Gross profit			47.5			35
Less: Provision for loss (see note)			—			80
Net profit/(loss)			47.5			(45)

Note: For alternative treatment, see (b) below:

(b) SSAP 9 requires that stocks should be valued at the 'lower of cost and net realisable value'. This is an example of the application of the concepts of prudence and matching, i.e., that a loss should be recognised as soon as it is foreseen and that no account should be taken of profits until earned.

Cost can be calculated in many ways but SSAP 9 requires that it should be as close as possible to **actual** cost and, therefore, replacement cost is not satisfactory under historic cost accounting. Two of the more commonly used methods of establishing cost are the averaging method and the First in First Out method. The latter was used in (a) above and it assumes that the items of closing stock will be those which were bought at the latest dates.

With regard to the possible default by a customer, once again the concept of prudence is applied, i.e., that a loss should be recognised as soon as it is foreseen. When there is doubt as to the recovery of a debt, a provision should be made to reduce the value of the debtor to the amount of cash that will be received. In (a) it has been assumed that **no** cost will be recovered. Alternatively it might be that the goods can be reclaimed: in which case the provision would only be £35, i.e., the gross profit earned on the sale.

23 RINGERS LTD

(a) Corrected stock valuation

	£
Stock valuation at 8 May 19X0	23,850
Less: Purchases, net of returns, in last 8 days	(3,700)
Add: Cost of goods sold in last 8 days (W1)	2,048
Less: Worthless stock	(700)
Less: Overcast of stock sheets	(140)
Less: Stationery stock	(1,400)
Add: Goods on sale or return	200
Stock valuation at 30 April 19X0	20,158

(b) Corrected gross and net profit

	£
Gross profit per draft accounts	158,000
Less: Adjustment to stock valuation	(3,692)
Add: Unrecorded sale $\frac{100}{80} \times £200$	250
Corrected gross profit	154,558

	£
Net profit per draft accounts	31,640
Less: Adjustment to stock valuation apart from stationery stock	(2,292)
Add: Unrecorded sale	250
Corrected net profit	29,598
Net current assets per draft accounts	24,600
Less: Adjustment to stock valuation apart from stationery stock	(2,292)
Add: Unrecorded debtor	250
Corrected net current assets	22,558

Working

1. Cost of goods sold from 30 April 19X0 to 8 May 19X0

	£
Sales	2,900
Returns	(340)
	2,560
Less: Gross profit of 20%	(512)
	2,048

24 PRICE

Rent

	£		£
Per T.B.	2,000	Profit and loss account	2,400
Accrual c/d	400		
	2,400		2,400
		Accrual b/d	400

Rates

Per T.B.	900	Prepayment c/d	150
		P & L Account	750
	900		900
Prepayment b/d	150		

Plant and machinery depreciation

	£		£
Depreciation provision	750	P & L Account	750

Depreciation provision

		Per T.B.	1,500
		Plant and machinery depreciation	750
			2,250

Stock

Per T.B.	3,600	Trading account	3,600
Trading account	4,000		

Insurance

Per T.B.	200	Prepayment c/d	50
		Profit and loss account	150
	200		200
Prepayment b/d	50		

Bad debts expense

Bad debt provision	50	Profit and loss account	50

Bad debt provision

		Per T.B.	350
		Bad debts expense	50
			400

4 Books of prime entry

This is a very short section as examination questions devoted entirely to the books of prime entry are very few in number. They are included so that when references are made to day books or journals in subsequent chapters, students will remember how these books are prepared.

The journal, however, is used as a tool in many examination questions as will be seen later, particularly in the chapters on suspense accounts and adjustments to profits, where the examiner often requires the answers in journal form.

QUESTIONS

1 ZOFF

Zoff started up a small business on 1 April 19X2. During the month of April the following transactions took place:

		£
1 April	Introduced cash as capital	10,000
1 April	Bought a second-hand typewriter for cash	300
2 April	Made purchases for cash	550
3 April	Made further purchases on credit from Conti	620
6 April	Made sales for cash	270
7 April	Paid three months' rent by cash	210
10 April	Made further sales on credit to Tardelli	400
13 April	Bought a van on credit from Graziani, paying a deposit of £500 and agreeing to pay the balance of £3,500 in May	4,000
15 April	Paid £620 to Conti in settlement of debt	620
20 April	Made further sales on credit to Tardelli	350
27 April	Received £300 cash from Tardelli	300

You are required to record the above transactions in journal form.

10 marks

2 DAWSON

Dawson has the following purchases and sales on credit for the month of February 19X7:

1 February	Purchased from Smith Bros – linen £37, silk £25.
4 February	Purchased from W. Mills – woollen goods £46, cotton goods £33.
8 February	Sold to A. Thompson – linen £21, cotton goods £26.
12 February	Purchased from F. Jackson – cotton goods £39, silk £28.
17 February	Sold to T. Robinson – linen £17, silk £18, cotton goods £24.
23 February	Sold to J. Williams – woollen goods £30, linen £14.

He also paid and received cash as follows:

10 February	Paid to Smith Bros £62
20 February	Received from A. Thompson £47
28 February	Paid to W. Mills £50

At 1 February 19X7 the balance on his cash account was a debit balance of £350.

You are required to enter the above transactions in the purchases day book, the sales day book and the cash book and to make the necessary postings to the personal accounts and to the purchases account and sales account. Your day books should include suitable analysis columns.

12 marks

3 MEADOWS

(a) You are required to enter the following transactions in a petty cash book, having analysis columns for motor expenses, sundry expenses, postage and stationery, and ledger accounts. The amount spent is reimbursed on the last day of each month.

19X2

1 April	Received cash float of £250
3 April	Paid £15 for petrol
4 April	Bought stationery £15
5 April	Paid postage £27
9 April	Paid J. Smith – ledger account – £8
11 April	Paid £13 for petrol
12 April	Paid garage bill of £15
16 April	Paid £8 for office cleaning
18 April	Paid £10 for petrol
19 April	Paid J. Jones – ledger account – £12
23 April	Paid window cleaner £10
24 April	Bought coffee, tea, sugar £20
24 April	Bought stationery £10
25 April	Paid £15 for petrol
29 April	Paid postage £25

(b) What postings will be made at the end of the month?

10 marks

ANSWERS

1 ZOFF

Date	Accounts		Debit £	Credit £
1 April	Debit	Cash	10,000	
	Credit	Capital		10,000
	being introduction of initial capital			
1 April	Debit	Typewriter	300	
	Credit	Cash		300
	being cash purchase of typewriter			
2 April	Debit	Purchases	550	
	Credit	Cash		550
	being cash purchases			
3 April	Debit	Purchases	620	
	Credit	Conti		620
	being credit purchases			
6 April	Debit	Cash	270	
	Credit	Sales		270
	being cash sales			
7 April	Debit	Rent	210	
	Credit	Cash		210
	being payment of 3 months' rent			
10 April	Debit	Tardelli	400	
	Credit	Sales		400
	being credit sales			
13 April	Debit	Van	4,000	
	Credit	Cash		500
		Graziani		3,500
	being purchase of van for £4,000, paying a deposit of £500			
15 April	Debit	Conti	620	
	Credit	Cash		620
	being settlement of debt to Conti			
20 April	Debit	Tardelli	350	
	Credit	Sales		350
	being credit sales			
27 April	Debit	Cash	300	
	Credit	Tardelli		300
	being receipt of cash from Tardelli in part settlement of debt			

2 DAWSON

Purchases day book

Date	Supplier	Goods inwards note	Total	Linen	Silk	Woollen goods	Cotton goods
			£	£	£	£	£
1 February	Smith Bros	321	62	37	25		
4 February	W Mills	322	79			46	33
12 February	F Jackson	323	67		28		39
			208	37	53	46	72

Sales day book

Date	Customer	Invoice	Total	Linen	Silk	Woollen goods	Cotton goods
			£	£	£	£	£
8 February	A Thompson	465	47	21			26
17 February	T Robinson	466	59	17	18		24
23 February	J Williams	467	44	14		30	
			150	52	18	30	50

Cash book

		£			£
1 Feb	Balance b/d	350	10 Feb Smith Bros		62
20 Feb	A Thompson	47	28 Feb W Mills		50
			28 Feb Balance c/d		285
		397			397
1 Mar	Balance b/d	285			

Personal accounts
Creditors

Smith Bros

Cash	62	PDB	62

W Mills

Cash	50	PDB	79
Bal c/d	29		
	79		79
		Bal b/d	29

F Jackson

		PDB	67

Debtors

A Thompson

SDB	47	Cash	47

T Robinson

SDB	59		

J Williams

SDB	44		

Nominal ledger

Purchases account

PDB	208		

Sales account

		SDB	150

3 MEADOWS

(a) **Petty cash book**

Debit			Credit						
		Total £			Total £	Motor expenses £	Sundry expenses £	Postage and stationery £	Ledger account £
1 April	Cash book	250	3 April	Petrol	15	15			
			4 April	Stationery	15			15	
			5 April	Postage	27			27	
			9 April	J Smith	8				8
			11 April	Petrol	13	13			
			12 April	Garage	15	15			
			16 April	Office cleaning	8		8		
			18 April	Petrol	10	10			
			19 April	J Jones	12				12
			23 April	Window cleaner	10		10		
			24 April	Coffee etc.	20		20		
			24 April	Stationery	10			10	
			25 April	Petrol	15	15			
			29 April	Postage	25			25	
					203	68	38	77	20
30 April	Cash book	203	30 April	Balance c/d	250				
		453			453				
1 May	Balance b/d	250							

90

(b) The postings to be made at the end of the month will be:

		£
Debit	Motor expenses	68
Debit	Sundry expenses	38
Debit	Postage and stationery	77
Debit	J Smith	8
Debit	J Jones	12

If Meadows maintains a purchase ledger control account then it will also be necessary to make the following posting:

		£
Debit	PLCA	20

5 Control accounts

This is a popular topic with examiners as it is a good test of a student's understanding of double entry. The typical question requires a reconciliation between the control account and the subsidiary ledger. The presentation of the answer is important: the errors in the control account must be corrected there and the adjustments to the ledger accounts should be shown as a reconciliation.

Throughout this book, it is assumed that the control account is the double entry (not the individual accounts in the subsidiary ledger) unless it is stated otherwise.

QUESTIONS

1 SARGENT

From the following information, you are required to write up the sales ledger control account and purchases ledger control account for Sargent:

		£
(a)	Amount due to suppliers 1 May 19X9	24,016
	Amounts due from customers 1 May 19X9	23,420

(b) Transactions for the month of May:

	£
Sales	13,120
Purchases	10,140
Cash paid to suppliers	8,650
Bills payable accepted	450
Cash received from customers	14,200
Discount from suppliers	480
New bills receivable	60
Purchases returns	70
Discount allowed to customers	540
Sales returns	130
Bad debts written off	70
Bills receivable dishonoured	240
Interest charged to customers	70
Cash paid to customers on outstanding credits	30
Empty containers returned to suppliers (charged originally as purchases)	210
Debtors and creditors accounts offset by contra	150

10 marks

2 EXCEL STORES LTD

The bookkeeper of Excel Stores Ltd prepared a schedule of balances of individual suppliers' accounts from the creditors ledger of 30 June 19X4 and arrived at a total of £86,538.28.

He passed the schedule over to the accountant who compared this total with the closing balance on the creditors ledger control account reproduced below:

Creditors ledger control

19X4		£	19X4		£
30 June	Purchases returns	560.18	1 June	Balance b/d	89,271.13
30 June	Bank	96,312.70	30 June	Purchases	100,483.49
30 June	Balance c/d	84,688.31	30 June	Discount received	2,656.82
			30 June	Debtors ledger control (contras)	3,049.75
		192,561.19			195,261.19
			1 July	Balance b/d	84,688.31

During his investigation into the discrepancy between the two figures, the accountant discovered a number of errors in the control account and the individual ledger accounts and schedule. You may assume that the total of each item posted to the control account is correct except to the extent that they are dealt with in the list below.

(a) One supplier had been paid £10.22 out of petty cash. This had been correctly posted to his personal account but has been omitted from the control account.

(b) The credit side of one supplier's personal account had been under-added by £30.00.

(c) A credit balance on a supplier's account had been transposed from £548.14 to £584.41 when extracted on to the schedule.

(d) The balance on one supplier's account of £674.32 had been completely omitted from the schedule.

(e) Discounts received of £12.56 and £8.13 had been posted to the wrong side of two individual creditors' accounts.

(f) Goods costing £39.60 had been returned to the supplier but this transaction had been completely omitted from the returns day book.

You are required to:

(a) Prepare an account starting with the original closing balance on the creditors ledger control account, then identifying and correcting the errors in that account and concluding with an amended closing balance. **9 marks**

(b) Prepare a statement starting with the original total of the schedule of individual creditors then identifying and correcting errors in that schedule and concluding with an amended total. **7 marks**

Total 16 marks

3 SEA FOODS

The sales ledger supervisor of Sea Foods has been taken ill and the inexperienced ledger clerk is having problems balancing the ledgers for the month of February. He presents you with the following information and asks for your help.

The balances on the individual accounts at 28 February are:

	£
R. Herring & Sons	100
S. Newt Ltd	1,160
C. Lion & Co Ltd	2,835
Fish Food Ltd	490
The Eating Plaice	195
Fred's Restaurant	235
H. Addock	180
Trout Farms	740
	5,935

The balance brought forward on the control account for 1 February is £6,830.

The clerk says he has entered the following items on the customers' accounts cards to get the above balances:

	Sales £	Cash received £	Discount allowed £	Goods returned £
R. Herring & Son	250	190		
S. Newt Ltd	490	960	40	
C. Lion & Co Ltd	365	745	15	125
Fish Food Ltd	45	85		30
The Eating Plaice	–	25		
Fred's Restaurant	70	50		
H. Addock	230	30		
Trout Farms	510	290	30	
	1,960	2,375	85	155

When he enters the above totals in the sales ledger control account it does not balance to the total of the customer's accounts.

On investigation you find that:

(a) Sales to S. Newt Ltd have been mistakenly entered on S. Newt's account in the creditors ledger.

(b) A contra has been entered on the account of Fred's Restaurant for £65 against his account on the creditors ledger. This has not been recorded on the control account.

(c) An invoice for £210 in respect of C. Lion & Co Ltd has been omitted from the list of sales and is not included in the individual account balances on 28 February.

(d) The account for Mr C. Horse showing a balance of £165 has been removed from the sales ledger as the debt has been proven to be bad.

(e) The cheque from R. Herring & Son has been returned by the bank marked 'refer to drawer'.

(f) A credit note for £450 has been posted to the account of Trout Farms Ltd but not to the control account.

(g) The cash received from C. Lion & Co had not been entered in the customer account card.

(h) The chief accountant has been looking at the account of Codds Ltd. You have reason to believe the customer account card showing a credit balance of £185 is locked in his filing cabinet.

You are required to:

(a) complete the sales ledger control account; and

(b) reconcile the list of individual debtors account balances to the control account balance.

15 marks

4 SOUTHERN APIARIES

The following information has been taken from the books of Southern Apiaries in respect of the year ended 31 March 19X9:

	£
Sales ledger control account balance at 1 April 19X8	49,251
Returns by credit customers	6,144
Credit sales	544,382
Cash sales	36,243
Settlement discounts allowed to credit customers	1,316
Cash received from credit customers	526,139

The following additional information has been established:

(a) The list of balances on the sales ledger at 31 March 19X9 totals £62,183; a similar list at 31 March 19X8 agreed with the sales ledger control account at that date.

(b) Credit balances on the sales ledger at 31 March 19X9 amounting to £1,066 were entered as debit balances on the list extracted at that date.

(c) An amount of £62, received during the year from Salmon & Co, a supplier, in settlement of a debit balance on the bought ledger was entered in the sales ledger column in the cash book, and was posted to the account of Solomon Brothers in the sales ledger.

(d) Cash received from customers includes £315 in respect of a debt which was written off at 31 March 19X8. This has not been posted to the sales ledger as no account exists.

(e) A sub-total of £3,456 in the sales day book total column has been carried forward as £3,654.

(f) A total in the sales ledger column of the cash book has been undersummed by £100.

(g) An amount of £39 received during the year from H. Brewer & Co Ltd, has been posted to the account of Brewer & Co (Holdings) Ltd.

(h) It was agreed during the year that an amount of £52 owing by M. Brent & Sons would be settled by contra with a similar balance on their account in the bought ledger. No entries have yet been made in respect of this contra.

You are required to prepare the sales ledger control account for the year ended 31 March 19X9 and to reconcile the balance with the list of debtors' balances.

15 marks

5   TOM BROWN LTD

The draft balance sheet at 31 March 19X9 of Tom Brown Ltd included the following items:

	£
Purchases ledger control account	24,782 net balance
Sales ledger control account	37,354 net balance

These control account figures however did not agree with the position at 31 March 19X9 as shown by the lists of balances extracted from the individual creditors' and debtors' accounts.

The list of purchases ledger balances at 31 March 19X9 included the following debit balances:

	£
G. Brook	167
K. River	89

The list of sales ledger balances at 31 March 19X9 included the following credit balances:

	£
L. Bridge	642
S. Tunnel	914

Subsequent investigations revealed the following accounting errors:

(a)   The sales day book for December 19X8 was overcast by £1,500.

(b)   A credit note for goods costing £160 returned to the supplier, T. Street, in September 19X8, was not recorded in the company's books, but the stock records have been adjusted correctly. According to the list of balances T. Street is owed £790 at 31 March 19X9.

(c)   A cheque for £900 received from a customer, P. Bridger Ltd, in February 19X9, was credited, in error, to L. Bridge.
   Note: The account of P. Bridger Ltd in the sales ledger shows a debit balance at 31 March 19X9 of £960.

(d)   In February 19X9, a debt due from T. Wood to the company of £600 was written off as a bad debt. Although the debt has been written off in T. Wood's personal account, no adjustment for this has been made in the relevant control account.

(e)   A payment of £420 to J. King, supplier, in June 19X8, was debited in the purchases account. The invoices making up this amount were correctly entered in the purchase day book.

You are required to produce:

(a) a computation of the corrected balances at 31 March 19X9 of the purchases ledger control account and the sales ledger control account;

(b) an extract of the balance sheet at 31 March 19X9 of Tom Brown Ltd showing the inclusion of the purchases ledger balances and sales ledger balances at 31 March 19X9;
14 marks

(c) explain the importance of control accounts in a modern accounting system.
5 marks
Total 19 marks

6 ABC COMPANY

ABC Company maintains a sales ledger control account in its nominal ledger and keeps the individual account for each customer in a subsidiary debtors ledger. There are 230 accounts in the debtors ledger. At 1 January the balances on the first six accounts were as follows:

	£
B. Archer	290
J. Atwood	456
S. Banks	–
R. Boole	187
F. Bragg	74
T. Charles	371

The total of the balances outstanding in the debtors ledger at 1 January (including the above) was £25,418, and a provision for doubtful debts of £550 was made at that time.

Transactions during January were:

	Sales £	Returns inwards £	Bad debts £	Cheques and cash received £	Cash discounts allowed £
B. Archer	140	20	–	265	10
J. Atwood	291	18	–	103	5
S. Banks	–	–	–	300	–
R. Boole	–	–	187	–	–
F. Bragg	–	–	–	74	–
T. Charles	518	41	–	320	15
All other accounts	14,660	720	470	14,111	470
	15,609	799	657	15,173	500

The cheque received from S. Banks for £300 was payment for a debt which had been written off last year.

98

A cheque for F. Bragg received and banked in the sum of £50 was returned by the bank marked 'refer to drawer'. It must be written back.

The ABC Company wish to provide a sum for doubtful debts equal to 2% of the closing debtors figure.

You are required to head up accounts for the sales ledger control, and the first six accounts in the debtors ledger, with a further account to represent all the other customer accounts. Enter the above transactions, balance all the accounts and check that the ledger agrees with the control account; and write up the provision for doubtful debts and the bad debts expense accounts.

16 marks

7 FERGUSON

(a) The following information has been obtained from the records of Ferguson, electrical retailers, for the year ended 31 March 19X1:

	£
Debtors balances at 1 April 19X0	15,150
Creditors balances at 1 April 19X0	9,803
Credit purchases, per day book	42,133
Cash purchases, per cash book	2,481
Cheque payments (after cash discount of £2,782) to suppliers	37,415
Credits for goods returned to suppliers	3,719
Cash received from debtors	52,144
Provision for doubtful debts at 1 April 19X0	1,534

The sales day book is missing but from various VAT calculations it has been noted that the output tax for the year on credit sales was £7,317. All sales were subject to VAT at 15% during the year.

You are required to write up the purchases ledger control account and sales ledger control account for the year ended 31 March 19X1.

(b) The total of the debtors' balances as listed at 31 March 19X1 was £22,135 and the total of the creditors' balances was £10,165. In attempting to reconcile the control accounts and the subsidiary ledger you discover the following:

(i) A purchase invoice for £1,078 was incorrectly entered in the day book as a credit note.

(ii) Amounts received from debtors include a sum of £3,003, being an income tax refund received and entered in the wrong cash book column.

(iii) An account of £875 was settled by contra between the sales and purchase ledgers but not recorded in the control account.

(iv) The total of a page in the purchase day book has been incorrectly carried forward as £2,351 instead of £3,215.

(v) No entries have been made in respect of the sums received in February and March from a credit card company who remit directly to the business bank account. An account is kept in the debtors ledger and the receipts for credit card sales for these two months were £2,078.

(vi) Credit balances in the debtors ledger of £452 have been listed at 31 March 19X1 as debit balances.

You are required to adjust the control accounts for the above items and to reconcile the adjusted accounts with the total per the list of balances from the subsidiary ledgers.

(c) (i) A company which was supplied during the year with goods to the value of £380 has gone into liquidation and the estimated statement of affairs indicates that no dividend will be paid to ordinary creditors.

(ii) The provision for bad debts at 1 April 19X0 of £1,534 consists of £625 in respect of specific debts and £909 in respect of a general provision. Debts totalling £716 which were outstanding at 1 April 19X0 are considered bad and are to be fully written off. An amount of £476 was previously specifically provided in respect of those debts.

(iii) The general provision for bad debts is to be adjusted to 5% of the debtors balances at 31 March 19X1 (excluding those specifically provided against).

You are required to write up the provision for doubtful debts, the bad debts expense and sales ledger control account to reflect the above items.

20 marks

ANSWERS

1 SARGENT

Sales ledger control account (total debtors)

	£		£
Balance b/d	23,420	Cash received from customers	14,200
Sales	13,120	Bills receivable	60
Dishonoured bills	240	Discount allowed to customers	540
Interest charged	70	Sales returns	130
Cash paid in respect of credit balances	30	Bad debts written off	70
		Contra with PLCA	150
		Balance c/d	21,730
	36,880		36,880
Balance b/d	21,730		

Purchases ledger control account (total creditors)

	£		£
Cash paid to suppliers	8,650	Balance b/d	24,016
Bills payable	450	Purchases	10,140
Discount from suppliers	480		
Purchase returns	70		
Containers returned	210		
Contra with SLCA	150		
Balance c/d	24,146		
	34,156		34,156
		Balance b/d	24,146

2 EXCEL STORES LTD

(a)

Creditors ledger control account

1984		£	1984		£
30 June	Discount—cancelled	2,656.82	30 June	Balance b/d	84,688.31
	Discount received	2,656.82		Incorrect addition—cr	200.00
	Contra—cancelled	3,049.75		Incorrect addition—dr	11,000.00
	Contra—Drs ledger	3,049.75		Difference in totals	2,700.00
	Petty cash (a)	10.22			
	Purchase return (f)	39.60			
	Balance c/d	87,125.35			
		98,588.31			98,588.31

(b) **Schedule of individual creditors**

	£
Original list per question	86,538.28
Error in addition (b)	30.00
Error in extraction (c)	(36.27)
Balance omitted	674.32
Discounts entered on wrong side — cancel	(12.56)
Discounts entered on wrong side — correct	(12.56)
Discounts entered on wrong side — cancel	(8.13)
Discounts entered on wrong side — correct	(8.13)
Return omitted	(39.60)
Adjusted total per control	87,125.35

3 SEA FOODS

(a) **Sales ledger control account**

	£		£
Balance b/d	6,830	Cash received	2,375
Sales	1,960	Discount allowed	85
		Goods returned	155
		Balance c/d	6,175
	8,790		8,790
Balance b/d	6,175	Contra with PLCA (b)	65
Invoice not recorded (c)	210	Bad debt (d)	165
Cheque dishonoured (e)	190	Credit note (f)	450
		Balance c/d	5,895
	6,575		6,575
Balance b/d	5,895		

(b) **Reconciliation with the individual accounts**

	£
Total per list of balances	5,935
Amount posted to S. Newt (a)	490
Invoice not recorded to C. Lion (c)	210
Cheque dishonoured (e)	190
Cash received (g)	(745)
Credit balance omitted (h)	(185)
Balance per SLCA	5,895

4 SOUTHERN APIARIES

Sales ledger control account

	£		£
Balance at 1 April 19X8	49,251	Returns	6,144
Credit sales	544,382	Cash received	526,139
		Discount allowed	1,316
		Balance c/d	60,034
	593,633		593,633
Balance b/d	60,034	Incorrect carry forward in SDB (e)	198
To bought ledger (c)	62	Undercast of cash received (b)	100
Bad debt recovered (d)	315	Contra with purchase ledger control account (h)	52
		Balance c/d	60,061
	60,411		60,411
Balance b/d	60,061		

Reconciliation with sales ledger balances

	£	£
Total per sales ledger		62,183
Credit balances shown as debits (b)		(2,132)
To Salmon & Co in bought ledger (c)		62
Brewer & Co (Holdings) (g)	39	
H. Brewer & Co (g)	(39)	
		—
Contra with bought ledger (h)		(52)
Balance per sales ledger control account		60,061

5 TOM BROWN LTD

(a) Purchases ledger control account

Credit note	160	Balance b/d	24,782
Payment to J. King	420		
Balance c/d	24,458	Balance c/d	256
	25,038		25,038
Balance b/d	256	Balance b/d	24,458

Sales ledger control account

	£		£
Balance b/d	37,354	Overcast of sales day book	1,500
		Bad debt written off	600
Balance c/d	914	Balance c/d	36,168
	38,268		38,268
Balance b/d	36,168	Balance b/d	914

(b) **Extracts from balance sheet at 31 March 19X9**

	£
Current assets	
Debtors (256 + 36,168)	36,424
Current liabilities	
Creditors (914 + 24,458)	25,372

(c) The size and complexity of many modern accounting systems necessitate integrated arrangements for sectional balancing. These procedures permit the books to be balanced expeditiously, not only at accounting year-ends, but also at various points throughout the year according to particular needs. For example, in banks daily balancing is practised.

The sheer volume of transactions and the large number of accounts requires the use of procedures for the balancing of each ledger so that errors may be located relatively quickly. Accordingly, every section of the accounts not included in the general ledger is represented in that ledger by a control (or total) account.

Control accounts may also facilitate certain aspects of financial control, for example by identifying the movement of debts in respect of a particular major classification of customer.

6 ABC COMPANY

Sales ledger control account

	£		£
Balance b/d	25,418	Returns	799
Sales	15,609	Bad debts expense	657
Cheque 'referred'	50	Cash	15,173
Bad debt recovered	300	Discount	500
		Balance c/d	24,248
	41,377		41,377
Balance b/d	24,248		

Provision for doubtful debts

	£		£
Bad debts expense (decrease in provision)	65	Balance b/d	500
Balance c/d	485		
	550		550
		Balance b/d	485

Bad debts expense

	£		£
LCA (Boole and others)	657	Bad debt recovered	300
		Provision reduced	65
		Profit and loss account	292
	657		657

Workings

Provision at 31 January	= 2% × £24,248
	= £485
Decrease in provision during January	= £485 − £550
	= £65

Sales ledger

Archer

	£		£
Balance b/d	290	Returns	20
Sales	140	Cash	265
		Discount	10
		Balance c/d	135
	430		430
Balance b/d	135		

Atwood

	£		£
Balance b/d	456	Returns	18
Sales	291	Cash	103
		Discount	5
		Balance c/d	621
	747		747
Balance b/d	621		

Boole

	£		£
Balance b/d	187	Bad debts expense	187

Bragg

	£		£
Balance b/d	74	Cash	74
Cheque 'referred'	50	Balance c/d	50
	124		124
Balance b/d	50		

Charles

	£		£
Balance b/d	371	Returns	41
Sales	518	Cash	320
		Discount	15
		Balance c/d	513
	889		889
Balance b/d	513		

Other debtors

	£		£
Balance b/d	24,040	Returns	720
Sales	14,660	Bad debts expense	470
		Cash	14,111
		Discount	470
		Balance c/d	22,929
	38,700		38,700
Balance b/d	22,929		

List of balances per sales ledger

Archer	135
Atwood	621
Bragg	50
Charles	513
Other debtors	22,929
Balance per SLCA	24,248

7 FERGUSON

(a) **Purchases ledger control account**

	£		£
Cheque payments	37,415	Balance b/d	9,803
Discount received	2,782	Credit purchases	42,133
Goods returned	3,719		
Balance c/d	8,020		
	51,936		51,936
Contra with SLCA (b)(iii)	875	Balance b/d	8,020
Balance c/d	10,165	Purchase invoice recorded as credit (a)	2,156
		Incorrect carry forward in PDB (b)(iv)	864
	11,040		11,040
		Balance b/d	10,165

Sales ledger control account

	£		£
Balance b/d	15,150	Cash received	52,144
Credit sales (115 × £7,317)	56,097	Balance c/d	19,103
15			
	71,247		71,247
Balance b/d	19,103	Contra with PLCA (b)(iii)	875
Income tax refund shown as		Credit card receipts (b)(v)	2,078
cash received (b)(ii)	3,003	Balance c/d	19,153
	22,106		22,106
Balance b/d	19,153	Bad debts expense (c)(i)	380
		Provision for doubtful	
		debts (c)(iii)	476
		Bad debt expense (c)(ii)	240
		Balance c/d	18,057
	19,153		19,153
Balance b/d	18,057		

(b) **Reconciliation with sales ledger**

	£
Total per list of balances	22,135
Credit card receipts	(2,078)
Credit balances shown as debit balances	(904)
Adjusted total before recording bad debts	
(which agrees with balance per SLCA)	19,153

Reconciliation with purchases ledger

Total per list of balances	
(which agrees with balance per PLCA)	10,165

(c) **Provision for doubtful debts**

	£		£
SLCA (ii)	476	Balance b/d	1,534
Bad debt expense (iii)		general £909	
(decrease in general provision)	14	specific £625	
Balance c/d	1,044		
	1,534		1,534
		Balance b/d	1,044
		general £895	
		specific £149	

Bad debts expense

	£		£
SLCA (i)	380	Decrease in general provision (iii)	14
SLCA (ii)	240	Profit and loss account	606
	620		620

Workings

1 General provision at 31 March 19X1 = 5% (18,057 − (625 − 476))
   = 5% × £17,908
   = £895

2 Decrease in general provision = £895 − £909 = £14

6 Bank reconciliations

Like control accounts this is a topic fairly frequently covered in examination questions. Once again the presentation of the answer is important: the errors in the cash book must be corrected there and the other outstanding items shown as part of a reconciliation statement.

QUESTIONS

1 WEST

The following were from the bank columns of the cash book of West:

Debit		£	Credit		£
19X0			19X0		
1 March	Balance b/f	150	8 March	A. Roe	30
6 March	Cash	75	16 March	T. Salmon	15
13 March	W. Wing	17	28 March	A. Bird	29
31 March	R. Nest	39	31 March	Balance c/d	207
		281			281

On 31 March 19X0 he received the following bank statement:

19X0		Debit £	Credit £	Balance £
1 March	Balance (credit)			150
6 March	Cash		75	225
10 March	A. Roe	30		195
13 March	W. Wing		17	212
15 March	Credit transfer – B. Egg		16	228
18 March	T. Salmon	15		213
31 March	Charges	10		203

You are required to:

(a) bring the cash book up-to-date, and state the new balance at 31 March 19X0; and

(b) prepare a statement to reconcile the difference between the new up-to-date balance in the cash book and the balance in the bank statement on 31 March 19X0.

10 marks

2 NORTH

The cash book of North, a trader, showed a balance of £970 at the bank on 30 September 19X4.

On investigation you find that:

(a) Cheques from customers amounting to £386 which were entered in the cash book on 30 September 19X4, were not credited by the bank until the following day.

(b)   Cheques drawn by J. North on 29 September 19X4, £618, in favour of trade creditors, entered in the cash book on that day, were paid by the bank in October.

(c)   On 17 August 19X4, a cheque for £196 was received from a customer and discount of £4 allowed. £200 had been entered in the bank column of the cash book and credited to the customer. No entry for the discount was made in the books.

(d)   In accordance with a standing order from North, the bank had paid £18 for a trade subscription on 20 September 19X4, but no entry had been made in North's books. The subscription is in respect of the year to 30 September 19X5.

(e)   On 21 September 19X4, a credit transfer of £64, in settlement of the balance in a customer's account, was received by the bank for the credit of J. North, but no entry had been made in North's books.

(f)   On 21 September 19X4, a cheque for £120 was received from a customer in settlement of his account and correctly entered in the books. This cheque was dishonoured and, on 26 September, the bank debited North's account, but no entry was made in North's books. It is considered that nothing will be recovered from this customer.

You are required to prepare:

(a)   a statement showing the balance which should appear in the cash book on 30 September 19X4, after making all necessary corrections; and

(b)   a statement reconciling the corrected cash book balance with the balance shown by the bank statement.

10 marks

3 SKINFLINT

Skinflint has employed the least expensive book-keeper he could find, but unfortunately he is both inexperienced and inefficient. He has written up the cash book for the month of May 19X9, but the balance shown by his work does not agree with the corresponding amount on the bank statement. Skinflint is worried by this situation and asks you to check the cash book for errors, reconcile it to the bank statement and comment briefly to him on any matters which you discover which might merit further investigation.

Josiah Skinflint & Co: Cash book May 19X9

Receipts

May	Account	£
5	Dawson & Co	37.50
6	Williams	39.29
14	Crawshaw	10.00
23	Duffield Ltd	60.00
23	Fineweather Ltd	46.32
27	Marstans	51.29
27	Richards	78.00
	Total lodgements	322.40
31	Balance c/f	2,497.59
		3,319.99

Payments

May	Cheque	Accounts	ref.	£
1		Opening balance b/d		2,761.75
5	473	T. Maine	M13	42.00
5	474	L. Brackett	B7	25.00
7	475	ICI Ltd	12	8.20
8	476	Clambake	C4	49.14
12	477	Cracker Ltd	C7	50.00
15	478	Lampard & Co	L17	39.98
18	479	Peat & Co	P42	100.25
19	480	Mandelle Ltd	M3	22.67
24	481	Petty Cash	PC14	50.00
26	482	Crumblecost	C5	36.00
26	483	Anderson	A7	30.00
28	484	Neighbour Ltd	N21	105.00
				3,319.99
June 1		Opening balance b/d		2,497.59

Natmid Bank Ltd
Statement of account with Josiah Skinflint & Co

Particulars	Debit	Credit	Date	Balance £
Balance forward			1 May 19X9	2,761.75 Dr
Lodged		37.50	8 May 19X9	2,724.25
476	49.14		9 May 19X9	2,773.39
473	42.00			
SO	16.32		11 May 19X9	2,831.71
477	50.00			
475	8.20		12 May 19X9	2,889.91
Lodged		39.29	19 May 19X9	2,850.62
478	39.98		22 May 19X9	2,890.60
SO	36.00		23 May 19X9	2,926.60
		60.00	24 May 19X9	2,866.60
CT		23.34	25 May 19X9	2,843.26
481	50.00			
9,437	21.50		26 May 19X9	2,914.76
482	36.00		29 May 19X9	2,950.76
CT		46.32	31 May 19X9	2,904.44

Legend: SO = Standing order
CT = Credit transfer

15 marks

4 MR LAKES

On 15 May 19X8, Mr Lakes received his monthly bank statement for the month ended 30 April 19X8. The bank statement contained the following details:

Mr Lakes Statement of Account with Baroyds Limited
(*Balance indicates account is overdrawn)

Date	Particulars	Payments £	Receipts £	Balance £
1 April	Balance			1,053.29
2 April	236127	210.70		842.59
3 April	Bank Giro credit		192.35	1,034.94
6 April	236126	15.21		1,019.73
6 April	Charges	12.80		1,006.93
9 April	236129	43.82		963.11
10 April	427519	19.47		943.64
12 April	236128	111.70		831.94
17 April	Standing order	32.52		799.42
20 April	Sundry credit		249.50	1,048.92
23 April	236130	77.87		971.05
23 April	236132	59.09		911.96
25 April	Bank Giro credit		21.47	933.43
27 April	Sundry credit		304.20	1,237.63
30 April	236133	71.18		1,166.45

For the corresponding period, Mr Lakes' own records contained the following bank account:

Date	Detail	£	Date	Detail	Cheque no.	£
1 April	Balance	827.38	5 April	Purchases	128	111.70
2 April	Sales	192.35	10 April	Electricity	129	43.82
18 April	Sales	249.50	16 April	Purchases	130	87.77
24 April	Sales	304.20	18 April	Rent	131	30.00
30 April	Sales	192.80	20 April	Purchases	132	59.09
			25 April	Purchases	133	71.18
			30 April	Wages	134	52.27
			30 April	Balance		1,310.40
		£1,766.23				£1,766.23

You are required to:

(a) prepare a statement reconciling the balance at 30 April as given by the bank statement to the balance at 30 April as stated in the bank account; *10 marks*

(b) explain briefly which items in your bank reconciliation statement would require further investigation. *4 marks*

Total 14 marks

5 ALBERT

Albert is having problems reconciling his bank account to his cash book at 30 September 19X9. The cash book at that date shows a credit balance of £1,389.

The reconciled bank balance as shown by the books at 1 October 19X8 was an overdraft of £2,612. The bank statement disclosed a debit balance of £987 at 30 September 19X9.

The following additional information has been obtained:

(a) On 2 July 19X9, Albert entered into a two-year leasing agreement in respect of certain shop-fittings, a monthly payment of £46 being due under the agreement. The first monthly payment fell due on 2 July, with subsequent payments being due on the second day of every month. All payments have been made by a bank standing order on the due dates, but no entries relating to the payments have been made in the cash book.

(b) A bank lodgement of £914 on 7 September 19X9 has been entered in the cash book as £897.

(c) Two cheques lodged in the bank during the year amounting in total to £78 were returned by the bank marked 'refer to drawer'. Neither cheque had been represented to the bank prior to 30 September 19X9 but both cheques were subsequently met. No adjustments have been made in the cash book in respect of the return of these cheques by the bank.

(d) A sub-total on the credit side of the cash book of £22,200 has been carried forward to the subsequent page as £22,020.

(e) The following cheques, all in respect of purchases and written on the dates stated, had not been presented at the bank prior to 30 September 19X9:

	£
3 January 19X9	14
28 March 19X9	87
17 April 19X9	49
28 August 19X9	15
14 September 19X9	196
25 September 19X9	526
26 September 19X9	20
28 September 19X9	79

(f) Bank charges of £85 and £120 have been debited by the bank in the bank statements on 31 March 19X9 and 30 September 19X9 respectively, but no entries for these amounts have been made in the cash book.

You are required to show the adjusted cash book and to prepare the bank reconciliation as at 30 September 19X9.

15 marks

ANSWERS

1 WEST

(a)   **Cash book**

	£		£
Balance b/d	207	Bank charges	10
Credit transfer	16	Balance c/d	213
	223		223
Balance b/d	213		

(b) **Bank reconciliation at 31 March 19X0**

	£
Balance per bank statement	203
Less: Unpresented cheque	29
	174
Add: Lodgement not yet credited	39
Balance per cash book	213

2 NORTH

(a)   **Cash book**

	£		£
Balance b/d	970	Discount allowed (c)	4
Credit transfer (e)	64	Standing order (d)	18
		Cheque dishonoured (f)	120
		Balance c/d	892
	1,034		1,034
Balance c/d	892		

(b) **Bank reconciliation at 30 September 19X4**

	£
Balance per bank statement (balancing figure)	1,124
Add: Lodgements not yet credited (a)	386
	1,510
Less: Unpresented cheques (b)	618
Balance per cash book	892

3 SKINFLINT

Cash book

	£		£
Credit transfer	23.34	Corrected balance b/d	2,997.59
		Standing order	16.32
Balance c/d	3,048.07	Standing order	36.00
		Cheque not entered (see note)	21.50
	3,071.41		3,071.41
		Balance b/d	3,048.07

Bank reconciliation at 31 May 19X9

Bank statement			2,904.44 O/D
Add: Unpresented cheques		25.00	
		100.25	
		22.67	
		30.00	
		105.00	
			282.92
			3,187.36
Less: Lodgements not yet credited		10.00	
		51.29	
		78.00	
			139.29
Balance per cash book			3,048.07

Notes

1 This cheque seems to be out of sequence. Is it a payment by Skinflint or has the bank debited it to his account in error?
   OR Is it a cheque which he had cancelled without properly informing the bank?

2 Why is the book-keeper taking so long to bank cheques received?

4 MR LAKES

(a)

Cash book

	£		£
Balance b/d	1,310.40	Charges	12.80
Credit not recorded	21.47	Standing order	32.52
Error in entry on 16 April	9.90	Balance c/d	1,296.45
	1,341.77		1,341.77

Bank reconciliation as at 30 April 19X8

	£	£
Balance per bank statement		1,166.45
Add: Lodgements not yet credited	192.80	
Cheque incorrectly debited	19.47	
		212.27
		1,378.72
Less: Cheques not yet presented	30.00	
	52.27	
		82.27
		1,296.45

(b) (i) Does cheque No. 427519 have anything to do with Mr Lakes? Because of the number of the cheque and the fact that it does not appear in the **opening** reconciliation, it would appear that the bank is in error in debiting the cheque to Mr Lakes' account. However, it could be an old cheque which Mr Lakes has written back in a previous period.

(ii) What is the correct amount for cheque 236130? The answer assumes that the bank is correct.

(iii) What is the standing order for?

(iv) From whom has the giro credit come?

Note: At 31 March 19X8 the only outstanding items appear to be cheques No. 236126 and 236127.

5 ALBERT

Cash book

	£		£
		Balance b/d	1,389
		Lease instalments July (a)	46
Incorrect recording of		August	46
lodgement	17	September	46
		Cheques returned (c)	78
		Incorrect carry forward (d)	180
		Bank charges March (f)	85
Balance c/d	1,973	September	120
	1,990		1,990
		Balance b/d	1,973

Reconciliation at 30 September 19X9

	£
Balance per bank statement	987
Unpresented cheques (e)	986
Balance per cash book	1,973 O/D

117

7 Suspense accounts, adjustments to profits and extended trial balances

In this section the student will find questions dealing with the correction of errors prior to the preparation of the final accounts. In practice the errors may be corrected by the use of a suspense account, by means of a journal, on an extended trial balance, or by any combination of these methods.

Questions on the use of an extended trial balance are very time-consuming and do not appear frequently in the examinations. However, as this general topic tests the students' knowledge of double entry and also their grasp of accounting principles, there are many questions on suspense accounts and the use of a journal for correcting errors. It is important that students should use the particular method requested by the question as marks will be awarded for presentation. In some cases the question will require a corrected balance sheet: this should obviously be in standard format rather than the draft, and probably incorrect, format given in the question.

QUESTIONS

1 RST LTD

The draft final accounts of RST Ltd for the year ended 30 April 19X5 showed a net profit for the year after tax of £78,263.

During the subsequent audit, the following errors and omissions were discovered. At the draft stage a suspense account had been opened to record the net difference.

(a) Trade debtors were shown as £55,210. However:

  (i) bad debts of £610 had not been written off;
  (ii) the existing provision for doubtful debtors, £1,300, should have been adjusted to 2% of debtors;
  (iii) a provision of 2% for discounts on debtors should have been raised.

(b) Rates of £491 which had been prepaid at 30 April 19X4 had not been brought down on the rates account as an opening balance.

(c) A vehicle held as a fixed asset, which had originally cost £8,100 and for which £5,280 had been provided as depreciation, had been sold for £1,350. The proceeds had been correctly debited to Bank but had been credited to Sales. No transfers had been made to disposals account.

(d) Credit purchases of £1,762 had been correctly debited to purchases account but had been credited to the supplier's account as £1,672.

(e) A piece of equipment costing £9,800 and acquired on 1 May 19X4 for use in the business had been debited to purchases account. (The company depreciates equipment at 20% per annum on cost.)

(f) Items valued at £2,171 had been completely omitted from the closing stock figure.

(g) At 30 April 19X5 an accrual of £543 for electricity charges and an insurance prepayment of £162 had been omitted.

(h) The credit side of the wages account had been under-added by £100 before the balance on the account had been determined.

Using relevant information from that given above, you are required to:

(a) prepare a statement correcting the draft net profit after tax;   *13 marks*

(b) Post and balance the suspense account. (*Note:* The opening balance of this account has not been given and must be derived.)   *4 marks*

                                                                          Total 17 marks

2 DEBBIE BROWN

When Debbie Brown extracted her trial balance at 31 March 19X2 she found that it did not agree. She opened a suspense account, prepared her trading and profit and loss account and drew up the following balance sheet:

				Cost	Dep'n	
Capital		£	£ Fixed assets	£	£	£
Balance 1 April 19X1		7,500	Shop fittings	1,500	300	1,200
Add: Profit for year		5,497	Delivery van	3,200	800	2,400
		12,997		4,700	1,100	3,600
Less: Drawings		5,000	Current assets			
			Stock		2,917	
		7,997				
Current liabilities			Debtors per sales ledger		2,154	
Sundry creditors	1,888		Bank		1,095	
Suspense account	9		Cash		128	
		1,897				6,294
		9,894				9,894

Subsequent checking of her records revealed the following errors which, when corrected, eliminated the suspense account:

(a) A cheque for £260 for the purchase of a new display stand on 31 March had been entered correctly in the cash book but had been entered in shop fittings account as £200.

(b) A credit note from XY Suppliers Ltd for £60 had been entered correctly in the returns outwards book but had been posted to XY's account as £66.

(c) Bank charges of £21 appeared in the cash book but had not been posted to the ledger.

(d) An invoice for £139 for goods sold to Thompson had been correctly entered in the sales day book but had been posted to Thompson's account as £193.

(e) The debit balance of £223 on Smith's account at 31 March 19X2 had been carried down as £253 and included in the trial balance at that figure.

You are required to:

(a) write up the suspense account showing the necessary correcting entries;
(b) prepare a statement showing the revised profit for the year;
(c) prepare a corrected balance sheet.

16 marks

3 WHITE LTD

After completing a draft profit and loss account for the year ended 30 April 19X2 of White Ltd the following balances remained and a suspense account entry was required for the difference which had arisen.

	£	£
Fixed assets: at cost	60,000	
provision for depreciation		31,000
Ordinary share capital		35,000
Profit and loss account		12,300
Stock in trade, at cost	14,000	
Sales ledger control account	9,600	
Purchases ledger control account		6,500
Balance at bank	1,640	
Difference on balances suspense account		440
	85,240	85,240

After investigation the following discoveries were made:

(a) A rent payment of £350 in March 19X2 had been debited in the sales ledger control account.

(b) Although instructed to do so, the accounts clerk had not set a debt due from B. Bell of £1,650 in the sales ledger control account against an amount due to B. Bell in the purchases ledger control account.

(c) Discounts allowed of £500 during the year ended 30 April 19X2 had not been recorded in the company's accounts.

(d) No entry had been made for the refund of £2,620 made by cheque to L. Green in March 19X2, in respect of defective goods returned to the company.
Note: The correct entries had been made previously for the return of the goods to White Ltd.

(e) The purchases day book for February 19X2 had been undercast by £300.

(f) A payment of £1,000 to K. Bloom in January 19X2 for cash purchases had been debited in the purchases ledger control account.
Note: The company does not maintain a credit account with K. Bloom.

(g) No entries had been made in the company's books for cash sales of £2,450 on 30 April 19X2 and banked on that date.

(h) No entries had been made in the company's books for bank charges of £910 debited in the company's bank account in December 19X1.

(i) The company's cash book (debit column) had been overcast by £1,900 in March 19X2.

(j) A cheque payment of £8,640 for new fixtures and fittings in April 19X2 had not been recorded in the company's books.

(k) A payment by cheque of £1,460 in June 19X1 for stationery had not been posted to the appropriate nominal account.

You are required to prepare:

(a) journal entries to reflect the above;
(b) the suspense account, clearing the balance; and
(c) a corrected balance sheet.

18 marks

4 BLACKHEATH LTD

The draft final accounts for the year ended 31 March 19X9 of Blackheath Ltd, car dealers, show the gross profit of £36,000 and a net profit of £9,000.

After subsequent investigations the following discoveries were made:

(a) Discounts received in August 19X8 of £210 have been credited, in error, to purchases.

(b) A debt of £300 due from P. Black to the company was written off as irrecoverable in the company's books in December 19X8. Since preparing the draft accounts, P. Black has settled the debt in full.

(c) The company's main warehouse was burgled in June 19X8, when goods costing £20,000 were stolen. This amount has been shown in the draft accounts as an overhead item 'Loss due to burglary'. Although the insurance company denied liability originally, in the past day or two that decision has been changed and Blackheath Ltd have been advised that £14,000 will be paid in settlement.

(d) On 2 January 19X9, a car which had cost the company £1,800 was taken from the showrooms for the use of one of the company's sales representatives whilst on company business. In the showrooms, this car had had a £2,400 price label. Effect has not been given to this transfer in the books of the company, although the car was not included in the trading stock valuation at 31 March 19X9. The company provides for depreciation on motor vehicles at the rate of 25% of the cost of vehicles held at the end of each financial year.

(e) Goods bought and received from L. Ring on 30 March 19X9 at a cost of £1,200 were not recorded in the company's books of account until early April 19X9. Although they were unsold on 31 March 19X9, the goods in question were not included in the stock valuation at that date.

(f) The company is hoping to market a new car accessory product in July 19X9. The new venture is to be launched with an advertising campaign commencing in April 19X9. The cost of this campaign is £5,000 and this has been debited in the company's profit and loss account for the year ended 31 March 19X9 and is included in current liabilities as a provision, notwithstanding the confident expectation that the new product will be a success.

(g) On 31 March 19X9 the company paid an insurance premium of £600, the renewal being for the year commencing 1 April 19X9. This premium was included in the insurances of £1,100 debited in the draft profit and loss account.

You are required to prepare:

(a) the journal entries necessary to adjust for items (c), (d) and (f) above. (**Note**: narratives are required.)

(b) a computation of the corrected gross profit and net profit for the year ended 31 March 19X9.

17 marks

5 NICHOLAS TANGLE

Nicholas Tangle is determined to cut costs to the bone in his business, and to this end, his wife has been called on to keep the books, and she has produced the following set of accounts.

Trading and profit and loss account for year to 31 July 19X5

	£		£
Opening stock	4,050	Sales	25,000
Purchases	17,750		
	21,800		
Less: Closing stock	4,800		
	17,000		
Gross profit c/d	8,000		
	25,000		25,000

	£		£
Expenses		Gross profit b/d	8,000
Rates	300		
Salaries and wages	3,500		
Stationery and postage	400		
Improvements	200		
Heat and light	600		
Depreciation	400		
Sundries	750		
Net profit	1,850		
	8,000		8,000

Balance sheet as at 31 July 19X5

Fixed assets	Cost £	Prior year depreciation £	This year depreciation £	£
Freehold property	7,000	–	–	7,000
Fixtures	4,000	2,400	400	1,200

Current assets		
Stock		4,050
Debtors		1,200
Cash		1,000
		6,250

Less			
Current liabilities			
Short-term loan	650		
Trade creditors	800	1,450	4,800
			13,000

Capital account		12,000
Profit for the year		1,850
		13,850

Mr Tangle suspects that the accounts are incorrect and asks you to investigate. After some enquiries you ascertain that:

(a) £2,000 which the proprietor had taken out as drawings was instead charged to salaries.

(b) Improvements have been written off to the profit and loss account.

(c) The charge for rates is £300 per annum but rates paid four months in advance at 31 July have been omitted from the balance sheet.

(d) A bill for heat and light relating to this accounting year, in the sum of £200, came in after the preparation of the accounts. One quarter of heat and light expense relates to private use.

(e) Credit sales were understated by £1,000 and these customers had not paid at the year end.

(f) The fixtures and fittings related entirely to the business, but depreciation had been calculated at a rate of 25% of written down value, not 25% of cost as in previous years.

(g) The opening stock figure had been included in the balance sheet.

You are required to:

(a) prepare a computation to show the effect of the seven notes above on profit and on the balance sheet as at 31 July; and *10 marks*

(b) make a brief comment on FOUR accounting principles violated by the original set of accounts. *4 marks*

Total 14 marks

6 LANCASTER

The following trial balance was extracted from the books of Lancaster, a trader, at 31 December 19X7:

	Dr	Cr
Capital account		19,364
Freehold land and buildings	12,500	
Furniture and fittings	1,680	
Provision for depreciation on furniture and fittings at 1 Jan 19X7		840
Motor car	950	
Provision for depreciation on motor car at 1 Jan 19X7		300
Purchases	46,982	
Sales		66,649
Rent received		360
Drawings	3,230	
Car expenses	396	
Stock in trade at 1 Jan 19X7	4,988	
Bad debts expense	422	
Provision for doubtful debts at 1 Jan 19X7		226
General expenses	827	
Rent and rates	1,162	
Trade debtors	7,921	
Trade creditors		6,933
Wages and salaries	8,983	
Discounts allowed	2,164	
Balance at bank	2,467	
	94,672	94,672

Investigation reveals the following:

(a) Stock in trade at 31 December 19X7 was £5,429.

(b) Wages and salaries accrued at 31 December 19X7 were £198.

(c) Rates paid in advance at 31 December 19X7 were £48.

(d) The provision for doubtful debts at 31 December 19X7 is to be £258.

(e) Depreciation is to be provided:

    (i) on the motor car at 20% pa on cost;
    (ii) on the furniture and fittings at 10% pa on cost.

(f) Part of the building is let to a tenant who owed £120 at 31 December 19X7.

(g) Lancaster rents a postal franking machine. Unused stamps at 31 December 19X8 were worth £47. Postages are part of general expenses.

You are required to:

(a) prepare an extended trial balance to reflect the above information;

(b) prepare Lancaster's trading and profit and loss account for 19X7 and a balance sheet as at 31 December 19X7.

28 marks

7 RODNEY

The following trial balance was extracted from the books of Rodney, a sole trader, at 31 December 19X7:

	Dr	Cr
Capital		20,271
Drawings	2,157	
Debtors	7,680	
Creditors		5,462
Sales		81,742
Purchases	62,101	
Rent and rates	880	
Lighting and heating	246	
Salaries and wages	8,268	
Bad debts expense	247	
Provision for doubtful debts at 31 Dec 19X6		326
Stock at 31 Dec 19X6	9,274	
Insurances	172	
General expenses	933	
Bank balance	1,582	
Motor vans at cost	8,000	
Provision for depreciation at 31 Dec 19X6		3,600
Disposal of van		250
Motor expenses	861	
Freehold property	10,000	
Discounts received		750
	112,401	112,401

The following matters are to be taken into account:

(a) Stocks at 31 December 19X7 were £9,884.

(b) Rent and rates include £160 for rates for the year ended 31 March 19X8.

(c) Lighting and heating has not been paid for the last quarter of 19X7. The charge is estimated to be £85.

(d) The provision for doubtful debts is to be 5% of debtors at the year end.

(e) Insurances includes £82 for motor insurance which is to be transferred to motor expenses.

(f) Rodney has taken goods, cost £370, from the business for his own private use.

(g) Depreciation has been and is to be charged on vans at 20% of cost. A full year's depreciation is charged in the year of purchase and none in the year of sale.

(h) During 19X7 a van, which was purchased during 19X4 for £1,000, was sold for £250. The only entry which has been made is to credit the £250 to a disposal account.

You are required to prepare:

(a) an extended trial balance to reflect the above information; and

(b) a trading and profit and loss account for 19X7 and a balance sheet at 31 December 19X7.

28 marks

ANSWERS

1 RST LTD

(a) **Statement of adjustment to profit**

	£	£	£
Net profit after tax			78,263
	−	+	
Bad debts written off	610		
Provision written back		208	
Provision for discount (W)	1,070		
Rates	491		
Reduction in sales	1,350		
Loss on disposal	1,470		
Reduction in purchases		9,800	
Depreciation on equipment	1,960		
Increase in closing stock		2,171	
Electricity accrual	543		
Insurance prepayment		162	
Wages undercast		100	
	7,494	12,441	+4,947
Adjusted profit			83,210

(b) **Suspense account**

	£		£
Balance b/f	301	Rates prepayment	491
Wages	100		
Supplier's account	90		
	491		491

Working

	£
Debtors	55,210
Bad debts written off	610
	54,600
Provision required: 2%	1,092
	53,508
Provision for discount	
2% × 53,508 =	1,070

2 DEBBIE BROWN

(a)   Suspense account

	£		£
XY Suppliers (b)	6	Balance b/d	9
Thompson (d)	54	Shop fittings	60
Smith (e)	30	Bank charges (c)	21
	90		90

(b)

	£
Profit per draft balance sheet	5,497
Bank charges	(21)
Adjusted profit	5,476

Note: No additional depreciation is provided on the extra £60 of shop fittings as they were purchased at the year-end.

(c) **Balance sheet at 31 March 19X2**

	Cost £	Depreciation £	£
Fixed assets			
Shop fittings	2,560	300	1,260
Delivery van	3,200	800	2,400
	4,760	1,100	3,660
Current assets			
Stocks		2,917	
Sundry debtors		2,070	
Bank		1,095	
Cash		128	
		6,210	
Current liabilities			
Sundry creditors		1,894	
			4,316
			7,976
Capital			
Balance 1 April 19X1			7,500
Profit for the year			5,476
			12,976
Less: Drawings			5,000
			7,976

3 WHITE LTD

(a) Journal entries

		Dr £	Cr £
(a)	Debit rent 　Credit SLCA being correction of rent payment recorded in SLCA	350	350
(b)	Debit PLCA 　Credit SLCA being contra between B. Bell's accounts in the sales and purchases ledgers	1,560	1,560
(c)	Debit discounts allowed 　Credit SLCA being discounts allowed, not recorded	500	500
(d)	Debit SLCA 　Credit balance at bank being refund to customer (L. Green)	2,620	2,620
(e)	Debit purchases 　Credit PLCA being correction of undercast of day book	300	300
(f)	Debit purchases 　Credit PLCA being cash purchases posted to PLCA	1,000	1,000
(g)	Debit balance at bank 　Credit sales being cash sales not recorded	2,450	2,450
(h)	Debit bank charges 　Credit balance at bank being bank charges not recorded	910	910
(i)	Debit suspense account 　Credit balance at bank being overcast of debits in cash book	1,900	1,900
(j)	Debit fixtures and fittings 　Credit balance at bank being fixtures and fittings bought just prior to the year end	8,640	8,640
(k)	Debit stationery 　Credit suspense account being posting of stationery (previously omitted)	1,460	1,460

(b) Suspense account

	£		£
Balance at bank (i)	1,900	Balance b/d	440
		Stationery (k)	1,460
	1,900		1,900

(c) Balance sheet at 30 April 19X2

	Cost	Depreciation	
	£	£	£
Fixed assets	68,640	31,000	37,640
Current assets			
Creditors (W3)	6,240		
Bank overdraft (W2)	9,980		
		16,220	
			7,590
			45,230
Capital and reserves			
Share capital			35,000
Profit and loss account (W4)			10,230
			45,230

Workings

SLCA

	£		£
Balance b/d	9,600	Rent (a)	350
Balance at bank (d)	2,620	PLCA (b)	1,560
		Discounts allowed (c)	500
		Balance c/d	9,810
	12,220		12,220
Balance b/d	9,810		

Balance at bank

	£		£
Balances b/d	1,640	SLCA (d)	2,620
Sales (g)	2,450	Bank charges (h)	910
Balance c/d	9,980	Suspense account (i)	1,900
		Fixtures and fittings (j)	8,640
	14,070		14,070
		Balance b/d	9,980

PLCA

	£		£
SLCA (b)	1,560	Balance b/d	6,500
		Purchases (e)	300
Balance c/d	6,240	Purchases (f)	1,000
	7,800		7,800
		Balance b/d	6,240

Profit

		£
Profit and loss account per question		12,300
Rent	(a)	(350)
Discount allowed	(c)	(500)
Purchases	(e)	(300)
Purchases	(f)	(1,000)
Sales	(g)	2,450
Bank charges	(h)	(910)
Stationery	(k)	(1,460)
Corrected profit and loss account		10,230

Note: No additional depreciation is provided on the additional fixtures and fittings as they were purchased at the year end.

4 BLACKHEATH LTD

			Dr £	Cr £
(a)	**Journal entries**			
	(c)	Debit Debtor — insurance company	14,000	
		Credit Loss due to burglary		14,000
		being part of burglary loss accepted by insurance company		
	(d)	Debit Fixed assets — motor vehicles	1,800	
		Credit Purchases (cost of goods sold)		1,800
		being car transferred from stocks to fixed assets		
		Debit Profit and loss — depreciation	450	
		Credit Provision for depreciation		450
		being 25% depreciation on above car		
	(f)	Debit Current liabilities — provision	5,000	
		Credit Profit and loss account — advertising		5,000
		being expenditure to be incurred and paid in next year		

(b)

		Gross profit		Net profit	
		£	£	£	£
	From draft accounts		36,000		9,000
(a)	Discounts deducted from purchases	(210)			210
(b)	Debt recovered				300
(c)	Insurance settlement				14,000
(d)	Car used as fixed asset	1,800			
	Depreciation				(450)
(e)	Stocks not recorded		—		—
(f)	Advertising for next year				5,000
(g)	Insurance for next year				600
			1,590		
	Corrected gross profit		37,590		
	Adjustments to gross profit c/f				1,590
	Corrected net profit				30,250

5 NICHOLAS TANGLE

			£	£
(a)	Net profit per the accounts			1,850
	Add: Drawings charged as salaries	(a)	2,000	
	Improvements capitalised	(b)	200	
	Credit sales	(e)	1,000	
				3,200
				5,050
	Less: Electricity accrued	(d)	150	
	Extra depreciation (W1)	(b)(f)	650	
				800
	Corrected profit			4,250

Balance sheet at 31 July 19X5

	Cost £	Depreciation £	Net £
Fixed assets			
Freehold property	7,000	–	7,000
Fixtures	4,200	3,450	750
	11,200	3,450	7,750

Current assets			
Stock		4,800	
Debtors		2,200	
Payment in advance		100	
Cash		1,000	
		8,100	
Current liabilities			
Loan	650		
Trade creditors	800		
Accrual	150		
		1,600	
			6,500
			14,250

Capital account			12,000
Add: Profit		4,250	
Less: Drawings		2,000	
			2,250
			14,250

(b) **Accounting principles violated include:**

(i) Drawings an appropriation of profit not a charge against it.
(ii) Capital versus revenue.
(iii) Matching concept – payment in advance omitted.
(iv) Matching concept – accrual omitted.
(vi) Consistency.

Workings

			£
1	Depreciation charged per P & L		400
	Correct depreciation 25% of (£4,000 + £200)		1,050
	Extra depreciation to be charged		650

6 LANCASTER

(a) Extended trial balance at 31 December 19X7

	Trial balance Dr £	Trial balance Cr £	Adjustments Dr £	Adjustments Cr £	Accruals £	Prepayments £	Profit & Loss a/c Dr £	Profit & Loss a/c Cr £	Balance sheet Dr £	Balance sheet Cr £
Capital		19,364								19,364
Freehold property	12,500								12,500	
Furniture and fittings	1,680								1,680	
Provision for depreciation		840		168(e)						1,008
Motor car	950								950	
Provision for depreciation		300		190(e)						490
Purchases	46,982						46,982			
Sales		66,649						66,649		
Rent received		360	120(f)					480		
Drawings	3,230								3,230	
Car expenses	396						396			
Stock	4,988						4,988			
Bad debts expense	422		32(d)				454			
Provision for doubtful debts		226		32(d)						258
General expenses	827					47(g)	780			
Rent and rates	1,162					48(c)	1,114			
Trade debtors	7,921								7,921	
Trade creditors		6,933								6,933
Wages and salaries	8,983				198(b)		9,181			
Discount allowed	2,164						2,164			
Balance at bank	2,467								2,467	
	94,672	94,672								
Stock – balance sheet			5,429(a)						5,429	
Stock – trading account				5,429(a)				5,429		
Depreciation expense			{190(e) 168(e) 120(f)}				358			
			5,939	5,939						
Debtor for rent									120	
					198	95				
							66,417	72,558		198
						Profit	6,141			6,141
							72,558	72,558	34,392	34,392

(b) **Trading and profit and loss account for the year ending 31 December 19X7**

	£	£
Sales		66,649
Less: Cost of goods sold		
Opening stock	4,988	
Purchases	46,982	
	51,970	
Closing stock	4,429	
		46,541
Gross profit		20,108
Rent receivable		480
		20,588
Less: Car expenses	396	
Bad debts expense	454	
General expenses	780	
Rent and rates	1,114	
Wages and salaries	9,181	
Discounts allowed	2,164	
Depreciation	358	
		14,447
Net profit		6,141

Balance sheet at 31 December 19X7

	Cost £	Depreciation £	£
Fixed assets			
Freehold property	12,500	—	12,500
Furniture and fittings	1,680	1,008	672
Motor car	950	490	460
	15,130	1,498	13,632
Current assets			
Stocks		5,429	
Trade debtors	7,921		
Less: Provision for doubtful debts	258		
		7,663	
Debtor for rent		120	
Prepayments		95	
Balance at bank		2,467	
		15,774	
Current liabilities			
Trade debtors	6,933		
Accruals	198		
		7,131	
			8,643
			22,275

	£
Proprietor's interest	
Capital at 1 January 19X7	19,364
Profit for the year	6,141
	25,505
Less: Drawings	3,230
	22,275

7 RODNEY

(a) Extended trial balance at 31 December 19X7

	Trial balance Dr £	Trial balance Cr £	Adjustments Dr £	Adjustments Cr £	Accruals £	Pre-payments £	Profit & Loss a/c Dr £	Profit & Loss a/c Cr £	Balance sheet Dr £	Balance sheet Cr £
Capital		20,271								20,271
Drawings	2,157								2,527	
Debtors	7,680								7,680	
Creditors		5,462								5,462
Sales		81,742						81,742		
Purchases	62,101						61,731			
Rent and rates	880		370(f)			40(b)	840			
Lighting and heating	246				85(c)		331			
Salaries and wages	8,268						8,268			
Bad debts expense	247		58(d)				305			
Provision for doubtful debts		326		58(d)						384
Stock at 31 Dec 19X6	9,274						9,274			
Insurances	172			82(e)			90			
General expenses	933						933			
Bank balance	1,582								1,582	
Motor vans	8,000								7,000	
Provision for depreciation		3,600	1,000(h)	1,000(h)						4,400
Disposal of van		250	600(h)	1,400(g)			150			
			82(e)	600(h)						
Motor expenses	861						943			
Freehold property	10,000								10,000	
Discounts received		750						750		
	112,401	112,401								
Stocks – profit and loss account				9,884(a)				9,884		
Stock – balance sheet			9,884(a)						9,884	
Depreciation expense			1,400(g)				1,400			
			13,394	13,394	85	40	84,265	92,376	38,713	8,111
							8,111			8,111
						Profit	92,376	92,376	38,713	38,713

138

(b) **Trading and profit and loss account for the year ending 31 December 19X7**

	£	£
Sales		81,742
Less: Cost of goods sold		
Opening stock	9,274	
Purchases	61,731	
	71,005	
Closing stock	9,884	
		61,121
Gross profit		20,621
Discounts received		750
		21,371
Less: Rent and rates	840	
Lighting and heating	331	
Salaries and wages	8,268	
Bad debts expenses	305	
Insurances	90	
General expenses	933	
Loss on disposal of van	150	
Motor expenses	943	
Depreciation	1,400	
		13,260
Net profit		8,111

Balance sheet at 31 December 19X7

	Cost	Depreciation	
	£	£	£
Fixed assets			
Freehold property	10,000	—	10,000
Motor car	7,000	4,400	2,600
	17,000	4,400	12,600
Current assets			
Stocks		9,884	
Debtors	7,680		
Less: Provision for doubtful debts	384		
		7,296	
Prepayments		40	
Balance at bank		1,582	
		18,802	
Current liabilities			
Creditors	5,462		
Accruals	85		
		5,547	
			13,255
			25,855

139

	£
Proprietor's interest	
Capital at 1 January 19X7	20,271
Profit for the year	8,111
	28,382
Less: Drawings	2,527
	25,855

8 Incomplete records

This term is used to describe any question where some of the information is missing. It is probably the most popular question at this level and is also often seen in subsequent examinations.

There are three standard techniques which are used in the questions. They are the use of control accounts, the preparation of a cash and bank account and the use of gross profit percentages. Each example in this section illustrates the use of one or more of these techniques.

The most difficult aspect of incomplete records questions is knowing where to start. The student must first decide what information is missing and then has to know how to find it: this, of course, demands a good understanding of double-entry bookkeeping and is the reason why questions on this topic are so highly favoured.

QUESTIONS

1 KINGSTON

(a) The stocks held by Kingston at their warehouse premises were damaged by fire on 1 September 19X1. The books of account show the following information at that date:

	£
Sales for the year to 31 July 19X1	264,000
Sales for the month of August 19X1	20,000
Purchases for the year ending 31 July 19X1	184,000
Purchases for the month of August 19X1	58,000
Stock at 1 August 19X0	21,320
Stock at 31 July 19X1	25,800

You are also advised that the gross profit to sales ratio has remained constant. Stock salvaged after the fire was sold for £30,000.

You are required to calculate the amount of the insurance claim.

(b) The information given is exactly the same as that in part (a) except that you are also told that one item of stock included in the valuation of stock on 31 July 19X1 was written down to £700 on 10 August 19X1 from its original cost price of £1,200 and was sold for £1,000 on 15 August 19X1.

You are required to calculate the amount of the insurance claim.

12 marks

2 SMITH

Smith has recently received a legacy from an aunt, and used it to buy a self-service petrol filling station. As he lives some distance from the site he has appointed a manager, Jones, to run the station for him at a salary of £90 per week, and five gallons of four star petrol per week for his own use. Jones was in charge from Monday 1 January, but on Friday 30 March, Smith received a telephone call from Brown, the cashier employed by Jones at the site, to say that Jones had absconded, taking all available funds with him. Brown also complained that his wages of £60 per week, had not been paid for the weeks ending 23 March and 30 March, and that four weeks site rent was outstanding.

Smith has asked you to compute the amount of Jones' defalcation. Your investigations reveal the following facts:

(a) The bank statement for the 13 weeks to 30 March shows lodgements of £41,327.

(b) Smith had entrusted Jones with a cash float of £200 on 1 January, and instructed him to pay his own salary and Brown's wages out of the takings. Jones was also instructed to pay the rent of the site at £70 per week, and petty cash expenses estimated at £15 per week, out of the till.

(c) Depreciation on buildings, plant and fixtures was £9,260 for the quarter.

(d) Three grades of petrol were sold: Four star at 95p per gallon
                                            Three star at 93p per gallon
                                            Two star at 89p per gallon.

(e) Stocks of petrol at 1 January and 30 March respectively were:
     Four star   4,000 gallons and 1,500 gallons
     Three star   1,800 gallons and 600 gallons
     Two star   1,400 gallons and 850 gallons

Deliveries from O Peck (Oil Supplies) Ltd during the period were Four star — 23,000 gallons, Three star — 11,000 gallons and Two star — 18,000 gallons.

(f) Smith has a credit note for 500 gallons of four star petrol returned to the suppliers as sub-standard, and unpaid bills for the site telephone for £28, and Electricity £79.

You are required to produce a statement computing the amount of Jones' defalcation.

Your workings should be shown, with reference to the reasons why you have excluded some of the information given above from your computation.

15 marks

3 SNOW

Snow is the sole distribution agent in the Branton area for Diamond floor tiles. Under an agreement with the manufacturers, Snow purchases the Diamond floor tiles at a trade discount of 20% off list price and annually in May receives an agency commission of 1% of his purchases for the year ended on the previous 31 March.

For several years, Snow has obtained a gross profit of 40% on all sales. In a burglary in January 19X1 Snow lost stock costing £4,000 as well as many of his accounting records. However, after careful investigations, the following information has been obtained covering the year ended 31 March 19X1:

1. Assets and liabilities at 31 March 19X0 were as follows:

	£
Building: at cost	10,000
provision for depreciation	6,000
Motor vehicles: at cost	5,000
provision for depreciation	2,000
Stock: at cost	3,200
Trade debtors (for sales)	6,300
Agency commission due	300
Prepayments (trade expenses)	120
Balance at bank in hand	4,310
Trade creditors	4,200
Accrued expenses (vehicle expenses)	230

2. Snow has been notified that he will receive an agency commission of £440 on 1 May 19X1.

3. Stock, at cost, at 31 March 19X1 was valued at £6,200.

4. In October 19X0 stock costing £1,000 was damaged by dampness and had to be scrapped as worthless.

5. Trade creditors at 31 March 19X1 related entirely to goods received whose list prices totalled £9,500.

6. Discounts allowed amounted to £1,620 whilst discounts received were £1,200.

7. Trade expenses prepaid at 31 March 19X1 totalled £80.

8. Vehicle expenses for the year ended 31 March 19X1 amounted to £7,020.

9. Trade debtors (for sales) at 31 March 19X1 were £6,700.

10. All receipts are passed through the bank account.

11. Depreciation is provided annually at the following rates:

    Buildings 5% on cost
    Motor vehicles 20% on cost.

12. Commissions received are paid direct to the bank account.

13. In addition to the payments for purchases, the bank payments were:

	£
Vehicle expenses	6,720
Drawings	4,300
Trade expenses	7,360

14. Snow is not insured against loss of stock owing to burglary or damage to stock caused by dampness.

You are required to prepare Snow's trading and profit and loss account for the year ended 31 March 19X1 and a balance sheet at that date.

22 marks

4 TOM SMITH

Since commencing business several years ago as a cloth dealer, Tom Smith has relied on annual receipts and payments accounts for assessing progress. These accounts have been prepared from his business bank account through which all business receipts and payments are passed.

Tom Smith's receipts and payments account for the year ended 31 March 19X2 is as follows:

	£		£
Opening balance	1,680	Drawings	6,300
Sales receipts	42,310	Purchases payments	37,700
Proceeds of sale of		Motor van expenses	2,900
grandfather clock	870	Workshop: rent	700
Loan from John Scott	5,000	rates	570
Closing balance	1,510	Wages – John Jones	3,200
	51,370		51,370

Additional information:

(a) The grandfather clock sold during the year ended 31 March 19X2 was a legacy received by Tom Smith from the estate of his late father.

(b) The loan from John Scott was received on 1 January 19X2; interest is payable on the loan at the rate of 10% per annum.

(c) In May 19X2. Tom Smith received from his suppliers a special commission of 5% of the cost of purchases during the year ended 31 March 19X2.

(d) On 1 October 19X1, Tom Smith engaged John Jones as a salesman. In addition to his wages, Jones receives a bonus of 2% of the business's sales during the period of his employment; the bonus is payable on 1 April and 1 October in respect of the immediately preceding six-month period.

Note: It can be assumed that sales have been at a uniform level throughout the year ended 31 March 19X2.

(e) In addition to the items mentioned above, the assets and liabilities of Tom Smith were as follows:

At 31 March	19X1	19X2
	£	£
Motor van, at cost	4,000	4,000
Stock in trade, at cost	5,000	8,000
Trade debtors	4,600	12,290
Motor vehicle expenses prepaid	–	100
Workshop rent accrued due	–	200
Trade creditors	2,900	2,200

(f) It can be assumed that the opening and closing balances in the above receipts and payments account require no adjustment for the purposes of Tom Smith's accounts.

(g) As from 1 April, 19X1, it has been decided to provide for depreciation on the motor van annually at the rate of 20% of the cost.

You are required to produce the trading and profit and loss account for the year ended 31 March 19X2, and a balance sheet at that date of Tom Smith.

17 marks

5 A. HIGHTON

A. Highton is in business as a general retailer. He does not keep a full set of accounting records; however it has been possible to extract the following details from the few records that are available:

Balances as at:	1 April 19X1 £	31 March 19X2 £
Freehold land and buildings, at cost	10,000	10,000
Motor vehicle (cost £3,000)	2,250	
Stock, at cost	3,500	4,000
Trade debtors	500	1,000
Prepayment — Motor vehicle expenses	200	300
— Property insurance	50	100
Cash at bank	550	950
Cash in hand	100	450
Loan from Highton's father	10,000	
Trade creditors	1,500	1,800
Accrual — Electricity	200	400
— Motor vehicle expenses	200	100

Extract from a rough cash book for the year to 31 March 19X2

RECEIPTS	£
Cash sales	80,400
PAYMENTS	**£**
Cash purchases	17,000
Drawings	7,000
General shop expenses	100
Telephone	100
Wages	3,000

Extract from the bank pass sheets for the year to 31 March 19X2

RECEIPTS	£
Cash banked	52,850
Cheques from trade debtors	8,750
PAYMENTS	**£**
Cheques to suppliers	47,200
Loan repayment (including interest)	10,100
Electricity	400
Motor vehicle expenses	1,000
Property insurance	150
Rates	300
Telephone	300
Drawings	1,750

Note: Depreciation is to be provided on the motor vehicle at a rate of 25% per annum on cost.

You are required to prepare a trading, and profit and loss account for the year to 31 March 19X2, and a balance sheet as at that date.

20 marks

6 VICTOR BINGHAM

Victor Bingham commenced business as a retail grocer on 1 November 19X0 but has not kept a proper set of books of account. Most of his sales are for cash, and a record of credit sales has been maintained.

A summary of the bank transactions for the year to 31 October 19X1 is as follows:

Lodgements	£	Payments	£
Introduction of capital	18,600	Fixtures & fittings	8,005
Net cash sales (i.e., after		Vehicles	4,000
payments)	86,800	Stationery & advertising	1,488
Receipts from credit sales	18,178	Personal expenses	930
		Electricity	521
		Purchases for resale	92,008
		Staff wages	8,184
		Rent & rates	2,108
		Insurance	620
		Legal costs	645

In addition to making the following cash payments before banking the takings, Bingham also withdrew £110 each week for living expenses.

Cash payments	£
Sundry expenses	496
Purchases for resale	248
Staff wages and insurance	2,654

The following additional information is also available:

(a)

	31 October 19X1
	£
Stock on hand	9,920
Debtors	2,554
Creditors	5,456
Heating & lighting accrued (electricity)	136
Rates paid in advance	164
Insurance paid in advance	10

(b) Goods costing £960 had been taken by Bingham from stock for his own use, and depreciation is to be provided for at the rate of 20 per cent on cost price per annum on fixtures and fittings, and on motor vehicles.

(c) Assume a 52 week year.

You are required to:

(a) prepare cash and bank accounts covering the year ended 31 October 19X1;
8 marks

(b) prepare a trading and profit and loss account for the year ended 31 October 19X1, together with a balance sheet as at that date. *15 marks*
Total 23 marks

7 BBB LTD

BBB Ltd owns a retail shop which is managed by Graham Smith. Graham has no knowledge of accountancy, and to help him the company accountant prepares and sends him every month a stock account. In this account, the purchases, stocks and all other items are shown at selling prices, the purpose being to enable Graham to see whether or not there are any stock shortages or surpluses.

The stock account for the year ended 31 December 19X4 is as follows:

	£000
Debit:	
Stock at 31 December 19X3, at selling prices	96
Debtors at 31 December 19X3	18
Purchases, at selling prices	981
	1,095
Credit:	
Cash sales	700
Cash received from debtors	185
Discounts allowed to debtors	4
Bad debts written off	7
Purchase returns, at selling prices	21
Debtors at 31 December 19X4	22
Stock at 31 December 19X4	144
Difference between book and physical stocks, at selling prices	12
	1,095

Other relevant information is as follows:

(a) The company's summarised cash account for the year ended 31 December 19X4 is:

	£000
Debit:	
Balance brought forward at 31 December 19X3	20
Cash sales	700
Debtors	185
	905
Credit:	
Creditors, after deducting cash discounts of £16,000	587
Salaries	60
Overhead expenses	119
Taxation	33
Dividends	25
Purchase of fixed assets	70
Balance carried forward at 31 December 19X4	11
	905

(b) All selling prices are calculated by adding a mark-up of 50% on cost. There were no sales which departed from this rule.

(c) The depreciation charge for the year is £27,000.

(d) Details of prepayments and accruals are as follows:

	31 December 19X3 £000	31 December 19X4 £000
Prepaid overhead expenses	3	4
Accrued overhead expenses	7	9

You are required to prepare the trading and profit and loss account of BBB Ltd, up to the figure of pre-tax profit or loss, for the year ended 31 December 19X4.

20 marks

8 JOHN BOWERS

The summarised balance sheet at 30 September 19X8, of John Bowers, retailer, is as follows:

	£		£	£
Capital account –		Fixtures and fittings:		
J. Bowers	15,600	At cost	11,000	
		Less: Aggregate depreciation	6,000	4,400
		Stock in trade		9,000
Trade creditors	2,130	Trade debtors		2,100
Accrued charges		Prepayments (rates)		260
(electricity)	230	Balance at bank		2,200
	17,960			17,960

Although John Bowers does not keep a full set of accounting records, his business transactions during the financial year ended 30 September 19X9, are summarised as follows:

(a) Sales totalled £95,830 and sales returns £880; trade debtors at 30 September 19X9, amounted to £4,400.

(b) Gross profit amounted to 2/9ths of net sales revenue.

(c) Stock in trade, at cost, at 30 September 19X9, shows an increase of £6,000 over that of a year earlier.

(d) Trade creditors at 30 September 19X9, amounted to £3,970; discounts received from suppliers totalled £450 for the year under review.

(e) Payments for rent, rates, light and heat totalled £6,830 and wages payments £8,250 for the year ended 30 September 19X9.

(f) At 30 September 19X9, rent prepaid amounted to £320 and electricity charges accrued due were £270.

(g) On 30 September 19X9, a loan of £2,000 was received from L. Pond.

(h) Additions to fixtures and fittings during the year cost £1,500 cash.

(i) Cash drawings amounted to £4,000 and, in addition, John Bowers withdrew from the business goods for his own use which had cost £310. Whilst these goods were paid for in the payments made to suppliers, the goods withdrawn by John Bowers for his own use were not included in the cost of the goods sold or sales.

(j) It has been decided to make a provision for doubtful debts at 30 September 19X9, of 2½% of trade debtors.

(k) Depreciation is provided annually on fixtures and fittings at the rate of 10% on the cost of assets held at the relevant accounting year end.

(a) From the figures and information above compile John Bowers' trading and profit and loss account for the year ended 30 September 19X9, and a balance sheet as at that date. *18 marks*

(b) Give reasons which could be advanced to John Bowers in favour of keeping a full set of accounting records. *4 marks*
Total 22 marks

9 EAST

The balance sheet of East, a long established trader, at 30 September 19X8 was as follows:

	£	£	£
Fixed assets, at cost			140,000
Less: Depreciation to date			96,000
			44,000
Current assets:			
Stock in trade		17,000	
Trade debtors		6,000	
Amounts prepaid		400	
Balance at bank		8,500	
		31,900	
Less: Current liabilities			
Trade creditors	6,200		
Accrued charges	700		
		6,900	
			25,000
			69,000

Representing:	£
Proprietor's interest	
Capital at 30 September 19X7	62,000
Profit for the year	16,000
	78,000
Less: Drawings	9,000
	69,000

Owing to a long illness, East has been obliged to leave the day-to-day operation of his business since early 19X9 in the hands of Peter Pink, a trusted employee.

Although his illness has prevented him keeping his accounting records up to date, East was able to make plans for the year ended 30 September 19X9 which showed that during the year the business bank account would never be in an overdraft situation.

A letter from the bank drawing East's attention to the fact that his business bank account was £5,000 overdrawn on 30 September 19X9 coincided with the sudden disappearance of Peter Pink. Subsequent investigations implicate Peter Pink whom it would appear has not paid into the business bank account all the monies received from trade debtors; however all necessary payments have been paid correctly through the business bank account.

It has always been the practice of East to bank all business receipts intact and to make all payments from the business bank account.

It can be assumed that there were no unpresented cheques at 30 September 19X9 and all amounts paid into the bank account on or before 30 September 19X9 were credited by that date.

East is now endeavouring to determine the amount of cash misappropriated and also prepare the annual accounts for the year ended 30 September 19X9. East is not insured against loss owing to the misappropriation of cash.

Accordingly, the following information has now been obtained concerning the year ended 30 September 19X9:

1. Stock in trade, at cost, at 30 September 19X9 was valued at £11,000.

2. Throughout the year, a uniform rate of gross profit was earned of one third of the cost of goods sold.

3. Payments for purchases totalled £110,700 whilst trade creditors at 30 September 19X9 were £3,300 more than a year previously.

4. Administrative expenses payments made during the year totalled £11,200 whilst the amount to be charged to the profit and loss account is £11,000.

5. Establishment expenses payments were £9,400 and establishment expenses prepaid at 30 September 19X9 amounted to £800.

6. Fixed assets bought and paid for amounted to £20,000.

7. Depreciation is provided annually at the rate of 5% of the cost of fixed assets held at the end of each financial year.

8. East's cash drawings totalled £10,000.

9. Trade debtors at 30 September 19X9 amounted to £6,500 and cash sales during the year under review amounted to £82,000.

10. Amounts prepaid at 30 September 19X8 of £400 related to establishment expenses.

11. Accrued charges at 30 September 19X8 of £700 related to administrative expenses.

You are required to prepare:

(a) a computation of the amount of cash misappropriated during the year ended 30 September 19X9; and

(b) East's trading and profit and loss account for the year ended 30 September 19X9 and a balance sheet at that date.

Note: the profit and loss account should include an item 'cash misappropriated'.
22 marks

10 MARTIN

Martin operates a stationery and book shop in Dundee. Separate stock records and trading accounts have not been maintained in respect of stationery and books.

On the night of 31 March 19X2 a fire destroyed the shop and all the stock was lost or damaged. As the accounting books and records are kept in Mr Martin's house they escaped destruction in the fire.

From the surviving books and other records, the following information is available:

1. The mark-up on stationery is $33\frac{1}{3}$% and on books is 50%.

2. The accounts for the year ended 30 June 19X1 included the following:

		£
Sales for the year		175,320
Purchases during the year	Stationery	57,100
	Books	68,550
Stock at 30 June 19X1	Stationery	5,500
	Books	12,650
Stock at 1 July 19X0	Stationery	4,200
	Books	12,100

3. During August each year Mr Martin holds a book sale of old stock on which he reduces his gross margin to 20%. Records of the sales of old stock in August 19X1 and August 19X0 show that the proceeds of these sales amounted to £6,250 and £5,400 respectively.

4. Purchases between 1 July 19X1 and 31 March 19X2 were:

	£
Stationery	55,640
Books	66,200

5. The value of sales (excluding the sale of old book stock in August) between 1 July 19X1 and 31 March 19X2 is estimated to have increased by 15% in respect of books and 12½% in respect of stationery as compared with the same period in the year ended 30 June 19X1. Sales arise evenly throughout the year, except for the sale of old book stocks in August.

6. Goods salvaged from the fire realised £2,000 of which £1,500 was in respect of books and £500 in respect of stationery.

7. Adequate insurance cover has been maintained since 1 July 19X1.

You are required to prepare a statement showing the amount to be claimed from the insurance company in respect of the stationery and books destroyed in the fire.

15 marks

ANSWERS

1 KINGSTON

Trading account for year ended 31 July 19X1

	£	£
Sales		264,000
Opening stock	21,320	
Purchases	184,000	
	205,320	
Closing stock	25,800	
		179,520
Gross profit		84,480

Gross profit as a percentage of sales is 32%.

Sales for the month of August 19X1	20,000
Gross profit (32%)	6,400
Cost of goods sold	13,600
Opening stock	25,800
Purchases	58,000
	83,800
Less: Closing stock (balance figure)	70,200
Cost of goods sold	13,600
Closing stock (cost)	70,200
Salvage value	30,000
Insurance claim	40,200

Calculation of cost of goods sold

Sales for August	20,000
Less: Sales at reduced price	1,000
Sales at normal gross profit percentage	19,000
Gross profit (32%)	6,080
Cost of sales at normal profit percentage	12,920
Cost of sales at reduced gross profit percentage	1,200
Cost of goods sold	14,120

Calculation of insurance claim

	£
Opening stock	25,800
Purchases	58,000
	83,800
Less: Closing stock (balancing figure)	69,680
Cost of goods sold	14,120
Cost of closing stock	69,680
Salvage value	30,000
Insurance claim	39,680

2 SMITH

Computation of sales

	4 star	3 star	2 star
Opening stock	4,000	800	1,400
Add: Purchases	22,500	11,000	18,000
	26,500	11,800	19,400
Less: Closing stock	1,500	600	850
	25,000	11,200	18,550
Less: Private use	65		
Gallons sold	24,935	11,200	18,550
Price	95p	93p	89p
Sales	£23,688	£10,416	£16,510

Total sales £50,614

Statement of Jones' defalcation

		£	£
Cash float			200
Sales			50,614
Less: Banked		41,327	
Spent:			
Salaries	13 × 90	1,170	
Wages	11 × 60	660	
Rent	9 × 70	630	
Expenses	13 × 15	195	(43,982)
Amount of Jones' defalcation			6,832

Note: Depreciation is a non-cash cost. Telephone and electricity bills are not yet paid so cannot affect the defalcation.

3 SNOW

Trading and profit and loss account for year ended 31 March 19X1

	£	£
Sales (W3)		60,000
Less: Cost of goods sold		
Stocks at 31 March 19X0	3,200	
Purchases (W2)	44,000	
	47,200	
Stocks at 31 March 19X0	6,200	
	41,000	
Stocks stolen or damaged	5,000	
		36,000
Gross profit		24,000
Add: Commission	440	
Discount received	1,200	
		1,640
		25,640
Less: Vehicle expenses	7,020	
Trade expenses (W5)	7,400	
Depreciation – buildings	500	
– motor vehicles	1,000	
Discounts allowed	1,620	
Stocks stolen	4,000	
Stocks damaged	1,000	
		22,540
Net profit		3,100

Balance sheet at 31 March 19X1

	Cost	Depreciation	
Fixed assets	£	£	£
Buildings	10,000	6,500	3,500
Motor vehicles	5,000	3,000	2,000
	15,000	9,500	5,500
Current assets			
Stock		6,200	
Debtors		6,700	
Commission due		440	
Prepayments		80	
Bank balance (W4)		4,810	
		18,230	
Carried forward		18,230	5,500

	Cost £	Depreciation £	£
Brought forward		18,230	5,500
Current liabilities			
Creditors	7,600		
Accruals (W6)	530		
		8,130	
			10,100
			15,600
Proprietor's interest			
Capital at 31 March 19X0 (W7)			16,800
Profit for year			3,100
			19,900
Less: Drawings			4,300
			15,600

Workings

1. **Sales ledger control account**

	£		£
Balance at 31 March 19X0	6,300	Discounts allowed	1,620
Sales (W3)	60,000	∴ cash received	57,980
		Balance at 31 March 19X1	6,700
	66,300		66,300
Balance at 31 March 19X1	6,700		

2. **Purchases ledger control account**

	£		£
Discounts received	1,200	Balance at 31 March 19X0	4,200
∴ payments to creditors	39,400	Purchases (Note 1)	44,000
Balance at 31 March 19X1 (Note 2)	7,600		
	48,200		48,200
		Balance at 31 March 19X1	7,600

Notes:

(1) Agency commission (1% of purchases) = £440
∴ purchases = £44,000

(2) Trade creditors at 31 March 19X1 relate to goods at list price of £9,500.
∴ creditors = 80% × £9,500 = £7,600

3.

	£
Stocks at 31 March 19X0	3,200
Purchases during year (W2)	44,000
	47,200
Less: Stock at 31 March 19X1	6,200
	41,000
Less: Stock stolen and damaged	5,000
Cost of goods sold	36,000

Sales = £36,000 × $\frac{100}{60}$ = £60,000

4. **Cash book**

	£		£
Balance at 31 March 19X0	4,310	Payments to creditors (W2)	39,400
Receipts from debtors (W1)	57,980	Vehicle expenses	6,720
Commission	300	Drawings	4,300
		Trade expenses	7,360
		Balance c/d	4,810
	62,590		62,590
Balance b/d	4,810		

5. **Trade expenses**

	£		£
Balance at 31 March 19X0	120	∴ profit and loss charge	7,400
Payments	7,360	Balance at 31 March 19X1	80
	7,480		7,480
Balance at 31 March 19X1	80		

6. **Vehicle expenses**

	£		£
Payments	6,720	Balance at 31 March 19X0	230
∴ balance at 31 March 19X1	530	Profit and loss charge	7,020
	7,250		7,250
		Balance at 31 March 19X1	530

7. **Balance sheet at 31 March 19X0**

	Cost £	Depreciation £	£
Fixed assets			
Buildings	10,000	6,000	4,000
Motor vehicles	5,000	2,000	3,000
	15,000	8,000	7,000
Current assets			
Stock		3,200	
Debtors		6,300	
Commission due		300	
Prepayments		120	
Bank balance		4,310	
		14,230	
Current liabilities			
Creditors	4,200		
Accruals	230		
		4,430	9,800
			16,800
Capital at 31 March 19X0			16,800

4 TOM SMITH

Trading and profit and loss account for the year ended 31 March 19X2

	£	£
Sales (W1)		50,000
Less: Cost of goods sold		
Opening stock	5,000	
Purchases (W2)	37,000	
	42,000	
Less: Closing stock	8,000	
		34,000
Gross profit		16,000
Commission received (5% × 37,000)		1,850
		17,850
Less: Expenses		
Workshop rent (700 + 200)	900	
Workshop rates	570	
Motor van expenses (2,900 − 100)	2,800	
Motor van depreciation (20% × 4,000)	800	
Wages	3,200	
Bonus (2% × 25,000)	500	
Loan interest (¼ × 10% × 5,000)	125	
		8,895
Net profit		8,955

Balance sheet at 31 March 19X2

	Cost £	Depreciation £	£
Fixed assets			
Motor van	4,000	800	3,200

Current assets		
Stock		8,000
Debtors		12,290
Prepayments		100
Commission receivable		1,850
		22,240

Current liabilities		
Creditors	2,200	
Accruals	200	
Bonus	500	
Interest due	125	
Bank overdraft	1,510	
		4,535

	£
	17,705
	20,905
Loan from John Scott	5,000
	15,905

Capital	
At 31 March 19X1 (W3)	12,380
Introduced during the year	870
Profit for the year	8,955
	22,205
Drawings	6,300
	15,905

Workings

1. **Sales ledger control account**

	£		£
Balance b/d	4,600	Cash received	42,310
Sales	50,000	Balance c/d	12,290
	54,600		54,600
Balance b/d	12,290		

2.   Purchases ledger control account

	£		£
Cash payments	37,700	Balance b/d	2,900
Balance c/d	2,200	Purchases	37,000
	39,900		39,900
		Balance b/d	2,200

3. Capital at 31 March 19X1

Net assets		£
Motor van		4,000
Stock		5,000
Debtors		4,600
Cash		1,680
		15,280
Creditors		2,900
Capital = Net assets =		12,380

5 A. HIGHTON

Trading and profit and loss account for the year to 31 March 19X2

	£	£
Sales		
Cash	80,400	
Credit (W2)	9,250	89,650
Cost of sales		
Opening stock	3,500	
Purchases (W3)	64,500	
	68,000	
Less: Closing stock	4,000	64,000
Gross profit		25,650
Expenses:		
General shop expenses	100	
Depreciation – Motor vehicle	750	
Electricity (W4)	600	
Loan interest	100	
Motor vehicle expenses (W4)	800	
Property insurance (W4)	100	
Rates	300	
Telephone	400	
Wages	3,000	6,150
Net profit		19,500

Balance sheet at 31 March 19X2

	Cost £	Depreciation £	Net book value £
Fixed assets			
Freehold land and buildings	10,000	–	10,000
Motor vehicle	3,000	1,500	1,500
	13,000	1,500	11,500
Current assets			
Stock, at cost	4,000		
Debtors	1,000		
Prepayments	400		
Cash at bank	950		
Cash in hand	450	6,800	
Less: Current liabilities			
Creditors	1,800		
Accruals	500	2,300	4,500
			16,000
Financed by:			
Capital as at 1 April 19X1 (W1)			5,250
Net profit for the year		19,500	
Less: Drawings		8,750	10,750
			16,000

Workings

1. Opening capital

		£
Freehold land and buildings		10,000
Motor vehicle		2,250
Stock		3,500
Trade debtors		500
Prepayments		250
Cash at bank and in hand		650
		17,150
Less:		
Loan	10,000	
Trade creditors	1,500	
Accruals	400	11,900
Capital as at 1 April 19X1		5,250

2. Credit sales

	£
Cheques received from trade debtors	8,750
Less: Trade debtors outstanding 1.4.X1	500
	8,250
Add: Trade debtors outstanding 31.3.X2	1,000
Credit sales for the year	9,250

3. Credit purchases

	£
Cheques to suppliers	47,200
Less: Trade creditors 1.4.X1	1,500
	45,700
Add: Trade creditors 31.3.X2	1,800
Credit purchases for the year	47,500

4.

Expenses	Electricity £	Motor vehicle expenses £		Property insurance £
Cheques paid	400	1,000		150
Less: Accrual 1.4.X1	200	200		–
Prepayment 31.3.X2	–	300	500	100
	200		500	50
Add: Accrual 31.3.X2	400		100	–
Prepayment 1.4.X1	–		200	50
Expenses for the year	600		800	100

Note: Workings 2, 3 and 4 could have been presented as control accounts.

6 VICTOR BINGHAM

(a) Bank and cash accounts for the year ended 31 October 19X1

	Bank £	Cash £		Bank £	Cash £
Capital	18,600		Drawings	930	5,720
Debtors	18,178		Staff wages etc.	8,184	2,654
Cash sales banked	86,800		Cash sales banked		86,800
∴ Cash sales		95,918	Petty expenses		496
			Purchases	92,008	248
			Fixtures & fittings	8,005	
			Vehicles	4,000	
			Stationery & advertising	1,488	
			Electricity	521	
			Rent & rates	2,108	
			Insurance	620	
			Legal fees	645	
			Balance	5,069	
	123,578	95,918		123,578	95,918

(b) Trading and profit & loss account for the year ended 31 October 19X1

	£	£	£	£
Sales (W2)				116,650
Less: Stock at beginning	—			
Plus: Purchases (W1)	96,752			
Less: Stock at end	9,920			
				86,832
Gross profit				29,818
Staff wages & insurance			10,838	
Rent & rates (W4)			1,944	
Insurance (W5)			610	
Electricity (W6)			657	
Legal fees			645	
Depreciation — Fixtures & fittings	1,601			
Vehicles	800			
			2,401	
Sundry expenses			496	
Stationery & advertising			1,488	
				19,079
Net profit				10,739

Balance sheet as at 31 October 19X1

Fixed assets	Gross £	Accumulated depreciation £	£
Fixtures & fittings	8,005	1,601	6,404
Motor vehicles	4,000	800	3,200
	12,005	2,401	9,604

Current assets			
Stock	9,920		
Debtors	2,554		
Prepayments	174		
Bank	5,069		
		17,717	
Less: Current liabilities			
Creditors	5,456		
Accruals	136	5,592	
			12,125
			21,729

	£
Victor Bingham	
Opening capital	18,600
Plus: Profit	10,739
	29,339
Less: Drawings (W3)	7,610
	21,729

Workings

1. Purchases

	£
Payments by cheque	92,008
Cash	248
	92,256
Add: Creditors – 31 October 19X1	5,456
	97,721
Less: Personal consumption	960
	96,752

165

2. Sales £
   Cash received 18,178
   Add: Debtors – 31 October 19X1 2,554
   Credit sales 20,732
   Cash sales (W1) 95,918
   116,650

3. Drawings
   Cash 930
   Cheque 5,720
   Personal consumption 960
   7,610

4. Rent & rates
   Payments 2,108
   Less: Prepaid 164
   1,944

5. Insurance
   Payments 620
   Less: Prepaid 10
   610

6. Electricity
   Payments 521
   Plus: Accrued 136
   657

7 BBB LTD

Trading, profit and loss account for the year ended 31 December 19X4

	£000	£000
Sales — credit (W2)	200	
cash	700	
		900
Opening stock (96 × 100/150)	64	
Purchase, less returns (W3)	640	
	704	
Closing stock (144 × 100/150)	(96)	
		608
Gross profit (after stock loss)		292
Discount received	16	
Carried forward		308

	£000	£000
Brought forward		308
Less expenses:		
Salaries	60	
Overhead expenses (W4)	120	
Discount allowed	4	
Bad debts	7	
Depreciation	27	
		218
Profit before taxation		90

Workings

1. **Price structure**

    Cost + mark-up = selling price
    100 + 50 = 150

2. **Debtors**

	£000		£000
Balance b/d	18	Cash	185
Credit sale		Discount allowed	4
(balancing figure)	200	Bad debts	7
		Balance c/d	22
	218		218

3. **Creditors**

	£000		£000
Cash	587	Purchases (981 × 100/150)	654
Discount received	16		
Purchase returns (21 × 100/150)	14		
Balance c/d			
(balancing figure)	37		
	654		654

4. **Overhead**

	£000		£000
Balance b/d (prepayments)	3	Balance b/d (accruals)	7
Cash	119	Profit and loss	
Balance c/d (accruals)	9	(balancing figure)	120
		Balance c/d (prepayments)	4
	131		131

Tutorial note

Since the mark-up is 50% of cost or 33.3% of sales, then on sales of £900,000:

	£000
Gross profit (50/150 × 900)	300
Less: Stock loss (100/150 × 12)	8
Actual gross profit	292

Had we used the book value for closing stock then from the gross profit we would need to deduct the stock loss, in order to:
(a) highlight as a separate item the loss in the profit and loss account; and
(b) adjust the closing stock value to the physical valuation for balance sheet purposes.

(The above answer eliminates the additional entries by taking directly the physical count figure.)

8 JOHN BOWERS

(a) **Trading and profit and loss account for the year ended 30 September 19X9**

	£	£
Sales		94,950
Less: Cost of goods sold		
Opening stock	9,000	
Purchases (balancing figure)	79,850	
	88,850	
Closing stock	15,000	
		73,850
Gross profit (2/9 of sales)		21,100
Discounts received		450
		21,550
Less: Expenses		
Rent, rates, light and heat (W1)	6,810	
Wages	8,250	
Depreciation (W2)	1,250	
Provision for doubtful debts	110	
		16,420
Net profit		5,130

Balance sheet at 30 September 19X9

	£	£	£
Fixed assets			
Fixtures and fittings – Cost			12,500
Depreciation			7,850
			4,650
Current assets			
Stock		15,000	
Trade debtors less provision		4,290	
Prepayments		320	
Carried forward		19,610	4,650

	£	£	£
Brought forward		19,610	4,650
Current liabilities			
Creditors	3,970		
Overdraft (W5)	1,600		
Accruals	270		
		5,840	
			13,770
			18,420
Loan – L. Pond			2,000
			16,420
Capital at 30 September 19X8			15,600
Profit for the year			5,130
			20,730
Less: Drawings			4,310
			16,420

(b) The maintenance of a full set of accountancy records would enable John Bowers to have an ongoing record of his position with regard to debtors and creditors as well as fixed assets and stock.

The existence of good accounting records would assist the operation of business planning, the determination of VAT and tax liabilities etc, and would give a good impression if John Bowers wished to raise a loan.

Workings

1. **Rent etc.**

Rent, rates, light and heat

	£		£
Balance b/d	260	Balance b/d	230
Cash paid	6,830	Profit and loss charge	6,810
Balance c/d	270	Balance c/d	320
	7,360		7,360
Balance b/d	320	Balance b/d	270

2. **Depreciation**

	£
Cost of fixtures at 30.9.19X8	11,000
Additions during year	1,500
	12,500
Depreciation	1,250

3. **Cash from debtors**

Sales ledger control account

	£		£
Balance b/d	2,100	Cash received	92,650
Sales	94,950	Balance c/d	4,400
	97,050		97,050
Balance b/d	4,400		

4. **Payments to creditors**

Purchases ledger control account

	£		£
Discounts received	450	Balances b/d	2,130
Cash paid	77,870	Purchases	79,850
Balance c/d	3,970	Goods for own use	310
	82,290		82,290
		Balance b/d	3,970

5. **Cash balance**

Cash book

	£		£
Balance b/d	2,200	Cash to suppliers (W4)	77,870
Cash from debtors (W3)	92,650	Cash for rent etc.	6,830
Loan	2,000	Wages	8,250
		Fixtures bought	1,500
Balance c/d	1,600	Drawings	4,000
	98,450		98,450
		Balance b/d	1,600

9 JOHN EAST

(a)

Cash book

	£		£
Balance b/d	8,500	Payments — purchases	110,700
Receipts (W1)	159,500	— admin expenses	11,200
		— est expenses	9,400
		Fixed assets bought	20,000
		Cash drawings	10,000
Balance c/d	5,000	Cash misappropriated (balancing figure)	11,700
	173,000		173,000
		Balance b/d	5,000

(b) **Trading and profit and loss account for year ended 30 September 19X9**

	£	£
Sales (W3)		160,000
Opening stock	17,000	
Purchases (W2)	114,000	
	131,000	
Less: Closing stock	11,000	
		120,000
Gross profit		40,000
Administrative expenses	11,000	
Establishment expenses (W5)	9,000	
Depreciation (5% × £160,000)	8,000	
Cash misappropriated ((a) above)	11,700	
		39,700
Net profit		300

Balance sheet at 30 September 19X9

	Cost £	Depreciation £	£
Fixed assets	160,000	104,000	56,000
Current assets:			
Stock		11,000	
Debtors		6,500	
Amounts prepaid		800	
		18,300	
Current liabilities:			
Trade creditors	9,500		
Accrued charges (W4)	500		
Bank overdraft	5,000		
		15,000	
			3,300
			59,300
Representing:			
Capital at 30 September 19X9			69,000
Add: Profit for year ended 30 September 19X0			300
			69,300
Less: Drawings			10,000
			59,300

171

Workings

1.   **Sales ledger control account**

	£		£
Balance b/d	6,000	Receipts (balancing figure)	159,500
Sales — cash	82,000		
— credit (W3)	78,000	Balance c/d	6,500
	166,000		166,000
Balance b/d	6,500		

2.   **Purchase ledger control account**

	£		£
Cash	110,700	Balance c/d	6,200
Balances c/d	9,500	Purchases (balancing figure)	114,000
	120,200		120,200
		Balance b/d	9,500

3.   Cost of goods sold =   17,000   Opening stock
                                   +114,000(W2)   Purchases

                                     131,000
                                    − 11,000   Closing stock
                                   120,000

       ∴ sales   160,000   (Cost plus one third)
          cash sales   82,000
          credit sales   78,000

4.   **Administrative expenses account**

	£		£
Paid	11,200	Balance b/d	700
∴ balance c/d	500	Profit and loss account	11,000
	11,700		11,700
		Balance b/d	500

5. Establishment expenses account

	£		£
Balance b/d	400	Profit and loss account	
Paid	9,400	(balancing figure)	9,000
		Balance c/d	800
	9,800		9,800
Balance c/d	800		

10 PETER MARTIN

Stationery

	£
Opening stock at 1 July 19X1	5,500
Purchases	55,640
	61,140
Less: Cost of goods sold (W2)	47,081
Closing stock at 31 March 19X2	14,059

Books

	£
Opening stock at 1 July 19X1	12,650
Purchases	66,200
	78,850
Less: Cost of goods sold (W2)	59,924
Closing stock at 31 March 19X2	18,926

Total stock at 31 March 19X2

	£
Stationery	14,059
Books	18,926
	32,985

Insurance claim

	£
Stocks at 31 March 19X2	32,985
Less: Salvage value	2,000
Insurance claim	30,985

Workings

1. **19X0–19X1**

    (a) **Stationery** £

    Cost of goods sold
    Opening stock 4,200
    Purchases 57,100

    61,300
    Closing stock 5,500

    Cost of goods sold 55,800

    Sales = £55,800 × $133\frac{1}{3}\%$ = 74,400

    (b) **Books**

    Cost of goods sold
    Opening stock 12,100
    Purchases 68,550

    80,650
    Closing stock 12,650

    Cost of goods sold 68,000

    Book sales at reduced margin 5,400

    Cost of these books = 80% × £5,400 = 4,320

    Cost of goods sold at normal mark-up
     = £68,000 − £4,320 = 63,680

    Sales at normal mark-up = £63,680 × 150% = 95,520

    (c) **Total sales for year** £
    Stationery 74,400
    Books — at reduced margin 5,400
     — at standard mark-up 95,520

    175,320

    Note: A **mark-up** is always on **cost** whereas a **margin** is on **selling price**.

2. **19X1–19X2**

   (a) **Stationery**

   Sales $= 112\tfrac{1}{2}\% \times \dfrac{9}{12} \times (19\text{X}0 - 19\text{X}1 \text{ sales})$

   $\phantom{\text{Sales }} = 112\tfrac{1}{2}\% \times \dfrac{9}{12} \times £64{,}400 \text{ (W1)}$

   $\phantom{\text{Sales }} = £62{,}775$

   Cost of goods sold $= \dfrac{100}{133\tfrac{1}{3}} \times £62{,}775 = £47{,}081$

   (b) **Books**

   Sales at normal mark-up $= 115\% \times \dfrac{9}{12} \times (19\text{X}0 - 19\text{X}1 \text{ sales})$

   $\phantom{\text{Sales at normal mark-up }} = 115\% \times \dfrac{9}{12} \times £95{,}520 \text{ (W1)}$

   $\phantom{\text{Sales at normal mark-up }} = £82{,}386$

   Cost of these sales $= \dfrac{100}{150} \times £82{,}386 = £54{,}924$

   Cost of sales at reduced margin $= 80\% \times £6{,}250$
   $\phantom{\text{Cost of sales at reduced margin }} = £5{,}000$

   Total cost of books sold $= £59{,}924$

9 Receipts and payments accounts

This term is used to describe the situation where the only records maintained by the organisation are those of receipts and payments. It is, therefore, a specific type of incomplete records question, the main problem being to distinguish between capital and revenue items.

The organisation concerned is most likely to be a non-profit-making organisation such as a sports club or trust fund. An opening balance sheet is rarely given and it is therefore necessary to reconstruct one in order to find the value of the fund at the beginning of the year.

QUESTIONS

1 GREEN BANK SPORTS CLUB

The following receipt and payments account for the year ended 31 March 19X3 for the Green Bank Sports Club has been prepared by the treasurer Andrew Swann:

Receipts	£	Payments	£
Balance brought forward		Painting of clubhouse	580
1 April 19X2		Maintenance of grounds	1,310
Cash in hand	196	Bar steward's salary	5,800
Bank current account	5,250	Insurances	240
Members' subscriptions:		General expenses	1,100
Ordinary	1,575	Building society investment	
Life	800	account	1,500
Annual dinner – ticket sales	560	Secretary's honorarium	200
Bar takings	21,790	Annual dinner – expenses	610
		New furniture and fittings	1,870
		Bar purchases	13,100
		Rent of clubhouse	520
		Balance carried forward	
		31 March 19X3	
		Bank current account	3,102
		Cash in hand	239
	30,171		30,171

The following additional information has been given:

1. Ordinary membership subscriptions. Received in advance at 31 March 19X2 £200. The subscriptions received during the year ended 31 March 19X3 included £150 in advance for the following year.

2. A life membership scheme was introduced on 1 April 19X1. Under the scheme life membership subscriptions are £100 and are apportioned to revenue over a ten year period. Life membership subscriptions totalling £1,100 were received during the first year of the scheme.

3. The club's building society investment account balance at 31 March 19X2 was £2,676; during the year ended 31 March 19X3 interest of £278 was credited to the account.

4. All the furniture and fittings in the club's accounts at 31 March 19X2 were bought in January 19X0 at a total cost of £8,000. It is the club's policy to provide depreciation annually on fixed assets at 10% of the cost of such assets held at the relevant year end.

5. Other assets and liabilities of the club were:

At 31 March	19X2	19X3
	£	£
Bar stocks	1,860	2,110
Insurance prepaid	70	40
Rent accrued	130	140
Bar purchase creditors	370	460

You are required to prepare:

(a) the bar trading and profit and loss account for the year ended 31 March 19X3; and

(b) the club's income and expenditure account for the year ended 31 March 19X3 and a balance sheet at that date.

20 marks

2 GREENFINGER GARDENERS' CLUB

The Greenfinger Gardeners' Club is a member of the Countryside Gardeners' Federation. The annual subscription payable by member clubs to the federation is 5% of the total subscription income plus 5% of any gross profit (or less any loss) arising from the sale of seeds and fertilisers.

The receipts and payments account for the year ended 31 December 19X8 of the Greenfingers Gardeners' Club is as follows:

	£		£
Balance at 1 January 19X8	196	Purchase of seeds and fertilisers	1,640
Subscriptions received	1,647		
Sales of tickets for visit to research centre	232	Cost of visit to research centre	247
Sale of seeds and fertilisers	1,928	Purchase of garden equipment	738
Annual garden show:		Repairs to garden equipment	302
Sale of tickets	829	Annual garden show:	
Competition fees	410	Hire of marquee	364
		Prizes	650
		Balances at 31 December 19X8	1,301
	5,242		5,242

The following additional information is given:

At 31 December	19X7	19X8
	£	£
Subscriptions due and unpaid	164	83
Subscriptions prepaid	324	248
Sale of seeds and fertilisers – debtors	220	424
Purchases of seeds and fertilisers – creditors	804	547
Stock of seeds and fertilisers – at cost	261	390

Depreciation of £225 for the year is to be charged on the garden equipment.

You are required to prepare:

(a) a computation of the membership subscription for 19X8 payable by the Greenfinger Gardeners' Club to the Countryside Gardeners' Federation; and

(b) an income and expenditure account for the year.

17 marks

3 COUNTRY COUSINS SPORTS CLUB

The following receipts and payments account for the year ended 31 October 19X4 has been prepared from the current account bank statements of the Country Cousins Sports Club:

19X3		£	19X4		£
1 Nov	Balance b/f	1,700	31 Oct	Clubhouse:	
19X4				Rates and	
31 Oct	Subscriptions	8,600		insurance	380
	Bar takings	13,800		Decorations and	
	Donations	1,168		repairs	910
	Annual dinner –			Annual dinner –	
	Sale of tickets	470		Catering	650
				Bar purchases	9,200
				Stationery and	
				printing	248
				New sports equipment	2,463
				Hire of films	89
				Warden's salary	4,700
				Petty cash	94
				Balance c/f	7,004
		25,738			25,738

The following additional information has been given:

At 31 October	19X3	19X4
	£	£
Clubhouse, at cost (bought 1 Nov 19X1)	15,000	15,000
Bar stocks, at cost	1,840	2,360
Petty cash float	30	10
Bank deposit account	600	730
Subscriptions received in advance	210	360
Creditors for bar supplies	2,400	1,900

The club provides for depreciation annually on the clubhouse at the rate of 10% of cost and on the new sports equipment at the rate of $33\frac{1}{3}\%$ of cost.

179

The petty cash float is used exclusively for postages.

The only entry in the bank deposit account during the year ended 31 October 19X4 concerns interest.

One quarter of the warden's salary and one half of the clubhouse costs, including depreciation, are to be apportioned to the bar.

The donations received during the year ended 31 October 19X4 are for the new coaching bursary fund which will be utilised for the provision of training facilities for promising young sportsmen and sportswomen. It is expected to make the first award during 19X5.

You are required to prepare:

(a) an account showing the profit or loss for the year ended 31 October 19X4 on the operation of the bar; and

(b) an income and expenditure account for the year ended 31 October 19X4 and a balance sheet at that date for the Country Cousins Sports Club.

18 marks

4 THE NODDINGTON MUSEUMS TRUST

The accounting records of the Noddington Museums Trust are maintained by the treasurer, a retired schoolmaster. He files paid bills meticulously, and compiles an analysis of payments and receipts to reflect movements into and out of the bank account.

Analysis of Bank Account – year to 31.12.X1

Receipts	£	Payments	£
Subscriptions – members	3,370	Rates	450
– groups	1,000	Rent	600
Tax rebate – 19X0	24	Grant to local dig	720
Investment income	56	Library shelving & files	640
Sales of pamphlets	400	General expenses	451
Rent received for flat	800	Insurance	1,500
Donations	415	Salaries – part-time	
Life members	1,500	museum staff	3,000
Grant from local authority	750	Printing and stationery	208
Advertisements in pamphlets	86	Post and telephone	412
Research fees	41	Cost of printing pamphlets	350
Annual appeal and garden party	2,001	Bookbinding for library	219
		Cost of meetings	860
		Committee travel and expenses	240
		Museum expenses	847
	10,443		10,497

The Trust is a charitable organisation which operates three small museums and an archaeological dig. During discussions with the treasurer the following information is revealed:

1. The bank account was overdrawn by £69 on 1 January 19X1, and during the year the bank has charged £28 for bank charges and interest.

2. Annual subscriptions are £10 for a member and £25 for a group. On 31 December 19X1 4 group members had paid in advance and 15 ordinary members were in arrears. There were no subscriptions in advance on 31 December 19X0, but 10 ordinary members were in arrears. The committee wish to provide £100 against subscriptions in arrears.

3. Amounts outstanding on 31 December 19X1: £150 is yet to be received for pamphlets sold, and £21 is owed by advertisers in the pamphlets. The treasurer holds unpaid bills for stationery £27, rates for the half year to 31 March 19X2 £250 and telephone £35. The treasurer says this is £10 more than he owed for the telephone a year ago. The committee suggest a fee for accountancy services of £40.

4. The flat over the museum had been let to a caretaker on 1 April 19X1 at an annual rental of £800. The insurance premium had been paid for the year to 31 May 19X2. The treasurer comments that the premium this year showed a two-thirds increase on last year's figure for the same period.

5. The lease of one museum building has been purchased for £2,400 on 31 December 19X0. The lease had twelve years to run from this date and the annual rent is £480 payable quarterly in advance from 1 January 19X1.

6. A life membership costs £300. There were ten life members at the beginning of the year, but three have died during the year.

7. Cash received from the annual appeal and garden party was banked after deducting payments of £180 general expenses and £29 postage. The treasurer paid these general bills out of the garden party cash. The treasurer usually has a cash float of £20 but this was permanently increased to £40 by retaining £20 of the garden party cash.

8. The Trust owns a freehold property which cost £20,000 3 years ago. At that time the land on which the building stands was reckoned to be worth £5,000. Depreciation has not so far been provided on this property but it is reckoned to last the Trust 50 years from 1.1.X1. The premises were purchased with the assistance of a loan of £10,000 interest free, none of which has yet been repaid.

9. The exhibits in the museum do not belong to the Trust, but fixtures and fittings with a book value of £2,700 on 1 January 19X1 are depreciated at 10% per annum by the reducing balance method.

10. The stock of pamphlets held on 1 January 19X1 was valued at cost as £250, with £200 as the value of the closing stock.

11. The Trust owns an investment of £1,000 in Local Authority stock which pays interest at 8% per annum. This interest is paid after deduction of income tax at 30p in the pound.

12. The life members fund and the accumulated fund vest in the general assets of the Trust.

You are required to draft a revenue statement for the year to 31 December 19X1 and a balance sheet as at that date, for presentation to the trust members at the next annual general meeting.

25 marks

5 DOHRAY AMATEUR MUSICAL SOCIETY

The Dohray Amateur Musical Society has a treasurer who is responsible for receipts and payments which he records in cash and bank books. Periodically, these books are handed over to the firm of certified accountants which employs you.

One of your tasks is to prepare the final accounts of the Society. As a preliminary step, you have prepared the receipts and payments account (rounded to the nearest £1) for the year ended 31 May 19X5. This is shown below, together with the explanatory notes which the treasurer has supplied to enable you to understand the nature of some of the items.

Dohray Amateur Musical Society receipts and payments account for year ended 31 May 19X5

Receipts	Cash £	Bank £	Payments	Cash £	Bank £
Opening balances b/d	31	309	Creditors: trade fixed assets (note 4)		
Debtors: members'			musical instruments		522
joining fees (note 1)	190	160	trophies		83
annual subscriptions (note 2)	285	70	Creditors: trade purchases for resale (note 4)		
Annual concert (note 3)			sheet music		118
takings	1,791		musical instruments		336
Sales of goods (note 4)			Annual concert (note 3)		
sheet music	140		hall booking fees		490
musical instruments	287		printing of publicity		
Prize moneys (note 7)	190		posters		112
Sponsorship grant (note 5)		300	hire of professional soloists		236
Refreshment sales	113		musicians		174
Raffle profits	64		adjudication fees		50
PAC grants (note 6)			Musical Festivals (note 7)		
revenue		100	entrance fees		250
capital		400	hire of buses		281
Transfers from cash a/c		2,910	Honoraria (note 8)		
			secretary		150
			treasurer		100
			RMFC affiliation fee (note 9)		72
			Rent of society's premises (note 10)		510
			Refreshment purchases	72	
			Bank charges		42
			Sundry expenses	60	
			Transfers to bank a/c	2,910	
			Closing balances c/d	49	723
	3,091	4,249		3,091	4,249

Explanatory notes supplied by the treasurer

1. On joining the society, members pay a non-returnable fee of £10 (before 1 June 19X2, the fee had been £5). It has been found from experience that, on average, members remain in the society for five years. On this basis, one fifth of each joining fee is credited to income and expenditure account each year.

New members' statistics are:

During year ended 31 May	Number of new members	Joining fees in suspense at 31 May 19X4 £
19X1	20	20
19X2	24	48
19X3	32	192
19X4	27	216
19X5	35	Nil
		476

2. Annual subscriptions are due on 1 June each year. It is the Society's policy to credit these to income and expenditure account on an actual receipts basis, not an accruals basis. However, if subscriptions are received in advance, the amounts are credited to income and expenditure account for the year for which they are paid.

3. The society's major money-raising event is its annual public concert. This is given in a large hall which the Society hires. The Society also hires professional musicians and soloists and has to pay the fees of the adjudicators (judges).

4. The Society buys trophies (silver bowls and shields) to present to the winners of the individual musical items at the annual concert. It also buys musical instruments some of which are for use by the members and others for resale to the members. Musical scores and sheets are also bought for resale to the members.

5. A local building company has given a grant to the Society for a period of three years in return for publicity. This sponsorship grant was received in full on 1 June 19X4 and is being credited to income and expenditure account in equal instalments in each of the three years to 31 May 19X7.

6. The Performing Arts Council (PAC) has awarded the Society an annual grant towards the running costs. In addition the PAC makes capital grants. The Society's policy is to hold capital grants in suspense and to release each year's grant to income and expenditure account over a period of five years, from the year of grant onwards. At 31 May 19X4 capital grants held in suspense were analysed as follows:

In respect of year ended 31 May	Capital grants suspense £
19X1	30
19X2	70
19X3	120
19X4	120
	340

7. Throughout the year, the Society competes at various musical festivals. Cash prizes won by individual members are retained by the Society and credited to income and expenditure account in order to reduce the cost of attending the festivals.

8. The offices of secretary and treasurer are unpaid but the Society gives each of them an *ex gratia* (honorary) cash award, termed an honorarium.

9. In order to participate in the musical festivals, the Society has to be affiliated to the Regional Musical Festival Committee (RMFC). The annual fee, which has remained the same for a number of years, is paid on 1 March in each year.

10. The Society pays rent for its premises. The rental, which is inclusive of rates, heating, lighting, cleaning, etc. is reviewed annually on 31 March. The payment shown in the receipts and payments account represents quarterly payments in advance, as follows:

19X4	Payment
30 June	120
30 September	120
31 December	120
19X5	
31 March	150
	510

Further information was supplied by the treasurer as follows:

		19X4	19X5
1.	Creditors at 31 May	£	£
	Fixed assets		
	musical instruments	79	119
	trophies	23	13
	Purchases for resale		
	sheet music	14	20
	musical instruments	45	39
2.	Subscriptions		
	Payments in advance included in the actual receipts for the year	30	40
3.	Stocks at 31 May		
	Goods for resale		
	sheet music	31	52
	musical instruments	70	94
	Refreshments	not brought into account on the grounds that it is not material in amount	

4. Fixed assets (at cost) at 31 May
   Musical instruments   1,378   to be
   Trophies   247   derived

   There were no fixed assets disposals during the year

5. Provision for depreciation at 31 May
   Musical instruments   704   to be
   Trophies   96   derived

   Depreciation is calculated on the cost of these assets at the end of the financial year. The straight-line method is employed using the following assumed asset lives:

   Musical instruments   5 years
   Trophies   10 years

   The Society was formed on 1 June 19X0.

You are required to prepare for the Dohray Amateur Musical Society:

(a) The income and expenditure account for year ended 31 May 19X5, showing the surplus or deficit on each of the activities:

    (i)   annual concert;
    (ii)   musical festivals;
    (iii)   sales of goods.

(b) The balance sheet at that date.

Note: Workings are an integral part of the answer and must be shown.

34 marks

ANSWERS

1 GREEN BANK SPORTS CLUB

(a) **Bar trading and profit and loss account for the year ended 31 March 19X3**

	£	£
Bar takings		21,790
Opening stocks	1,860	
Purchases (W1)	13,190	
	15,050	
Closing stocks	2,110	
		12,940
Gross profit		8,850
Less: Bar steward's salary		5,800
Bar profit		3,050

(b) **Income and expenditure account for the year ended 31 March 19X3**

	£		£
Maintenance of grounds	1,310	Bar profit	3,050
Painting of clubhouse	580	Subscriptions – ordinary (W4)	1,625
Insurances (W2)	270	– life (W5)	190
General expenses	1,100	Interest on investment	
Loss on annual dinner	50	account	278
Rent of clubhouse (W3)	530		
Secretary's honorarium	200		
Depreciation (W6)	987		
Excess of income over			
expenditure	116		
	5,143		5,143

Balance sheet at 30 March 19X3

	Cost	Depreciation	
	£	£	£
Fixed assets	9,870	3,387	6,483
Current assets			
Stocks		2,110	
Insurances prepaid		40	
Cash in hand		239	
Bank current account		3,102	
Investment account (W8)		4,454	
Carried forward		9,945	6,483

187

	£	£	£
Brought forward		9,945	6,483
Current liabilities			
Bar creditors	460		
Rent accrued	140		
Ordinary subscriptions prepaid	150		
		750	
			9,195
			15,678
Life subscriptions not yet credited to income (W9)			1,600
			14,078
Accumulated fund			
Balance at 31 March 19X2			13,962
Excess of income over expenditure for the year			116
Balance at 31 March 19X3			14,078

Workings

1. **Bar creditors**

	£		£
Payments	13,100	Balance b/d	370
		∴ purchases	13,190
Balance c/d	460		
	13,560		13,560
		Balance b/d	460

2. **Insurance**

	£		£
Balance b/d	70	Charge for year	270
Payments	240		
		Balance c/d	40
	310		310
Balance b/d	40		

3. **Rent**

	£		£
Payments	520	Balance b/d	130
Balance c/d	140	Charge for year	530
	660		660
		Balance b/d	140

4. ### Subscriptions – ordinary

	£		£
Income for year	1,625	Balance b/d	200
Balance c/d	150	Receipts during year	1,575
	1,775		1,775
		Balance b/d	150

5. **Life subscriptions**

	£
Received during 19X1–19X2	1,100
Received during 19X2–19X3	800
	1,900
Income for year ($\frac{1}{10}$th)	190

6. **Depreciation of furniture and fittings**

	£
Cost at 31 March 19X2	8,000
Bought during year	1,870
Cost at 31 March 19X3	9,870
Depreciation (10%)	987

7. **Accumulated fund at 31 March 19X2**

	Cost £	Depreciation £	£
Fixed assets	8,000	2,400	5,600
Current assets			
Stocks		1,860	
Insurance prepaid		70	
Cash in hand		196	
Bank current account		5,250	
Investment account		2,676	
		10,052	
Current liabilities			
Bar creditors	370		
Rent accrued	130		
Ordinary subscriptions prepaid	200		
		700	
			9,352
Carried forward			14,952

	£
Brought forward	14,952
Life subscriptions not yet credited to income	990
	13,962
Accumulated fund at 31 March 19X2	13,962

8. **Investment account**

	£		£
Balance b/d	2,676		
Interest	278		
From current account	1,500	Balance c/d	4,454
	4,454		4,454
Balance b/d	4,454		

9. **Life subscriptions**

	£		£
To income 19X1–19X2	110	Received during 19X1–19X2	1,100
Balance c/d (31 March 19X2)	990		
	1,100		1,100
To income 19X2–19X3	190	Balance b/d (31 March 19X2)	990
Balance c/d (31 March 19X3)	1,600	Received during 19X2–19X3	800
	1,790		1,790
		Balance b/d	1,600

2 GREENFINGER GARDENERS' CLUB

(a) **Subscription income for 19X8**

Subscriptions

	£		£
Balance b/d	164	Balance b/d	324
Income for year	1,642	Subscriptions received	1,647
Balance c/d	248	Balance c/d	83
	2,054		2,054
Balance b/d	83	Balance b/d	248

Profit on sale of fertilisers and seeds

	£	£
Sales (W1)		2,132
Less: Cost of goods sold		
Opening stock	261	
Purchases (W2)	1,383	
	1,644	
Less: Closing stock	390	
		1,254
Gross profit		878

Subscription to Federation = 5% × (£1,642 + £878)
= £126

(b) **Income and expenditure account for the year ended 31 December 19X8**

	£			£
Repairs to garden equipment	302	Subscription income		1,642
Depreciation of garden		Gross profit on sale of		
equipment	225	fertilisers and seeds		878
Subscription to federation	126	Garden show		
Excess of income over		Income	1,239	
expenditure	2,077	Expenses	1,014	
				225
		Research centre		
		Sales	232	
		Costs	247	
				(15)
	2,730			2,730

Workings

1   **Sales ledger control account**

	£		£
Balance b/d	220	Amounts received	1,928
∴ sales	2,132	Balance c/d	424
	2,352		2,352
Balance b/d	424		

2   **Purchases ledger control account**

	£		£
Cash paid	1,640	Balance b/d	804
Balance c/d	547	∴ purchases	1,383
	2,187		2,187
		Balance b/d	547

3 COUNTRY COUSINS SPORTS CLUB

(a) Bar profit for year

	£	£
Bar takings		13,800
Less: Cost of goods sold		
Opening stocks	1,840	
Purchases (W1)	8,700	
	10,540	
Less: Closing stock	2,360	
		8,180
		5,620
Less: Share of warden's salary (¼)	1,175	
Share of clubhouse costs (½)(W2)	1,395	
		2,570
Bar profit		3,050

(b) Income and expenditure account for year

	£			£
Clubhouse costs	1,395	Bar profit		3,050
Warden's salary	3,525	Subscription income (W3)		8,450
Depreciation of sports		Annual dinner		
equipment	821	Tickets	470	
Stationery and printing	248	Costs	650	(180)
Hire of films	89			
Postage (W4)	114	Interest on deposit account		130
Excess of income over				
expenditure	5,258			
	11,450			11,450

Balance sheet at 31 October 19X4

	Cost	Depreciation	
	£	£	£
Fixed assets			
Clubhouse	15,000	4,500	10,500
Sports equipment	2,463	821	1,642
	17,463	5,321	12,142
Current assets			
Stocks		2,360	
Balance on deposit		730	
Current account		7,004	
Petty cash		10	
Carried forward			
		10,104	12,142

		£	£	£
Brought forward			10,104	12,142
Current liabilities				
Bar creditors		1,900		
Subscriptions in advance		360		
			2,260	
				7,844
				19,986
Accumulated fund				
At 31 October 19X3 (W5)				13,560
Excess of income over expenditure for year				5,258
At 31 October 19X4				18,818
Coaching bursary fund				1,168
				19,986

Workings

1. Bar creditors

	£		£
Payments	9,200	Balance b/d	2,400
Balance c/d	1,900	∴ purchases	8,700
	11,100		11,100
		Balance b/d	1,900

2. Clubhouse costs

	£
Rates and insurance	380
Decorations and repairs	910
Depreciation of clubhouse	1,500
	2,790

3. Subscriptions

	£		£
∴ subscription income	8,450	Balance b/d	210
Balance c/d	360	Subscriptions received	8,600
	8,810		8,810
		Balance b/d	360

4.   Petty cash

	£		£
Balance b/d	30	∴ postage	114
From bank account	94	Balance c/d	10
	124		124
Balance b/d	10		

5.   **Accumulated fund at 31 October 19X3**

	£	£
Net assets		
Clubhouse (NBV)		12,000
Stocks		1,840
Deposit account		600
Current account		1,700
Petty cash		30
		16,170
Subscriptions in advance	210	
Bar creditors	2,400	
		2,610
Net assets = accumulated fund		13,560

4   THE NODDINGTON MUSEUMS TRUST

Revenue account year ended 31 December 19X1

	£
Income	
Subscriptions – Individuals (W3)	3,420
– Groups (W3)	900
Appeal and Garden Party	
(2,001 + 180 + 29 + 20)	2,230
Rent for flat (800 − 200)	600
Donations	415
Sale of pamphlets – surplus (W8)	150
Investment income (gross)	80
Grant from local authority	750
Advertisements in pamphlets (86 + 21)	107
Research fees	41
Total income	8,693

	£	£	£
Expenses – Museum			
Depreciation of building (W7)		300	
Depreciation of fixtures and fittings (W7)		334	
Amortisation of lease (2400 ÷ 12)		200	
Rates (W4)		475	
Rent		480	
Insurance (W5)		1,250	
Book binding		219	
Museum expenses		847	
		4,105	
Administration			
Grant to dig	720		
Salaries	3,000		
Printing (208 + 27)	235		
Post and telephone (412 + 29 + 35 − 25)	451		
Meetings	860		
Committee expenses	240		
General expenses (451 + 180)	631		
Accounting charge	40		
Bank charges	28		
Provision for subscriptions in arrears	100		
		6,305	
Total expenses			10,410
Deficit of expense over income			(1,717)

Balance sheet as at 31 December 19X1

	Cost	Depreciation	
Fixed assets	£	£	£
Freehold premises	20,000	300	19,700
Leasehold premises	2,400	200	2,200
Fixtures and fittings – book value	–	–	3,006
Local Authority Loan Stock, at cost	–	–	1,000
			25,906
Current assets			
Stock of pamphlets		200	
Subscriptions in arrears	150		
Less: Provision	100		
		50	
Debtors (150 + 21)		171	
Payment in advance (625 + 120)		745	
Income tax rebate		24	
Cash		40	
Carried forward		1,230	25,906

	£	£	£
Brought forward		1,230	25,906
Current liabilities			
Creditors – Rent	200		
– Subscriptions in advance	100		
Accrued expenses (125 + 40 + 27 + 35)	227		
Overdraft (W1)	151		
		678	552
			26,458
Long-term interest-free loan			10,000
			16,458
Accumulated fund			
At 1 January 19X1 (W2)			13,675
Transfer from life members' fund			900
Deficit for the year			(1,717)
			12,858
Life membership fund			3,600
			16,458

Workings

1.	Bank		£
	Opening Balance overdrawn		(69)
	Add: receipts		10,443
	Less: Payments		(10,497)
	Less: Charges		(28)
	Closing Balance		(151)

2.	Accumulated fund at 31.12.X0		
		Assets	Liabilities
		£	£
	Leasehold	2,400	
	Freehold	20,000	
	Fixtures and fittings	2,700	
	Subscriptions in arrear	100	
	Insurance prepaid	375	
	Investment	1,000	
	Tax rebate on investment income	24	
	Rates outstanding		100
	Telephone		25
	Pamphlet stock	250	
	Cash	20	
	Bank		69
	Long term loan		10,000
	Life fund		3,000
	Fund = £13,675	26,869	13,194

3. Subscriptions	Individuals £	Groups £
Cash	3,370	1,000
Less: Opening arrears	100
	3,270	1,000
Add: Closing arrears	150
Less: Closing in advance		100
	3,420	900

4. **Rates**

	£
Cash paid	450
½ year to 30 September	250
∴ ½ year to 31 March 19X1	200

∴ Rates in arrears at 31.12.X0 = £200 ÷ 2 = £100
∴ Rates in arrears at 31.12.X1 = £250 ÷ 2 = £125
Cost for year £450 − £100 + 125 = £475

5. **Insurance**

	£
Cash paid for year to 31.5.X2	1,500
Prepaid 5/12	625
	875
Previous year £1,500 × 3/5 = 900	
Paid to 31.5.X1 £900	
∴ Paid in advance at 31.5.X1 £900 × 5/12	375
Cost for the year	1,250

6. **Life fund**

	£
Opening balance	3,000
Less: Transferred £300 × 3	900
	2,100
Plus: New members	1,500
	3,600

7. **Depreciation**

Freehold £20,000 − £5,000 = £15,000 ÷ 50 =	£300
N.B. Assume: 50 year life	
Leasehold £2,400 ÷ 12 =	£200
Fixture and fittings	
£2,700 + £640 = £3,340 ÷ 10 =	£334

8. **Pamphlets**   £
    Opening stock   250
    Purchases   350

                                                         600
    Less: Closing stock   200

    Cost of sales   400
    Sales (400 + 150)   550

    Surplus   150
                                                         ===

5 DOHRAY AMATEUR MUSICAL SOCIETY

(a) **Dohray Amateur Musical Society income and expenditure account for the year ended 31 May 19X5**

	£	
Income from members		
Joining fees (W3)	232	
Subscriptions (W2)	345	577
Income from activities		
Surplus on annual concert (W6)	729	
Surplus on sale of goods (W7)	18	
Surplus on refreshments	41	
Raffle profits	64	852
Income from grants and sponsorships		
PAC grant — revenue	100	
PAC grant — capital (W10)	215	
Sponsorship (W5)	100	415
Total income		1,844
Expenditure		
Deficit on musical festivals (W8)	413	
Honoraria — treasurer	100	
— secretary	150	
Rent (W11)	500	
Bank charges	42	
Sundry expenses	60	
Depreciation — musical instruments (W12)	388	
— trophies (W12)	32	
Total expenditure		1,685
Surplus of income over expenditure carried to accumulated fund		159

(b) **Dohray Amateur Musical Society balance sheet as at 31 May 19X5**

	Cost £	Depreciation £	£
Fixed assets (W12)			
Musical instruments	1,940	1,092	848
Trophies	320	128	192
	2,260	1,220	1,040
Current assets			
Stocks — sheet music		52	
— musical instruments		94	
Prepayments		50	
Cash and bank		772	
		968	
Current liabilities			
Creditors	191		
Subscriptions in advance	40		
	—	231	
		—	737
			1,777
Deferred income in suspense			
Joining fees (W9)		594	
PAC capital grant (W10)		525	
Sponsorship (W5)		200	
		—	1,319
			458
Accumulated fund			
Balance at 1 June 19X4 (W1)			299
Surplus of income over expenditure for the year			159
Balance carried forward 31 May 19X5			458

Workings

Opening balance sheet as at 31 May 19X4

	Cost	Depreciation	
	£	£	£
Fixed assets			
Musical instruments	1,378	704	674
Trophies	247	96	151
	1,625	800	825
Current assets			
Stock — sheet music		31	
— musical instruments		70	
Prepayment		40	
Cash and bank		340	
		481	
Current liabilities			
Creditors	161		
Subscriptions in advance	30		
		191	
			290
			1,115
Deferred income			
Joining fees		476	
PAC grant		340	
			816
Accumulated fund: 31 May 19X4			299

2.   **Subscriptions account**

	£		£
I & E account	345	Balance b/d	30
Balance c/d	40	Cash	285
		Bank	70
	385		385

3.   **Joining fees**

	£		£
I & E account	232	Balance b/d	476
Balance c/d	594	Cash	190
		Bank	160
	826		826

4. **PAC capital grant**

	£		£
I & E account	215	Balance b/d	340
Balance c/d	525	Bank	400
	740		740

5. **Sponsorship grant**

	£		£
I & E account	100	Bank	300
Balance c/d	200		
	300		300

6. **Annual concert account**

	£	£
Takings £1,791		1,791
Hall booking fees	490	
Printing posters	112	
Soloists	236	
Musicians	174	
Adjudication fees	50	
		1,062
		729

7. **Sale of goods**

	Sheet music		Musical instruments	
	£	£	£	£
Sales		140		287
Opening stock	31		70	
Purchases	118		336	
Adjust for creditors	−14		−45	
	+20		+39	
Closing stock	(52)		(94)	
	103		306	
	37		(19)	

8. **Music festivals**

		£
Prizes		190
Entrance fees	250	
Hire of buses	281	
RMFC fee	72	
	—	603
		(413)

9. **Joining fees**

		c/d £	I & E account £
19X1	20		20
19X2	24	24	24
19X3	32	128	64
19X4	27	162	54
19X5	35	280	70
	138	594	232

10. **PAC capital grant**

	c/d £	I & E account £
19X1	—	30
19X2	35	35
19X3	80	40
19X4	90	30
19X5	320	80
	525	215

11. **Rent, etc. account**

	£		£
Balance b/d	40	I & E account	500
Bank	510	Balance c/d ⅓ × 150	50
	550		550

12. **Fixed assets**

Musical instruments

19X4		£	19X4		£
1 June	Balance b/d	1,378	1 June	Creditor b/d	79
	Bank	522	19X5		
19X5			31 May	Balance c/d	1,940
31 May	Balance creditors c/d	119			
		2,019			2,019

Trophies

19X4		£	19X4		£
1 June	Balance b/d	247	1 June	Creditor b/d	23
	Bank	83	19X5		
19X5			31 May	Balance c/d	320
31 May	Balance creditors c/d	13			
		343			343

	£
Depreciation:	
Musical instruments £1,940 × 1/5 =	388
Balance b/d	704
Balance c/d	1,092
Trophies £320 × 1/10 −	32
Balance b/d	96
Balance c/d	128

10 Company accounts

Questions on company accounts at this level do not require a full set of published accounts complying with the Companies Acts. The examples, therefore, are similar to those in previous sections and the student merely needs to understand the issue of share capital and the specific formats used for the profit and loss account and balance sheet of a company. The formats used in the solutions comply, as far as possible, with those suggested in the Companies Act 1985 although they are, in some cases, in a simplified format.

QUESTIONS

1 BLM LTD

Although the trial balance of BLM Ltd appears to be correct because the totals are equal, it contains several errors. You are required to draw up the trial balance correctly.

Trial balance at 30 June 19X6

	£	£
Ordinary share capital		100,000
Preliminary expenses	10,000	
Share premium account	3,000	
General reserve		40,000
Goodwill		6,000
Retained profits at 1 July 19X5		700
Deferred taxation		17,000
10% Debentures (secured on fixed assets)		20,000
Bank overdraft	4,000	
Sundry creditors		30,000
Fixed assets, at cost	100,000	
Depreciation for the year		10,000
Provision for depreciation of fixed assets	30,000	
Provision for bad debts	1,600	
Stock of materials	29,000	
Work-in-progress	7,000	
Stock of finished products	71,000	
Sundry debtors	51,000	
Trade investment	12,000	
Sales		360,000
Purchases	149,000	
Wages and salaries	45,000	
Rent, rates and insurance	33,000	
Discount received	2,900	
Returns outwards	1,400	
Income from investments	800	
Carriage inwards		5,000
Bad debts written off	600	
Discount allowed		7,100
Selling expenses	37,000	
Rent received	1,000	
Returns inwards		5,600
Dividends paid	15,000	
Carriage outwards		11,000
Office expenses	5,000	
Lighting and heating	3,100	
	612,400	612,400

15 marks

2 LEDGERS

You are required to explain what the information given in each of the following ledger accounts conveys to you.

(a) **Payroll control**

		£			£
Dec 31	Bank	30,801	Jan 1	Balance b/d	571
Dec 31	National insurance		Dec 31	Wages	40,312
	creditor	2,607			
Dec 31	PAYE creditor	6,833			
Dec 31	Balance c/d	642			
		40,883			40,883

The above account does not include company's costs, such as its national insurance contribution.

(b) **RCM Ltd**

		£			£
Jan 3	Sales	1,000	Feb 17	Bank	975
Feb 25	Bank	975	Feb 17	Discount allowed	25
Feb 25	Discount allowed	25	Oct 3	Bank	150
			Oct 3	Bad debts	850
		2,000			2,000

(c) **Provision for doubtful debts**

		£			£
Dec 31	Sales ledger control	536	Jan 1	Balance b/d	2,019
Dec 31	Balance c/d	2,258	Dec 31	Bank	74
			Dec 31	Profit and loss	701
		2,794			2,794

(d) **Purchase ledger control**

		£			£
Dec 31	Purchase returns	574	Jan 1	Balance b/d	3,001
Dec 31	Bank	34,025	Dec 31	Purchases	36,449
Dec 31	Discount received	872			
Dec 31	Sales ledger control	413			
Dec 31	Balance c/d	3,566			
		39,450			39,450

(e) **Plant and machinery**

		£			£
Jan 1	Balance b/d	95,000	Aug 13	Disposal of plant	8,000
May 27	Bank	13,000	Dec 31	Balance c/d	100,000
		108,000			108,000

Provision for depreciation of plant and machinery

		£			£
Aug 13	Disposal of plant	7,200	Jan 1	Balance b/d	46,300
Dec 31	Balance c/d	49,000	Dec 31	Profit and loss	9,900
		56,200			56,200

Disposal of plant

		£			£
Aug 13	Plant and machinery	8,000	Aug 13	Provision for depreciation of plant and machinery	7,200
Dec 31	Profit and loss	100	Aug 13	Bank	900
		8,100			8,100

(f) **Rent and rates**

		£			£
Jan 1	Balance b/d	248	Jan 1	Balance b/d	100
Feb 28	Bank	300	Dec 31	Profit and loss	2,258
Apr 21	Bank	540	Dec 31	Balance c/d	270
May 31	Bank	300			
Aug 31	Bank	300			
Oct 24	Bank	540			
Nov 30	Bank	300			
Dec 31	Balance c/d	100			
		2,628			2,628

(g) **Ordinary share capital**

		£			£
Mar 31	Share premium	100,000	Jan 1	Balance b/d	500,000
Dec 31	Balance c/d	700,000	Mar 31	Bank	300,000
		800,000			800,000

Debentures

		£			£
Jun 30	Bank	110,000	Jan 1	Balance b/d	100,000
			Jun 30	Share premium	10,000
		110,000			110,000

Share premium

		£			£
Jun 30	Debentures	10,000	Mar 31	Ordinary share capital	100,000
Dec 31	Balance c/d	90,000			
		100,000			100,000

3 STEADFAST STORES LTD

The following is the draft balance sheet at 31 March 19X1 of Steadfast Stores Ltd:

	£	£		Cost £	Aggregate depreciation £	£
Capital:			Fixed assets:			
Ordinary shares of £1, fully paid		30,000	Freehold property	20,000	3,000	17,000
Share premium account		5,000	Fixtures and fittings	24,000	9,000	15,000
Profit and loss account		9,000				
		44,000		44,000	12,000	32,000
Current liabilities:			Current assets:			
Trade creditors	7,100		Stock in trade, at cost		9,500	
Proposed dividends	3,000	10,100	Trade debtors		7,700	
			Balance at bank		4,900	22,100
		54,100				54,100

Since preparing the above balance sheet, it has been discovered that:

(a) Goods received from B. Brown in February 19X1 on a sale or return basis and all unsold at 31 March 19X1 have been regarded as outright purchases at the pro forma invoice 'cost' of £4,000 by the accountant of Steadfast Stores Ltd.

(b) No entry has been made in the books for the following unpresented cheques at 31 March 19X1:

		£
	L. Barnes – Stationery	160
	K. Keeper – Payment in advance for goods to be delivered in June 19X1	240

(c) The annual stocktaking took place on 6 April 19X1 instead of on the accounting year end. During the period from 31 March 19X1 to 6 April 19X1:

	£
Sales were	16,000
Sales returns were	300
Purchases were	4,700
Purchases returns were	180

Note: Steadfast Stores Ltd obtains a uniform rate of gross profit of 25% on selling price.

(d) The company acquired a quantity of stationery in March 19X1 at a special price of £1,000. The acquisition of this stationery, none of which has been used yet, has been charged to fixtures and fittings.

Note: It can be assumed that the depreciation charge for the year ended 31 March 19X1 has not been affected by this item.

(e) One of the stock sheets prepared on 6 April 19X1 was undercast by £300.

(f) Adjustments have not been made in the accounts for discounts received from suppliers of £340 during the year ended 31 March 19X1.

You are required to prepare the corrected balance sheet at 31 March 19X1 of Steadfast Stores Ltd.

17 marks

4 PILLAR TRADERS LTD

The summarised draft trading and profit and loss account for the year ended 30 September 19X9, and draft balance sheet at that date of Pillar Traders Ltd are as follows:

Draft trading and profit and loss account for the year ended 30 September 19X9

	£	£
Sales		100,000
Less: Cost of sales		71,000
Gross profit		29,000
Less: Establishment and administrative expenses	8,000	
Sales and distribution expenses	6,000	14,000
Net profit		15,000

Draft balance sheet as at 30 September 19X9

		£
Share capital — Authorised and issued, fully paid		
50,000 Ordinary shares of £1 each		50,000
10,000 6% Redeemable preference shares of £1 each		10,000
		60,000
Reserves — Retained earnings		44,000
		104,000

Represented by:

Fixed assets:	At cost	Aggregate depreciation	
	£	£	£
Freehold property	51,000	—	51,000
Fixtures and fittings	9,000	3,600	5,400
Motor vehicles	12,000	6,000	6,000
	72,000	9,600	62,400

Current assets	£	£	
Stock, at cost		24,500	
Trade debtors		29,100	
		53,600	
Less: Current liabilities			
Bank overdraft	5,000		
Trade creditors and accruals	7,000	12,000	41,600
			104,000

It now appears that the following items have not been taken into account in the above draft accounts:

(a) Goods received by the company on a sale or return basis in July 19X9, and unsold at the accounting year end have been included in the stock, at cost, at 30 September 19X9, at £5,000.

(b) On 29 September 19X9, a cheque for £3,000 was received from P. Parkes, debtor; this receipt was not recorded in the company's books of account until 2 October 19X9.

(c) A motor vehicle, which was debited to motor vehicles, at cost, when bought in August 19X9 at a cost of £4,000 for the company's delivery fleet, was included wrongly in stock, at cost, at 30 September 19X9.

(d) During the year under review, the company received from its suppliers cash discounts totalling £600; however, no entry has been made in the books of account for these discounts.

(e) Establishment and administrative expenses consist of:

	£
Depreciation – fixtures and fittings	900
Building maintenance	700
Property insurance	600
Administrative expenses	5,800

The property insurance of £600 covers the 18 month period from 1 October 19X8: the annual premium has not changed since 1 October 19X7.

(f) A receipt of £2,000 in May 19X9, from D. Peacock, credit customer, was credited to sales.

Control accounts for purchases and sales ledgers are maintained.

It is the policy of the company to provide depreciation annually as follows: on fixtures and fittings – 10% on cost of assets held at the year ended; on motor vehicles – 25% on cost of assets held at the year end.

You are required to prepare:

(a) The journal entries correcting items (a), (d) and (f) above (**Note**: Journal narratives are required.)

(b) The corrected summarised trading and profit and loss account for the year ended 30 September 19X9, and summarised balance sheet as at that date of Pillar Traders Ltd.

17 marks

5 KEYSTALL LTD

The following balances at 30 April 19X1 have been extracted from the books of Keystall Ltd:

	£
Ordinary share capital, £1 ordinary shares issued and fully paid	50,000
Profit and loss account at 30 April 19X0	11,700
Freehold property, at valuation at 30 April 19X0	30,000
Fixtures and fittings: at cost	19,000
provision for depreciation at 30 April 19X0	7,600
Motor vehicles: at cost (used for distribution)	16,000
provision for depreciation at 30 April 19X0	5,500
Stock in hand, at cost, at 30 April 19X0	12,100
Trade debtors	13,500
Provision for doubtful debts, at 30 April 19X0	70
Balance at bank	8,500
Trade creditors	3,700
General rates	1,300
Wages and salaries	29,000
Returns inwards	3,200
Returns outwards	5,700
Sales	128,000

	£
Advertising	1,800
Purchases	74,000
Heat, light and power	9,220
Loan stock interest, to 31 October 19X0	400
Insurances	2,300
General expenses	1,900
8% Loan stock 19Y0-Z2	10,000

Additional information, with particular reference to the accounting year ended 30 April 19X1:

1. Since preparing the above list of balances, the company has been advised that the following outstanding trade debt is irrecoverable: K. Booker — £400. It has been decided to write off this debt.

2. The provision for doubtful debts is maintained at 2% of trade debtors at the relevant account year end.

3. No entry has been made in the accounts concerning the sale of one of the company's vehicles on 19 March 19X1. This vehicle was acquired by the company on 19 March three years earlier at a cost of £3,000; the proceeds of the sale amounting to £250 were received on 13 May 19X1.

4. It is policy to provide for depreciation annually on the cost or value of fixed assets held at the end of each accounting year at the following rates:

Freehold property	5%
Fixtures and fittings	10%
Motor vehicles	25%

5. Included in the advertising charge of £1,800 is £300 for the preparation of a brochure for a staff recruitment campaign to commence in July 19X1. The remaining advertising is entirely for distribution.

6. The charge for insurance includes a payment of £2,000 for the year ending 31 July 19X1.

7. The company has now received a demand for rates of £2,400 for the year ending 31 March 19X2.

8. The stock in hand at 30 April 19X1 has been valued at cost at £15,300.

9. The directors are recommending that a dividend of 5% be paid on the ordinary share capital for the year ended 30 April 19X1.

10. Apart from bad debts, depreciation of motor vehicles and advertising, the expenses are 50% administrative and 50% distribution.

You are required to prepare the profit and loss account for the year ended 30 April 19X1 and a balance sheet as at that date of Keystall Ltd.

Ignore taxation.

20 marks

ANSWERS

1 BLM LTD

Trial balance at 30 June 19X6

	£	£
Ordinary share capital		100,000
Preliminary expenses	10,000	
Share premium account		3,000
General reserve		40,000
Goodwill	6,000	
Retained profits, at 1 July 19X5		700
Deferred taxation		17,000
10% Debentures (secured on fixed assets)		20,000
Bank overdraft		4,000
Sundry creditors		30,000
Fixed assets, at cost	100,000	
Depreciation for the year	10,000	
Provision for depreciation of fixed assets		30,000
Provision for bad debts		1,600
Stock of materials	29,000	
Work-in-progress	7,000	
Stock of finished products	71,000	
Sundry debtors	51,000	
Trade investment	12,000	
Sales		360,000
Purchases	149,000	
Wages and salaries	45,000	
Rent, rates and insurance	33,000	
Discount received		2,900
Returns outwards		1,400
Income from investments		800
Carriage inwards	5,000	
Bad debts written off	600	
Discount allowed	7,100	
Selling expenses	37,000	
Rent received		1,000
Returns inwards	5,600	
Dividends paid	15,000	
Carriage outwards	11,000	
Office expenses	5,000	
Lighting and heating	3,100	
	612,400	612,400

2 LEDGERS

(a) Payroll control

The account shows that on 1 January, the beginning of the year, the business owed £571 in respect of wages earned at the end of the previous financial year. During the year ended 31 December, the business incurred wage costs amounting to £40,312 but, of this amount, £642 was owing at the year end. From the gross wages payable, £2,607 was deducted for the employee's National Insurance contributions and £6,833 for their PAYE Income Tax, for payment to the Collector of Taxes. The balance, £30,801, was paid as net wages to the employees during the year.

(b) RCM Ltd

On 3 January goods worth £1,000 were sold by the business to RCM Ltd who sent a cheque for £975 on 17 February, being allowed £25 cash discount for prompt payment. The bank did not honour RCM's cheque so RCM's account was debited with £975 in respect of the bad cheque and £25 in respect of cash discount to reflect that this company still owed the full £1,000 for goods purchased. On 3 October, the business received payment by cheque for £150 and decided to write off the balance of the debt, £850, as irrecoverable.

(c) Provision for doubtful debts

At 1 January £2,019 had been provided from the profits of previous years to allow for debts which might not be paid to the business. During the year, £536 was written off as definite bad debts and £74 received in respect of debts previously thought to be bad and, consequently, written off. A further £701 was provided from the profit of the year ended 31 December to increase the provision to the required level of £2,258.

(d) Purchase ledger control

On 1 January the business owed £3,001 to its suppliers. During the year to 31 December it purchased goods valued at £36,449 and returned to its suppliers goods to the value of £574. During the year the business also paid £34,025 to its suppliers and was allowed £872 cash discount for prompt payment. It offset debts of £413 against sales of the same amount made to suppliers. At the end of the year it owed a balance of £3,566.

(e) Plant and machinery, provision for depreciation, disposal

At 1 January the business owned plant and machinery which had cost (or been revalued at) £95,000. On 27 May it bought new plant costing £13,000 and on 13 August it sold plant which had cost £8,000. At the end of the year the business owned plant and machinery which had cost (or been revalued at) £100,000. After allowing for £7,200 depreciation no longer required on the plant which had been sold and a further charge against the year's profits of £9,900 for wear and tear on the plant and machinery which had been used, the provision for depreciation (reflecting the lessening in value of plant and machinery) carried forward was £49,000. The plant which had been sold had originally cost £8,000. It had been depreciated by £7,200 and, therefore, had a book value of £800. The cash proceeds from its sale were £900 so that its disposal gave rise to a book profit of £100.

(f) **Rent and rates**

At the beginning of the year, three months' rates had been paid in advance and one month's rent had been accrued. During the year, two half-yearly payments of £540 made in advance for rates, leaving a balance of £270 to be carried forward as it relates to the first three months of the next year. Four quarterly payments of £300 each were made for rent which left one month's rent of £100 to be accrued and carried forward as a liability. The combined annual charge for rent and rates amounted to £2,258 and was transferred to the profit and loss account.

(g) **Ordinary share capital, debentures, share premium**

On 31 March the company received £300,000 for new ordinary shares issued. £200,000 of this amount, the nominal value of the shares, was added to the ordinary share capital to increase this to £700,000. £100,000 was credited to the share premium account. On 30 June, debentures, whose nominal value was £100,000, were redeemed, at a premium, for cash amounting to £110,000. £10,000 of the share premium account was applied to write off the 'premium on redemption of debentures' leaving the balance to be carried forward on the share premium account of £90,000.

3 STEADFAST STORES LTD

Balance sheet at 31 March 19X1

	Cost £	Depreciation £	£
Fixed assets			
Freehold property	20,000	3,000	17,000
Fixtures and fittings	23,000	9,000	14,000
	43,000	12,000	31,000
Current assets			
Stock in trade (W1)		13,055	
Stock of stationery		1,000	
Prepayments		240	
Trade debtors		7,700	
Balance at bank (W2)		4,500	
		26,495	
Current liabilities			
Trade creditors (W3)	2,760		
Proposed dividends	3,000		
		5,760	
			20,735
			51,735

	£
Capital and reserves	
Ordinary shares of £1, fully paid	30,000
Share premium account	5,000
Profit and loss account (W4)	16,735
	51,735

Workings

1. Stocks

	£
Per draft balance sheet	9,500
Less: Goods on sale or return	(4,000)
Less: Purchases received after year-end	(4,520)
Add: Cost of goods sold after year-end	11,775
Add: Undercast of stocks sheets	300
	13,055

2. Cash

	£
Per draft balance sheet	4,900
Less: Unpresented cheques (160 + 240)	(400)
	4,500

3. Creditors

	£
Per draft balance sheet	7,100
Less: Discounts received	(340)
Less: Goods on sale or return	(4,000)
	2,760

4. Profit and loss account

	£
Per draft balance sheet	9,000
Less: Extra stationery expense	(160)
Add: Adjustment to closing stock (11,775 − 4,520)	7,255
Add: Mistake in closing stock	300
Add: Discounts received	340
	16,735

4 PILLAR TRADERS LTD

(a) **Journal entries**

			Dr £	Cr £
(a)	Debit	Cost of goods sold	5,000	
	Credit	Stock at cost		5,000

being goods held on a sale or return basis at the year end and incorrectly counted in the stock figure.

			Dr £	Cr £
(d)	Debit	Purchases ledger control	600	
	Credit	Discount received		600

being dicounts received from suppliers. (It will also be necessary to debit the individual creditors' accounts.)

			Dr £	Cr £
(f)	Debit	Sales	2,000	
	Credit	Sales ledger control		2,000

being an amount received from a debtor which had incorrectly been credited to sales. (The individual account must also be credited.)

(b) **Trading and profit and loss account for the year ended 30 September 19X9**

	£	£
Sales		98,000
Less: Cost of sales (W1)		80,000
Gross profit		18,000
Less: Establishment and administrative expenses	7,800	
Sales and distribution expenses	6,000	
	13,800	
Less: Discounts received	600	
		13,200
Net profit		4,800

Balance sheet at 30 September 19X9

Fixed assets	At cost £	Aggregate depreciation £	£
Freehold property	51,000	–	51,000
Fixtures and fittings	9,000	3,600	5,400
Motor vehicles	12,000	6,000	6,000
	72,000	9,600	62,400

		£	£	£
Brought forward				62,400
Current assets				
Stock at cost (W4)			15,500	
Trade debtors and prepayments (W5)			24,300	
			39,800	
Current liabilities				
Bank overdraft (W6)		2,000		
Trade creditors and accruals (W7)		6,400	8,400	31,400
				93,800
Capital and reserves				
Ordinary shares of £1 each				50,000
6% Redeemable preference shares of £1 each				10,000
Profit and loss account (W3)				33,800
				93,800

Workings

1. Cost of goods sold

	£
Per draft P & L	71,000
Goods on sale or return (a)	5,000
Motor vehicle (c)	4,000
	80,000

2. Establishment and administrative expenses

	£
Per draft P & L	8,000
Prepayment on insurance	(200)
	7,800

3. Profit and loss account

	£
Per draft balance sheet	44,000
Adjustment to current year's profit (15,000 − 4,800)	(10,200)
	33,800

		£	£
4.	Stock at cost at 30 September 19X9		
	Per draft balance sheet		24,500
	Less: Reduction re goods on sale or return basis	5,000	
	Reduction re motor vehicle, a fixed asset, included in stock at 30 September 19X9	4,000	
			9,000
			15,500
5.	Trade debtors at 30 September 19X9	£	£
	Per draft balance sheet		29,100
	Plus: Insurance prepayment		200
			29,300
	Less: Adjustment for receipt from P. Parkes	3,000	
	Adjustment for receipt from D. Peacock	2,000	5,000
			24,300
6.	Bank overdraft at 30 September 19X9		£
	Per draft balance sheet		5,000
	Less: Adjustment for cheque from P. Parkes		3,000
			2,000
7.	Trade creditors and accruals at 30 September 19X9		£
	Per draft balance sheet		7,000
	Less: Adjustment re discounts received		600
			6,400

5 KEYSTALL LTD

Profit and loss account for the year ended 30 April 19X1

	£	£
Turnover		124,800
Less: Cost of sales (W1)		65,100
Gross profit		59,700
Less: Distribution costs (W2)	29,252	
Administrative costs (W2)	23,410	
		52,622
Trading profit		7,038
Interest payable		800
Profit		6,238
Dividends		2,500
Retained profit for the year		3,738

Balance sheet at 30 April 19X1

	Cost or valuation £	Depreciation £	£
Fixed assets			
Freehold property	30,000	1,500	28,500
Fixtures and fittings	19,000	9,500	9,500
Motor vehicles	13,000	6,500	6,500
	62,000	17,500	44,500
Current assets			
Stock		15,300	
Debtors	13,100		
Less: Provision	262		
		12,838	
Prepayments		800	
Amount receivable for motor		250	
Balance at bank		8,550	
		37,738	
Current liabilities			
Trade creditors	3,700		
Accrued expenses	200		
Accrued interest	400		
Proposed dividend	2,500		
		6,800	
			30,938
			75,438
Loan stock (19Y0–19Z2)			10,000
			65,438
Capital and reserves			
Ordinary share capital			50,000
Profit and loss account			
Balance at 30 April 19X0		11,700	
Retained profit for year		3,738	
			15,438
			65,438

Workings

1. Cost of sales

	£
Opening stock	12,100
Purchases	68,300
	80,400
Closing stock	15,300
Cost of sales	65,100

2. Distribution costs and administrative expenses
Expenses (sundry)

	£
Rates $(1{,}300 + (\frac{1}{12} \times 2{,}400))$	1,500
Wages and salaries	29,000
Insurances $(2{,}300 - (\frac{3}{12} \times 2{,}000))$	1,800
Heat, light and power	9,220
General expenses	1,900
Depreciation of property and fixtures (W3)	3,400
	46,820

Distribution costs

	£
Advertising $(1{,}800 - 300)$	1,500
Bad debts – written off	400
– increase in provision	192
Depreciation of motor vehicles (W3)	3,250
50% of sundry expenses	23,410
Loss on disposal (W4)	500
	29,252

Administrative expenses

	£
50% of sundry expenses	23,410

3. Depreciation

	£
Freehold $(5\% \times £30{,}000)$	1,500
Fixtures and fittings $(10\% \times £19{,}000)$	1,900
	3,400
Motor vehicles $(25\% \times £13{,}000$ (W4))	3,250

4. Vehicle sold. Necessary entries are:

	Debit £	Credit £
Debit Debtors	250	
Credit Disposal		250
with proceeds		
Debit Disposal	3,000	
Credit Motor vehicles (cost)		3,000
with original cost of vehicle		
Debit Motor vehicles (provision for depreciation)	2,250	
Credit Disposal		2,250
with 3 years depreciation provided to beginning of this year.		

This gives | £
Loss on disposal | 500
Motor vehicle (cost) | 13,000
Motor vehicle (depreciation)
– prior to this year's charge | 3,250

11 Manufacturing accounts

Questions on the preparation of manufacturing accounts appear in most of the syllabuses at this level. The business concerned can be a sole trader, a limited company or a partnership: questions of the first two types appear in this section and there are questions involving manufacturing partnerships in a later section.

There is no required format for a manufacturing account, although certain rules should be obeyed such as the emphasis of prime cost and factory cost: the answers in this section illustrate these points.

QUESTIONS

1 YMB PLC

The trial balance of YMB plc at 30 June 19X5 was as follows:

	Dr £000	Cr £000
Ordinary shares of £0.25 each, fully paid		50,000
6% preference shares of £1.00 each, fully paid		2,000
Share premium		8,000
Retained profit at 30 June 19X4		36,120
Freehold land and buildings at cost	15,000	
Plant and equipment at cost	80,000	
Motor vehicles at cost	10,000	
Depreciation provisions at 30 June 19X4:		
Freehold land and buildings		7,200
Plant and equipment		12,500
Motor vehicles		2,000
Stocks at 30 June 19X4:		
Materials	13,000	
Work-in-progress	84	
Finished products	9,376	
Packaging materials	18	
Trade debtors	23,000	
Provision for bad debts		1,000
Cash at bank	2,000	
Trade creditors		6,000
Sales		200,000
Purchases of materials	62,000	
Manufacturing wages	29,500	
Variable manufacturing overhead expenses	20,000	
Fixed manufacturing overhead expenses	34,895	
Variable distribution costs	2,702	
Fixed distribution costs	2,970	
Variable administration expenses	4,000	
Fixed administration expenses	14,155	
Preference dividend	120	
Interim ordinary dividend	2,000	
	324,820	324,820

You are given the following information:

1. There were no additions to fixed assets during the year.

2. Freehold land and buildings are to be depreciated at the rate of 2% per annum by the straight-line method, assuming no residual value.

3. Plant and equipment are to be depreciated at the rate of 10% per annum on cost.

4. Motor vehicles are to be depreciated at the rate of 25% per annum by the diminishing (reducing) balance method.

5. The annual depreciation charges are to be allocated as follows:

	Land and buildings	Plant and equipment	Motor vehicles
Fixed manufacturing overhead expenses	75%	80%	—
Fixed distribution costs	10%	5%	80%
Fixed administration expenses	15%	15%	20%

6. The bad debts provision is to be increased by an amount equal to 1% of sales. This item is to be regarded as a variable distribution cost.

7. Stocks at 30 June 19X5, valued at full manufacturing cost where appropriate, were:

	£000
Materials	15,000
Work-in-progress	80
Finished products	10,900
Packaging materials (variable distribution costs)	20

8. Prepayments and accruals at 30 June 19X5 were:

	Prepayments £000	Accruals £000
Manufacturing wages	—	500
Fixed administration expenses	900	1,100
Variable distribution costs	100	400

9. Provision is to be made for corporation tax at the rate of 50% of the net profit (advance corporation tax is to be ignored) and a final ordinary dividend of £0.02 per share.

You are required to prepare, for YMB plc's internal purposes, the following historic cost financial statements:

(a) a manufacturing, trading and profit and loss account, in vertical and columnar form, for the year ended 30 June 19X5;

22 marks

(b) a balance sheet, in vertical and columnar form, as at that date.   *18 marks*

Total 40 marks

2 SELBRIGHT LTD

From the following information prepare the manufacturing, trading and profit and loss account of Selbright Ltd for the year to 31 October 19X9 and a balance sheet as at that date for presentation to the management of the firm.

	£	£
Salesmen's salaries	32,000	
Office rates	3,200	
Salaries	80,000	
Factory rates	10,080	
Postage and telephone	2,880	
Wages	219,200	
Printing and stationery	800	
Purchases	520,000	
Commission	12,000	
Sales		1,233,760
Factory heat and light	9,600	
Bank	136,000	
Office heat and light	4,000	
Retained profits		49,440
Repairs to plant	13,600	
General reserves		80,000
Insurance — Factory	4,800	
— Office	800	
Share premium account		58,240
Debenture interest for year to 31 October 19X9	24,000	
Dividends received		60,800
Stock — Finished goods — 1 November 19X8	20,320	
— Raw material — 1 November 19X8	149,120	
Tax reserve certificates	128,000	
Goodwill	160,000	
Investments	300,000	
Furniture and fittings	35,200	
10% Debenture stock		240,000
Plant and machinery	192,000	
Debtors and creditors	171,200	80,000
Land and buildings	358,720	
Work in progress at 1 November 19X8	14,720	
Issued share capital		800,000
	2,602,240	2,602,240

Notes

(a) Stocks at 31 October 19X9 were:

Finished goods	64,160
Work in progress	20,480
Raw materials	122,240

(b) Depreciation is to be charged on plant and machinery and furniture and fittings at a rate of 20% and 10% respectively.

(c) Provide for a dividend of 10% on the issued share capital.

(d) Provide £128,000 for corporation tax on the profits of the year.

(e) The authorised and issued share capital consists of 800,000 ordinary shares of £1 each, fully paid.

25 marks

3 PGW LTD

You are required to correct where necessary the manufacturing, trading, profit and loss, and appropriation accounts of PGW Ltd for the year ended 31 December 19X4, and the balance sheet as at that date.

Manufacturing, trading, profit and loss, and appropriation accounts of PGW Ltd for the year ended 31 December 19X4

	£000	£000	£000
Sales			10,100
Less: Returns outwards			60
			10,040
Stock of materials, at 31 December 19X4			700
Purchase of materials		3,210	
Less: Returns inwards		100	
			3,110
			3,810
Less: Stock of materials, at 31 December 19X3			650
Materials consumed			3,160
Carriage outwards			22
Manufacturing wages			850
Manufacturing expenses			1,275
Depreciation			380
Increase in work-in-progress			20
Cost of goods manufactured			5,707
Decrease in stock of finished goods			900
Cost of goods sold			6,607
Gross profit			3,433
Add: Income from investments			80
Carriage inwards			15
Discount allowed			240
Carried forward			3,768

		£000	£000	£000
Brought forward				3,768
Less: Administration expenses				
	Office salaries and expenses		860	
	Rent received		20	
	Depreciation		50	
				930
Less: Marketing expenses:				
	Advertising		1,010	
	Salaries and commission		360	
	Discount received		70	
	Bad debt recovered	10		
	Less: Bad debts written off	13		
			(3)	
	Decrease in bad debt provisions		5	
	Depreciation		50	
				1,492
Less: Debenture interest payable				80
Net profit before tax				1,266
Taxation				500
				766
Net profit after tax				
Less: Dividends paid			100	
	Dividends proposed		200	
				300
Added to Reserves				466

Balance sheet as at 31 December 19X4

	£000	£000	£000
Fixed assets, at cost		4,800	
Less: Depreciation provision		1,800	
			3,000
Current assets:			
Stock of materials		650	
Work-in-progress		50	
Stock of finished goods		680	
Creditors	400		
Less: Bad debts provision	40		
		360	
Accrued expenses		20	
Bank overdraft		80	
		1,840	
Less: Current liabilities:			
Debtors	900		
Prepaid expenses	10		
Taxation	500		
Dividend paid	100		
		1,510	
			330
			3,330
Ordinary share capital			2,000
Reserves:			
Balance, at 31 December 19X3		1,800	
Add: Balance of unappropriated			
profit for year		466	
			2,266
Debentures			1,000
Investments			900
			6,166

In correcting these accounts you are to assume that:

1. the descriptions of all items are correct;

2. all values are correct except for profits before and after tax, profit added to reserves, and certain totals and differences;

3. the dates of items quoted in the profit and loss account are correct.

20 marks

4 TLM LTD

Using the information given below you are required to prepare for TLM Ltd:

(a) manufacturing, trading, profit and loss and appropriation accounts for the year ended 30 June 19X6;

(b) a balance sheet as at 30 June 19X6.

Balance sheet of TLM Ltd as at 30 June 19X5

	£	£	£
Fixed assets, at cost		835,000	
Less: Depreciation to date		549,000	
			286,000
Current assets:			
Stock of materials		191,000	
Work-in-progress		30,000	
Stock of finished products		200,000	
Debtors		408,000	
Cash at bank		10,000	
		839,000	
Less: Current liabilities:			
Creditors	190,000		
Taxation	50,000		
Proposed dividends	40,000		
		280,000	
			559,000
			845,000
Share capital, ordinary shares of £1 each fully paid			400,000
Retained profit			445,000
			845,000

The following information is also given:

1. During the year ended 30 June 19X6 movements in the accounts were:

	£	£
Net operating profit, before tax, for the year		180,000
Depreciation, for the year: manufacturing		80,000
administration and marketing		20,000
Issue for cash of 100,000 ordinary shares of £1 each at a price of £1.20 each		120,000
Sale of fixed assets		2,000
Increase in creditors		10,000
Reduction in work-in-progress		5,000
Reduction in cash at bank		40,000
Purchase of fixed assets	215,000	
Increase in stock of materials	34,000	
Increase in stock of finished products	50,000	
Increase in debtors	42,000	
Tax paid	51,000	
Dividends paid	65,000	
	457,000	457,000

2. There was a profit of £1,000 on the sale of the fixed assets, which originally cost £50,000. This profit is not included in the net operating profit before tax for the year, and is independent of the depreciation charge.

3. Purchases of materials during the year amounted to £784,000.

4. Wages amounted to 30% of materials consumed.

5. Gross profit (sales less the manufacturing cost of goods sold) was 20% of annual sales.

6. The liability for taxation at 30 June 19X6 was £70,000.

7. The amount charged against the appropriation account for dividends during the year to 30 June 19X6 was £75,000.

8. Manufacturing expenses during the year were £430,000. Administration and marketing expenses during the year were £160,000. These amounts do not include depreciation.

25 marks

ANSWERS

1 YMB PLC

(a) **Manufacturing, trading and profit and loss account for the year ended 30 June 19X5**

	£000	£000	£000
Material consumed			
Opening stock		13,000	
Purchases		62,000	
		75,000	
Closing stock		15,000	
			60,000
Manufacturing wages		29,500	
Accruals		500	
			30,000
Variable manufacturing overhead expenses			20,000
			110,000
Prime cost			
Fixed manufacturing overhead expenses		34,895	
Depreciation (W1)		6,625	
			41,520
			151,520
Work-in-progress—opening		84	
—closing		80	
			4
			151,524
Cost of goods manufactured			
Finished goods—opening		9,376	
—closing		10,900	
			1,524
Cost of goods sold			150,000
Sales			200,000
Gross profit			50,000
Less:			
Distribution costs:			
Variable cost (W3)		3,002	
Packaging stock—opening	18		
—closing	20		
	—	(2)	
Bad debt provision (W2)		1,000	
Carried forward		4,000	50,000

	£000	£000	£000
Brought forward		4,000	50,000
Fixed costs	2,970		
Depreciation (W1)	2,030		
		5,000	
		9,000	
Administration costs:			
Variable		4,000	
Fixed costs (W4)	14,355		
Depreciation (W1)	1,645		
		16,000	
		20,000	
Total distribution and administration costs			29,000
Net profit			21,000
Corporation tax (50%)			10,500
			10,500
Dividends — preference paid		120	
— interim paid	2,000		
— final proposed	4,000		
		6,000	
			6,120
Retained profit for the year			4,380

Statement of retained profit	£000
Retained profit for the year	4,380
Retained profit brought forward	36,120
Retained profit carried forward	40,500

(b) **Balance sheet as at 30 June 19X5**

	Cost £000	Depreciation £000	£000
Tangible fixed assets (note 1)			
Freehold land and building	15,000	7,500	7,500
Plant and equipment	80,000	20,500	59,500
Motor vehicles	10,000	4,000	6,000
	105,000	32,000	73,000
Carried forward			73,000

		£000	£000
Brought forward			73,000
Current assets			
Stocks (note 2)		26,000	
Debtors (note 3)		22,000	
Cash at bank		2,000	
		50,000	
Less: Creditors amounts falling due within one year (note 4)		22,500	
			27,500
Total assets less current liabilities			100,500
Capital and reserves:			
Called-up share capital (note 5)			52,000
Share premium			8,000
Profit and loss account			40,500
			100,500

Notes

1. Depreciation is provided as follows:
   - Freehold land and building — 2% p.a. straight-line basis
   - Plant and equipment — 10% p.a. straight-line basis
   - Motor vehicles — 25% p.a. reducing-balance basis

2. Stocks

	£000
Raw materials	15,000
Work-in-progress	80
Finished goods	10,900
Packing materials	20
	26,000

3. Debtors

	£000	£000
Trade		23,000
Less: Provision for bad debts		2,000
		21,000
Prepayments — distribution	100	
— administration	900	
		1,000
		22,000

4.	Creditors		£000	£000
	Trade			6,000
	Corporation tax			10,500
	Proposed dividends			4,000
	Accruals — wages		500	
	— administration		1,100	
	— distribution		400	
				2,000
				22,500

5.	Called-up share capital	£000
	Ordinary shares of £0.25 each fully paid	50,000
	6% preference shares of £1 each fully paid	2,000
		52,000

Workings

1.	Depreciation	Manufacture £000	Distribution £000	Administration £000
	Freehold land and building: 2% × £15,000 = £300 (75:10:15)	225	30	45
	Plant and equipment: 10% × £80,000 = 18,000 (80:5:15)	6,400	400	1,200
	Motor vehicles: 25% × £(10,000 − 2,000) = £2,000 (—:80:20)	—	1,600	400
		6,625	2,030	1,645

2.	Bad debt provision	£000
	Balance required at 30 June 19X5 (1% × £200,000)	2,000
	Less: Balance at 30 June 19X4	1,000
	Increase required	1,000

3.	Variable distribution costs:	£000
	per question	2,702
	plus accruals	400
		3,102
	less prepayments	100
		3,002

4. Fixed administration expenses:

	£000
per question	14,155
plus accruals	1,100
	15,255
less prepayments	900
	14,355

2 SELBRIGHT LTD

Manufacturing, trading and profit and loss accounts for the year ended 31 October 19X9

	£	£	£
Sales			1,233,760
Less:			
Materials			
Opening stock at 1 November 19X8	149,120		
Plus: Purchases	520,000		
	669,120		
Less: Closing stock	122,240		
Materials consumed		546,880	
Labour		219,200	
Prime cost		766,080	
Factory expenses			
Depreciation	38,400		
Repairs	13,600		
Rates	10,080		
Heat and light	9,600		
Insurance	4,800	76,480	
		842,560	
Opening work in progress	14,720		
Closing work in progress	20,480		
		(5,760)	
Cost of goods produced		836,800	
Opening stock of finished goods	20,320		
Closing stock of finished goods	64,160		
		(43,840)	
Cost of goods sold			792,960
Gross profit			440,800
Add: Dividends received			60,800
carried forward			501,600

	£	£	£
Brought forward			501,600
Less:			
Administrative expenses			
Salaries	80,000		
Heat and light	4,000		
Depreciation	3,520		
Rates	3,200		
Postage	2,880		
Printing	800		
Insurance	800	95,200	
Selling expenses			
Commission	12,000		
Salaries	32,000	44,000	
Financial expenses			
Debenture interest		24,000	163,200
Net profit before tax			338,400
Corporation tax on the profits for the year			128,000
Net profit after tax			210,400
Retained profits brought forward			49,440
			259,840
Appropriations			
Ordinary dividend – 10% Proposed			80,000
Undistributed profits carried forward			179,840

Balance sheet as at 31 October 19X9

Fixed assets	Cost £	Accumulated depreciation £	Net £
Land and buildings	358,720	–	358,720
Plant and machinery	192,000	38,400	153,600
Fixtures and fittings	35,200	3,520	31,680
	585,920	41,920	544,000
Goodwill			160,000
Investments			300,000
Current assets			
Stocks		206,880	
Debtors		171,200	
Bank		136,000	
Tax reserve certificates		128,000	
Carried forward		642,080	1,004,000

	£	£	£
Brought forward		642,080	1,004,000
Less: Current liabilities			
Creditors	80,000		
Corporation tax	128,000		
Proposed dividends	80,000	288,000	354,080
			1,358,080
Long term loans			
10% debentures			240,000
			1,118,080

	Authorised £	Issued £
Share capital		
Ordinary shares of £1 each fully paid	800,000	800,000

Reserves		
Share premium account	58,240	
General reserve	80,000	
Undistributed profits	179,840	
		318,080
		1,118,080

3 PGW LTD

Manufacturing, trading, profit and loss, and appropriation accounts for the year ended 31 December 19X4

	£000	£000	£000
Sales			10,100
Less: Returns inwards			100
			10,000
Stock of materials at 31 December 19X3			650
Purchase of materials		3,210	
Less: Returns outwards		60	
			3,150
Carriage inwards			15
Less: Stock of materials, at 31 December 19X4			700
Materials consumed			3,115
Manufacturing wages			850
Manufacturing expenses			1,275
Depreciation (assumed factory)			380
Carried forward			5,620

	£000	£000	£000
Brought forward			5,620
Less: Increase in work-in-progress			20
Cost of finished goods manufactured			5,600
Decrease in stock of finished goods			900
Cost of goods sold			6,500
Gross profit			3,500
Less: Carriage outwards		22	
Marketing expenses:			
Advertising	1,010		
Salaries and commission	360		
Depreciation	50		
Bad debts written off	13		
Bad debts recovered	(10)		
Decrease in bad debts provision	(5)		
		1,418	
Administration expenses:			
Office salaries and expenses	860		
Depreciation	50		
		910	
Discounts allowed	240		
Less: Discounts received	70		
		170	
			2,520
Operating profit			980
Add: Rents received		20	
Income from investments		80	
			100
			1,080
Less: Debenture interest payable			80
Profit before taxation			1,000
Taxation			500
			500
Profit after taxation			
Less: Dividends paid		100	
Dividends proposed		200	
			300
Added to reserves			200

Balance sheet as at 31 December 19X4

	£000	£000	£000
Net assets employed			
Fixed assets at cost		4,800	
Less: Depreciation		1,800	
			3,000
Investments			900
Current assets			
Stock of materials		700	
Work-in-progress		50	
Stocks of finished goods		680	
Debtors, less provision		860	
Prepayments		10	
		2,300	
Current liabilities			
Creditors	400		
Accruals	20		
Bank overdraft	80		
Current taxation	500		
Proposed dividends	200		
		1,200	
			1,100
			5,000
Debentures			1,000
			4,000
Financed by:			
Ordinary share capital			2,000
Reserves:			
Balance at 31 December 19X3		1,800	
Added for the year		200	
			2,000
			4,000

4 TLM LTD

(a) **Accounts for the year ended 30 June 19X6 — Manufacturing account**

	£000	£000
Materials consumed:		
Purchases	784	
Increase in stocks	34	
		750
Wages		225
Manufacturing expenses		430
Depreciation		80
Cost of production		1,485
Reduction in work-in-progress		5
Cost of finished goods produced		1,490

Trading and profit and loss accounts

	£000	£000
Sales		1,800
Cost of goods sold:		
Finished goods produced	1,490	
Increase in stocks	50	
		1,440
Gross profit		360
Administration and marketing expenses	160	
Depreciation	20	
		180
Operating profit		180
Profit on sale of fixed assets		1
Profit before taxation		181
Taxation:		
On the year's profit	70	
Underprovided in previous year	1	
		71
		110
Dividends:		
Interim – paid	25	
Final – proposed	50	
		75
Retained for the year		35
Balance brought forward		445
Balance carried forward		480

(b) **Balance sheet as at 30 June 19X6**

	£000	£000	£000
Fixed assets, at cost		1,000	
Less: Depreciation		600	
			400
Current assets:			
Stocks and work-in-progress		500	
Debtors		450	
		950	
Current liabilities			
Trade creditors	200		
Bank overdraft	30		
Taxation	70		
Proposed dividends	50		
		350	
			600
			1,000

Financed by:
Share capital and reserves: £000
    Ordinary shares of £1 each, fully paid 500
    Share premium account 20
    Retained profit 480
    1,000

12 Interpretation of accounts

The questions in this section cover the calculation of the standard ratios used in the interpretation of accounts. Students should remember three very important rules:

(a) to consider the interests of the person from whose viewpoint the accounts are being reviewed: is it a shareholder, management, creditor etc.;

(b) to use all of the information in the question and to show how it has been used; and

(c) to appreciate that there is probably not a right answer as assumptions may have to be made and therefore answers should not be too dogmatic.

QUESTIONS

1 MEMORIAL LTD

The condensed financial statements of Memorial Ltd are given below.

Profit and loss account for the year ending 31 October 19X1

	£	£
Sales		112,000
Less: Cost of goods sold		90,000
Gross profit		22,000
Operating expenses	12,000	
Interest	2,000	
		14,000
Net profit before tax		8,000
Taxation		4,000
Net profit after tax		4,000

Balance sheet as at 31 October 19X1

Fixed assets	Gross £	Accumulated depreciation £	£
Plant and equipment	44,000	4,000	40,000
Motor vehicles	11,000	1,000	10,000
	55,000	5,000	50,000

Current assets			
Stock	22,500		
Debtors	16,000		
Prepayments	1,000		
Bank	4,000		
		43,500	
Less: Current liabilities			
Creditors		18,000	
			25,500
			75,500

Represented by	Authorised £	Issued £
Share capital		
Ordinary shares of £1 each fully paid	30,000	20,000
Undistributed profits		30,500
		50,500
8% Debenture stock (19X3–19X5)		25,000
		75,500

Assuming that the levels of stock and debtors and creditors have all remained constant throughout the year, you are required to calculate the following ratios:

(a)	current ratio;	*1 mark*
(b)	debt/equity ratio;	*2 marks*
(c)	collection period;	*2 marks*
(d)	payment period;	*2 marks*
(e)	stock turnover;	*2 marks*
(f)	times interest earned;	*2 marks*
(g)	earnings per share;	*2 marks*
(h)	book value per share.	*2 marks*
		15 marks

2 CONE

Cone is in business as a motor factor. His condensed financial accounts for the last three years are summarised below:

Profit and loss accounts for the year to 31 March	19X0 £'000s	19X0 £'000s	19X1 £'000s	19X1 £'000s	19X2 £'000s	19X2 £'000s
Sales (all on credit)		400		630		870
Less: Cost of goods sold:						
Opening stock	20		25		50	
Purchases	325		550		790	
	345		575		840	
Less: Closing stock	25	320	50	525	100	740
Gross profit		80		105		130
Less: Expenses	40		50		60	
Loan Interest	–	40	–	50	10	70
Net profit		40		55		60

Balance sheets as at 31 March	19X0 £'000s	19X0 £'000s	19X1 £'000s	19X1 £'000s	19X2 £'000s	19X2 £'000s
Fixed assets		89		93		101
Current assets						
Stocks	25		50		100	
Trade debtors	50		105		240	
Cash at bank	10	85	5	160	–	340
		174		253		441
Financed by:						
Capital		100		118		141
Add: Net profit for the year	40		55		60	
Add: Drawings (all on 31 March)	22	18	32	23	36	24
		118		141		165
Loan		–		–		100
Current liabilities						
Creditors	56		112		166	
Bank overdraft	–	56	–	112	10	176
		174		253		441

You are required to:

(a) compute the following ratios for 19X0, 19X1 and 19X2:

    (i) gross profit on sales;
    (ii) gross profit on cost of goods sold;
    (iii) stock turnover;
    (iv) return on capital employed;
    (v) current ratio;
    (vi) liquidity (or quick) ratio;
    (vii) debtor collection period; and   *14 marks*

(b) comment briefly on the results of the business over the last three years using the ratios you have computed in answer to part (a) of the question.   *6 marks*

                                                                            20 marks

3 MORGAN LTD

The following are summarised comparative balance sheets of Morgan Ltd as at 30 November 19X8 and 19X9:

	£	19X9 £	£	19X8 £
Fixed assets				
Land and buildings		60,000		60,000
Equipment		50,000		40,000
Depreciation		(25,000)		(20,000)
		85,000		80,000
Intangible assets		25,000		30,000
Current assets				
Stock	75,000		60,000	
Prepaid expenses	2,000		1,000	
Debtors	50,000		45,000	
Marketable securities	10,000		20,000	
Cash at bank	28,000	165,000	14,000	140,000
		275,000		250,000
		£		£
Share capital				
Ordinary £1 shares, fully paid		120,000		100,000
Undistributed profits		55,000		80,000
		175,000		180,000
Current liabilities				
Creditors	95,000		60,000	
Accrued charges	5,000	100,000	10,000	70,000
		275,000		250,000

You are required to:

(a) Calculate the following for the years 19X8 and 19X9

    (i) working capital;
    (ii) current ratio;
    (iii) acid-test ratio;
    (iv) ratio of current assets to total assets;
    (v) ratio of cash to current liabilities. *10 marks*

(b) Evaluate the changes in each of the above. *5 marks*

Total 15 marks

4 BUSBY LTD

John Holt is interested in obtaining shares in Busby Ltd, and is at present examining financial data in respect of the past three years, derived from published accounts.

Before acquiring shares he approaches you for assistance in obtaining the answers to the following questions concerning the trend over the period.

(a) Is the company more able to pay its creditors?

(b) Do the shareholders gain any advantages from financial leverage?

(c) Are debtors settling their accounts quickly?

(d) Are the total debtors increasing?

(e) What has happened to the price/earnings ratio over the period?

(f) Are the earnings per share increasing?

(g) What trend can be seen in the movement of the market price of the company's shares?

(h) What movement is there on the level of stock held?

You are required to answer each of the above questions, using the following data, giving reasons for your answer.

Selected financial data for the years	19X4	19X3	19X2
Sales trend (as percentages)	120	107	100
Stock turnover	4.7 times	5.3 times	6.4 times
Dividend per share	Unchanged over the three year period		
Dividend yield	5%	4%	3%
Dividend payout ratio	35%	45%	55%
Debtors turnover	8.3 times	9.1 times	10.0 times
Return on total assets	6.3%	5.6%	5.2%
Acid test ratio	0.5:1	0.7:1	1.2:1
Return on shareholders' capital employed	7.6%	5.5%	4.4%
Working capital ratio	2.4:1	2.1:1	1.7:1

20 marks

5 WES WINDLE & CO

You are called in to advise a client who is proposing to buy a business at balance sheet value of £12,000. The balance sheet in question is as follows:

Liabilities	£	£	Fixed assets	£	£
Partners' capital			Goodwill		15,000
Wes	5,000		Plant and		
Share of profit for year	1,000		machinery	10,000	
		6,000	Less: Depreciation	2,000	8,000
			Stock		6,000
					29,000
			Current assets		
Windle	5,000		P & L Bal b/f		12,000
Share of profit for year	1,000		Debtors		20,000
		6,000	Bank		2,000
		12,000			
Creditors		51,000			
		63,000			63,000

Your client has been given the following information by the vendors:

(a) Fixed expenses are low since depreciation is only 5% on a straight line basis.

(b) Net profit this year is 20% of sales and gross profit 50% of sales.

(c) The high ratio of current assets to fixed assets shows that the company is using its capital efficiently.

(d) The goodwill figure is built up of £10,000 paid when the company was purchased and £5,000 because the partners waived £2,500 of salary each this year.

(e) Stock is conservatively stated since £3,000 of goods at cost, on sale or return, have not been included. However these goods were counted as sales of £3,000 in the profit computation for 1976, and treated as a Debtor in the Balance Sheet.

Your client asks for advice on matters which are of doubtful validity in this balance sheet in the light of the above information. Discuss briefly **six** specific points you would raise with your client. Ignore taxation.

16 marks

6 MARTIN SMITH

For a number of years Martin Smith has been employed as the works manager of a company which manufactures cardboard cartons.

He has now decided to leave the company and to set up a similar business of his own on 1 January 19X6 but, before taking this step he wants to see what his financial results are likely to be for his first year of operations.

In order to do this, he has obtained certain 'average industry' ratios from his trade association, the Cardboard Carton Manufacturers' Association (CCMA), which he wants to use as his norm for predicting the first year's results.

At this stage he consults you, asks for your professional assistance and supplies the following information.

	CCMA statistics 19X4 (based on year-end figures)
Sales/Net assets employed	2.8 times
Gross profit/Sales	28.0%
Net profit/Sales	10.0%
Fixed assets/Working capital	1.5:1
Current assets/Current liabilities	2.25:1
Debtors collection period	36.5 days
Creditors payment period	58.4 days

He informs you that he is able to contribute £40,000 as capital and has been promised a long-term loan of £6,000 from a relative.

Initially, he intends to acquire a stock of materials at a cost of £20,000 but his (simple) average stock for the first year will be £18,500. Purchases of materials for the year, excluding the initial purchase of stock, £20,000, will be £97,800. All purchases and sales will be on credit.

Sundry accruals at 31 December 19X6 are estimated at £350 and bank and cash balances at £5,000.

He proposes to withdraw £10,000 during the year for living expenses.

You are required to prepare, in as much detail as can be elicited from the information supplied, a forecast trading and profit and loss account for Martin Smith's proposed business for the year ended 31 December 19X6, and a forecast balance sheet at that date.

All figures should be stated to the nearest £10.

Marks will be awarded for workings which must be shown.

18 marks

7 INTERPRETATION OF ACCOUNTS

'Interpretation of accounts may be defined as the art and science of translating the figures therein in such a way as to reveal the financial strength and weaknesses of a business and the causes which have contributed thereto.'

(Source: *Spicer and Pegler's Book-keeping and Accounts,* 18th ed. pp. 241-2.)

You are required to:

(a) State those areas which you would consider to be important as an interpreter of such figures, identifying a few of the key questions to be asked in each area.

(b) Give an example of data (e.g. a ratio) from each of these areas which you consider might be useful to you in your interpretation.

20 marks

ANSWERS

1 MEMORIAL LTD

Ratio calculations

(a)	Current ratio		43,500:18,000 = 2.4:1	241%
(b)	Debt/equity ratio	(i)	25,000:50,500	49.5%
		or (ii)	43,000:50,500	85.1%
(c)	Collection period		(16,000 ÷ 112,000) × 365	52.1 days
(d)	Payment period		(18,000 ÷ 90,000) × 365	73 days
(e)	Stock turnover	(i)	90,000 ÷ 22,500	4 times
		or (ii)	(22,500 ÷ 90,000) × 365	91.25 days
(f)	Times interest earned		(8,000 + 2,000) ÷ 2,000	5 times
(g)	Earnings per share		4,000 ÷ 20,000	20p
(h)	Book value per share		50,500 ÷ 20,000	£2.52

2 CONE

(a) **Ratios**

(i) gross profit on sales: $\dfrac{\text{gross profit}}{\text{sales}} \times 100$

19X0 $\dfrac{80}{400} \times 100 = \underline{20.0\%}$

19X1 $\dfrac{105}{630} \times 100 = \underline{16.7\%}$

19X2 $\dfrac{130}{870} \times 100 = \underline{14.9\%}$

(ii) gross profit on cost of goods sold: $\dfrac{\text{gross profit}}{\text{cost of goods sold}} \times 100$

19X0 $\dfrac{80}{320} \times 100 = \underline{25.0\%}$

19X1 $\dfrac{105}{525} \times 100 = \underline{20.0\%}$

19X2 $\dfrac{130}{740} \times 100 = \underline{17.6\%}$

(iii) stock turnover: $\dfrac{\text{cost of goods sold}}{\text{½ (opening and closing stock)}}$

19X0 $\dfrac{320}{\text{½ }(20+25)} = \underline{\underline{14.2}}$

19X1 $\dfrac{525}{\text{½ }(25+50)} = \underline{\underline{14.0}}$

19X2 $\dfrac{740}{\text{½ }(50+100)} = \underline{\underline{9.9}}$

(iv) return on capital employed:

$$\dfrac{\text{profit before interest}}{\text{fixed assets + current assets - current liabilities}} \times 100$$

19X0 $\dfrac{40}{(89+85)-56} \times 100 = \underline{\underline{33.9\%}}$

19X1 $\dfrac{50}{(93+160)-112} \times 100 = \underline{\underline{35.5\%}}$

19X2 $\dfrac{60-10}{(100+340)-176} \times 100 = \underline{\underline{18.9\%}}$

(v) Current ratio: $\dfrac{\text{current assets}}{\text{current liabilities}}$

19X0 $\dfrac{85}{56} = \underline{\underline{1.5}}$

19X1 $\dfrac{160}{112} = \underline{\underline{1.4}}$

19X2 $\dfrac{340}{176} = \underline{\underline{1.9}}$

(vi) liquidity (or quick) ratio: $\dfrac{\text{current assets - stock}}{\text{current liabilities}}$

19X0 $\dfrac{85-25}{56} = \underline{\underline{1.1}}$

19X1 $\dfrac{160-50}{112} = \underline{\underline{1.0}}$

19X2 $\dfrac{240-100}{176} = \underline{\underline{0.8}}$

(vii) debtor collection period: $\dfrac{\text{closing debtors}}{\text{credit sales}} \times 365$

19X0 $\dfrac{50}{400} \times 365 = \underline{\underline{46 \text{ days}}}$

19X1 $\dfrac{105}{630} \times 365 = \underline{\underline{61 \text{ days}}}$

19X2 $\dfrac{240}{870} \times 365 = \underline{\underline{101 \text{ days}}}$

(b) Cone's mark-up on cost of goods sold has fallen sharply over the three years — from 25.0% in 19X0 to 17.6% in 19X2, as has his gross profit on sales — from 20.0% in 19X0 to 14.9% in 19X2. It is possible that this was caused by Cone cutting his profit margin and thereby increasing his sales.

Sales and profits have increased in absolute terms over the three years, but for the amount of capital invested in the business, the return on capital employed in 19X2 is well down on the 19X0 figure — 18.9% compared with 33.9%, and nearly half the return of 35.5% achieved in 19X1.

It would appear that Cone's rapid growth of sales in 19X2 has been at the expense of the efficient use of resources, e.g., stock turnover has fallen from 14.2 in 19X0 to 9.9 in 19X2. Whilst this also has had the effect of improving the current ratio (up from 1.5 to 1.9), as can be ascertained from the liquidity ratio (1.1 down to 0.8), Cone might be in difficulty in settling his creditors if they press for immediate payment. Indeed, he seems to have allowed an increasingly lengthy period before his debtors are required to settle their debts — from 46 days in 19X0 to 101 days in 19X1.

By borrowing £100,000 he has been able to finance the expansion of trade in 19X1, but even then his healthy bank balance of £32,000 at the end of 19X1 had become an overdraft of £10,000 just twelve months later.

3 MORGAN LTD

			19X9	19X8
(a)	(i)	Working capital	£65,000	£70,000
	(ii)	Current ratio	1.65:1	2.0:1
	(iii)	Acid test ratio	0.88:1	1.13:1
	(iv)	Ratio of current assets to total assets	0.60:1	0.56:1
	(v)	Ratio of cash to current liabilities	0.28:1	0.20:1

(b) (i) **Working capital** has decreased by £5,000.
The reason is:

	Increase £	Decrease £
Stock	15,000	
Prepaid expenses	1,000	
Debtors	5,000	
Marketable securities		10,000
Cash	14,000	
Creditors	(35,000)	
Accrued charges		(5,000)
	0	5,000

Enquiries are needed into the increase in stock levels and creditors; prima facie it appears that the period taken has extended.

(ii) **Current ratio**

The increase in creditors over 19X8 by 58% has caused the current ratio to fall. Explanations are required as under (i) above.

(iii) **Acid test ratio**

As for the current ratio, the disproportionate increase in the creditors has reduced the acid test ratio from 1.13 to 0.88:1. However, it is difficult to evaluate the change without reference to the cash budgets prepared by the business and to the average industry ratio.

(v) **Current assets to total assets**

The relationship can be affected by the treatment of such items as intangible items and depreciation. For example, the intangible assets have been reduced by £5,000 which would have the immediate effect of improving the current assets to total asset ratio. It is difficult to discuss the ratio without information on turnover to allow one to form views on asset utilisation.

(v) **Ratio of cash to current liabilities**

The ratio was calculated at 0.20:1 and 0.28:1. However, it might be more meaningful to include the marketable securities as part of the cash figure. This would then show:

	19X8 £	19X9 £
Marketable securities	20,000	10,000
Cash	14,000	28,000
	34,000	38,000
Creditors	70,000	100,000
Inclusive ratio	0.48:1	0.38:1
Cash only ratio	0.20:1	0.28:1

i.e., it discloses a completely different trend. As for (ii) it will be necessary to take a close look at the cash budget in order to be able to assess fully.

4 BUSBY LTD

(a) Debtors and stock are both turning over more slowly, indicating that they are an increasing element of the current assets. This is emphasised when it is noted that although working capital has increased over the period, the short term cash and cash equivalents which are used to pay creditors are diminishing as witnessed by the yearly fall in the acid test ratio. As a result it would appear that the company is less able to pay its creditors when due.

(b) 19X4 was the first year when shareholders gained any benefit from financial leverage, since in that year the return on shareholders' equity was in excess of the return on total assets.

(c) Collection of outstanding debtors has slowed down in 19X4, as evidenced in the decline in debtors' turnover, which if converted into days resulted in 36.5 days in 19X2; 40.1 days in 19X3; and 43.9 days in 19X4.

(d) As mentioned in (c) above collection of debts has slowed down, and this coupled with an increase in total sales leads one to understand that the total debtors are increasing.

(e) (f) (g) Dividend yield is increasing, at the same time as dividends themselves remain unchanged, reflecting a decline in the market price of the shares. In addition a decreasing dividend payout ratio coupled with stable dividends points to an increase in the earnings per share. Finally with earnings per share increasing, and a falling market price per share the price earnings ratio must be decreasing.

(h) A higher level of average stock holding must be required to service the increased volume of sales which have moved from 100 in 19X2 to 120 in 19X4. This coupled to the slowing down in stock turnover (from 57 days in 19X2 to 78 days in 19X4) reflects a larger average stock holding.

5 WES WINDLE & CO

Points to be raised would include:

(a) Arrangement of assets on balance sheet is wrong. Stock is a current asset. Debit balance of profit and loss represents past losses and is not an asset. Ratio of FA:CA = 8,000:2,800. This may be too high a ratio of FA:CA and such imbalance may not represent efficiency.

(b) Depreciation at 5% straight line implies a twenty year life for the plant which is now four years old. This may be an unrealistic life assumption. If depreciation is too low, past profits have been overstated, and losses understated.

(c) If net profit is 20% of sales then sales must be £10,000, and gross profit at 50% is £5,000. Thus overheads other than depreciation are £2,500 – 50% of the cost of sales. Sales of £10,000 on a capital employed of £51,000 do not represent an efficient use of capacity.

(d) If losses to date are deducted from partners' capital, there is nothing left. The business is trading entirely on creditors' funds.

(e) Stock on sale or return is wrongly treated in the accounts. Debtors must be reduced and stocks increased. There is no change in the profit figure.

(f) Ratio of debtors to sales (17,000:10,000) is absolutely unreasonable. Ratio of stocks to cost of sales (9,000:5,000) is absolutely unreasonable.

(g) The profit of £2,000 is changed to a loss of £3,000 if management salaries are charged. If this is done the accumulated loss becomes £15,000, and on this basis the existence of goodwill as an asset must be questionable.

Note: The question asks for only six points to be raised.

6 MARTIN SMITH

Forecast profit and loss account for the year ended 31 December 19X6

	£	£
Sales (100%)		140,000
Opening purchase of stock	20,000	
Other purchases	97,800	
	117,800	
Closing stock	17,000	
Cost of sales (72%)		100,800
Gross profit (28%)		39,200
Expenses (18%)		25,200
Net profit (10%)		14,000

Forecast balance sheet as at 31 December 19X6

	£	£
Fixed assets		30,000
Current assets		
Stock	17,000	
Debtors	14,000	
Bank and cash	5,000	
Carried forward	36,000	30,000

	£	£
Brought forward	36,000	30,000
Creditors		
Trade creditors	15,650	
Accruals	350	
	16,000	
Net current assets		20,000
Net assets employed		50,000
Long-term loan		(6,000)
		44,000
Capital introduced		40,000
Profit for the year		14,000
Drawings		(10,000)
		44,000

Workings

1. Closing stock
   - Average stock = (Opening + Closing) ÷ 2 = 18,500
   - Opening stock = 20,000
   - Closing stock = (2 × 18,500) − 20,000
     = 37,000 − 20,000
     = 17,000

2. Net assets employed = Sales ÷ 2.8
   = 140,000 ÷ 2.8
   = 50,000

3. Fixed assets and net current assets
   - Fixed assets = 1.5
   - Net current assets = 1
   - Total 2.5 = £50,000
   - Net current assets = (50,000 ÷ 2.5) × 1 = 20,000
   - Fixed assets = (50,000 ÷ 2.5) × 1.5 = 30,000

4. Current assets and current liabilities
   - Current assets = 2.25
   - Current liabilities = 1
   - Total 1.25 = £20,000
   - Current assets = (20,000 ÷ 1.25) × 2.25 = 36,000
   - Current liabilities = (20,000 ÷ 1.25) × 1 = 16,000

5. Debtors = (Sales per annum ÷ Days per annum) × 36.5
            = (140,000 ÷ 365) × 36.5
            = 14,000

6. Creditors
   Current liabilities = 16,000
   Accruals   =   350
                         ―――――
   Trade creditors   15,650
                         ―――――

   Check calculation
   Trade creditors = (97,800 ÷ 365) × 58.4 = 15,648

7 INTERPRETATION OF ACCOUNTS

(a) The important areas to be considered in interpreting a set of accounts would include the following:

   (i)   profitability;
   (ii) liquidity;
   (iii) capital structure;
   (iv) security of returns;
   (v)   management effectiveness;
   (vi) long-term trends in the business.

Looking at each of these areas in turn we can identify the following key questions.

Profitability

Does the company make a profit?
Is the profit reasonable in relation to the capital employed in the business?
What is the reason for any change in the relative level of profitability?
Could the profitability be increased?
Are the profits adequate to meet the returns required by the providers of capital, the maintenance of the business and to provide for growth?
How are the profits shared?

Liquidity

Has the business sufficient liquid resources to meet immediate demands from creditors?
Has the business sufficient resources to meet the requirements of creditors due for payment in the next 12 months, i.e., creditors payable within one year?
Has the business sufficient resources to meet the demands of its fixed asset replacement programme and its commitments to providers of long-term capital falling due for repayment in, say, the next five years?

Capital structure

What sort of capital has the company issued?
Who owns the capital?
What is the cost of the capital in terms of interest or dividend?
What proportion of the capital has a fixed return (gearing or leverage)?
Is the mix of capital optimum for the company?
Is further capital available if required?

Security of returns

How variable are the profits before interest and tax?
How many times can the interest be paid from the available profit?
How many times can the existing dividend be paid from the available profit?

Management effectiveness

Does management control the costs of the business well?
Which costs, if any, have changed significantly, thus reducing or improving apparent profitability?
Does management control the investment in assets well?
Are fixed assets sufficient for the current level of activity? Are they replaced on a regular basis and adequately maintained?
Are the stock levels adequate for the level of activity, or excessive?
Are debtors collected promptly?
Are creditors paid within a reasonable period of time?
Are surplus cash resources invested to increase overall returns?

Long-term trends in the business

Are profits increasing or decreasing?
Is the size of the business growing faster or slower than inflation?
How has past growth been financed?
Are the levels of stocks, debtors and creditors consistent with the long-term growth of the business?
Are dividends increasing?
Have any radical changes occurred in the past, giving rise to major changes in the business?

(b) Data which might be useful in interpreting the accounts would include:

Profitability: return on capital employed

This may be calculated on a before tax and interest basis in order to make comparisons with other organisations with different capital structures. Calculated on an 'after tax and interest' basis it reveals the level of profitability enjoyed by the shareholders after taking account of any benefits from loan capital.

Liquidity: current assets ratio and quick assets ratio

These are both useful, firstly, in measuring the medium-term ability of the organisation to meet its liabilities, and secondly as a useful measure of the short-term liquidity of the business.

Capital structure: gearing or leverage ratio

This measures the relationship between capital having a right to a fixed return and capital on which no return is guaranteed. Often expressed as the percentage which fixed interest capital bears to total capital.

Security of return: interest cover and dividend cover

These two measures indicate the relative security of interest and dividend payments.

Management effectiveness

The two secondary ratios initially measure two of the most important functions of management. **Net profit as a percentage of turnover** indicates control of costs which make up the difference between these two figures. **Asset utilisation**, that is, turnover per £ of net assets, measures the level of overall investment in assets relative to the level of activity in the business.

Long-term trends

These can be established by comparing growth of turnover from year to year, but it must be remembered that some increase would occur without any genuine increase in the level of activity where inflation causes an automatic increase in selling prices.

13 Source and application of funds statements

The questions in this section involve the preparation of simple statements of source and application of funds. The format used in the answers follows that suggested by Statement of Standard Accounting Practice Number 10.

QUESTIONS

1 A. GREEN

A. Green carries on business in the retail trade and has prepared the following balance sheets for both the current and previous years.

Balance sheets as at 30 June

Assets employed	19X1		19X0	
Fixed assets	£	£	£	£
Freehold property, at cost		100,000		100,000
Furniture and fittings, at cost	16,000		15,000	
Less: Depreciation	11,600		10,000	
		4,400		5,000
		104,400		105,000
Current assets				
Stocks	18,000		17,000	
Debtors and prepayments	25,000		17,000	
Cash at bank and in hand	2,000		1,000	
	45,000		35,000	
Less: Current liabilities				
Trade and accrued expenses	12,000		10,000	
		33,000		25,000
		137,400		130,000
Loan account (M. Green)		10,000		—
		127,400		130,000
Capital account		127,400		130,000

Note: The net profit for 19X1 was £20,000 and A. Green charged a salary of £8,000. His drawings amounted to £22,600.

You are required to:

(a) prepare a source and application of funds statement for the year to 30 June 19X1; *14 marks*

(b) explain briefly why the cash at the bank and in hand has only increased by £1,000 over the year, although the net profit for the same period was £20,000. *4 marks*

Total 18 marks

2 ANTIPODEAN ENTERPRISES

The balance sheets of Antipodean Enterprises at the end of two consecutive financial years were:

Balance sheets as at

31 December 19X2			31 December 19X3	
$	$		$	$
		Fixed assets at written-down value		
38,000		Premises	37,000	
17,600		Equipment	45,800	
4,080		Cars	18,930	
	59,680			101,730
	17,000	Investments (long-term)		25,000
		Current assets		
27,500		Stocks	19,670	
14,410		Debtors and prepayments	11,960	
3,600		Short-term investments	4,800	
1,800		Cash and bank balances	700	
47,310			37,130	
		Current liabilities		
20,950		Creditors and accruals	32,050	
—		Bank overdraft	28,200	
20,950			60,250	
	26,360	Working capital		(23,120)
	$103,040	Net assets employed		$103,610
		Financed by:		
67,940		Opening capital	75,040	
4,000		Capital introduced/(withdrawn)	(6,500)	
15,300		Profit/(loss) for year	25,200	
(12,200)		Drawings	(15,130)	
	75,040	Closing capital		78,610
		Long-term liability		
	28,000	Business development loan		25,000
	$103,040			$103,610

263

Profit for the year ended 31 December 19X3 ($25,200) is after accounting for:

	$
Depreciation — premises	1,000
— equipment	3,000
— cars	3,000
Profit on disposal of equipment	430
Loss on disposal of cars	740

The writen-down value of the assets at date of disposal was:

	$
Equipment	5,200
Cars	2,010

You are required to:

(a) Prepare a statement of sources and applications of funds for Antipodean Enterprises for the year ended 31 December 19X3. *14 marks*

(b) Comment on the financial position of the business as revealed by your answer to (a) and by the balance sheet as at 31 December 19X3. *7 marks*

Total 21 marks

3 LIGHT ENGINEERING COMPANY LTD

The Light Engineering Company Ltd has balance sheets for the last two years as follows:

Draft balance sheets as at 31 December

	19X0 £	19X1 £
Fixed assets		
Goodwill	25,000	20,000
Land and buildings	199,000	296,000
Plant	83,500	71,500
Vehicles	9,300	16,683
Fixtures and fittings	16,880	17,841
	333,680	422,024
ACT recoverable	10,286	8,572
Current assets		
Stock	31,219	21,304
Debtors	41,406	46,360
Bank	18,612	–
	435,203	498,260

Capital

Share capital	100,000	200,000
Share premium	–	27,250
Unappropriated profit	149,617	21,315
14% Redeemable preference shares	100,000	–
Capital redemption reserve fund	–	100,000
Deferred taxation	–	10,000

Long term loans

16% Loan stock	–	70,000

Current liabilities

Creditors	33,840	15,317
Overdraft	–	516
Proposed dividend on ordinary shares	10,000	20,000
Tax payable	31,460	25,290
ACT payable	10,286	8,572
	435,203	498,260

Note to the accounts:

(i) 100,000 ordinary shares of £1 each were issued at a premium of 30p a share. £70 of 16% loan stock was issued at a discount of 2½%. The preference shares were redeemed at a premium of 1%. The premium and the discount have been written off to the share premium account.

(ii) A provision of £20,000 was made for future corporation tax of which £10,000 was transferred to deferred taxation account.

(iii) £5,000 was written off goodwill to the profit and loss account.

(iv) Analysis of fixed assets

	Building £	Plant £	Vehicles £	Fittings £
Opening balance	220,000	147,000	28,512	36,240
Purchases	100,000	23,000	16,418	4,602
Disposals	–	31,000	18,460	–
Closing balance	320,000	139,000	26,470	40,842
Depreciation				
Opening balance	21,000	63,500	19,212	19,360
Profit and loss A/c	3,000	28,000	4,890	3,641
Disposals	–	24,000	14,315	–
Closing balance	24,000	67,500	9,787	23,001
Net book value	296,000	71,500	16,683	17,841

During the year plant was sold for £11,000 and vehicles were sold for £2,800.

You are required to:

(a) compute the trading profit, and taxation paid during the year by reconstructing the profit and loss appropriation account and the taxation account;
8 marks

(b) draft a funds flow statement for the year to 31 December 19X1, in accordance with SSAP 10;
12 marks

(c) comment briefly on what the statement reveals.
5 marks
Total 25 marks

4 GLS LTD

From the information given below relating to GLS Ltd you are required to list all the sources from which the company obtained finance during the year ended 31 August 19X8 and to show the amount raised from each source.

Balance sheets of GLS Ltd at 31 August

	19X7		19X8	
	£000	£000	£000	£000
Fixed assets:				
Freehold land and building at cost	100		—	
Less: Depreciation	20		—	
		80		
Leasehold land and buildings, at cost	—		50	
Less: Depreciation	—		1	
				49
Plant and equipment, at cost	300		1,200	
Less: Depreciation	250		320	
		50		880
		130		929
Investments, at cost		60		
Current assets:				
Stocks and work-in-progress	300		200	
Debtors	100		100	
Cash at bank	10		—	
Carried forward	410	190	300	929

	19X7		19X8	
	£000	£000	£000	£000
Brought forward	410	190	300	929
Less:				
Current liabilities:				
Creditors	40		70	
Bank overdraft	–		94	
Taxation	60		60	
Acceptance credits	–		5	
	100		229	
Net current assets		310		71
		500		1,000
Share capital:				
Preference shares of £1 each, fully paid	–		50	
Ordinary shares of £1 each, fully paid	200		320	
		200		370
Reserves:				
Capital redemption reserve fund	40		–	
Share premium	20		40	
Surplus on sale:				
freehold land and buildings	–		120	
investments	–		20	
Government grants	30		50	
Retained profits	210		250	
		300		480
Debentures		–		100
Loan: ICFC		–		50
		500		1,000

You are given the following information:

1. No plant and equipment was sold or scrapped during the year.
2. On 1 September 19X7 the freehold land and buildings were sold and leased back from the purchaser.
3. A bonus issue of ordinary shares on the basis of one new share for every five held has been made. The capital redemption reserve fund was used for this purpose.
4. The preference shares were issued for cash at par.
5. An issue of £1 ordinary shares was made at a price of £1.25 per share.
6. The debentures were issued at par.
7. The tax charge for the year was £60,000 and no dividends were paid or proposed for the year.

16 marks

ANSWERS

1 A. GREEN

(a) **Source and application of funds for the year ended 30 June 19X1**

	£	£
Source of funds:		
Profit		20,000
Adjustment for item not involving the movement of funds:		
Depreciation		1,600
Total generated from operations		21,600
Funds from other sources		
Loan from M. Green		10,000
		31,600
Application of funds:		
Purchase of furniture and fittings	1,000	
A. Green's drawings	22,600	
		23,600
		8,000
Increase/Decrease in working capital:		
Increase in stocks	1,000	
Increase in debtors	8,000	
(Increase) in creditors	(2,000)	
Movement in net liquid funds:		
Increase in bank and cash balances	1,000	
		8,000

(b) By using the accrual system of accounting, it does not necessarily follow that the level of net profit will be matched by a corresponding increase in liquid funds. Net profit is calculated by allowing for accruals and prepayments at the beginning and end of the financial year. Furthermore, some items of income and expenditure charged to the profit and loss account, e.g., profits on the sale of fixed assets, or depreciation, do not affect the movement of cash. In addition, items regarded as capital, e.g., the purchase of fixed assets, do not appear in the profit and loss account.

In the case of A. Green, the main reason why the cash at bank and in hand has increased by only £1,000, whereas the net profit has increased by £20,000 is because Green has drawn substantial amounts of cash out of the business during the year. Indeed, if M. Green had not loaned him £10,000, he would have been overdrawn at the bank. Another reason is that Green has invested more of the business funds in working capital, largely because of an increase in the amount owing from debtors.

These events are clearly highlighted in the source and application of funds statement which provides additional information beyond that ordinarily disclosed in the profit and loss account and the balance sheet.

2 ANTIPODEAN ENTERPRISES

Statement of sources and applications of funds for the year ended 31 December 19X3

Sources	$	$	$
Profit before tax			25,200
Adjust for items not involving movement of funds:			
Depreciation		7,000	
Loss on disposal		740	
Profit on disposal		(430)	7,310
Total generated from operations			32,510
Other sources			
Disposal of equipment (W3)		5,630	
Disposal of cars (W5)		1,270	6,900
			39,410
Applications			
Drawings		15,130	
Capital withdrawn		6,500	
Repayment of loan		3,000	
Purchase of long-term investments		8,000	
Purchase of equipment (W2)		36,400	
Purchase of cars (W4)		19,860	88,890
			(49,480)
Increase (Decrease) in working capital			
Decrease in stocks		(7,830)	
Decrease in debtors		(2,450)	
Increase in creditors		(11,100)	
Movement in net liquid funds			
Increase in short-term investments	1,200		
Decrease in cash and bank	(1,100)		
Increase in overdraft	(28,200)		
		(28,100)	
			(49,480)

Workings

1. **Premises**

	$		$
Opening balance	38,000	P & L account —	
		depreciation	1,000
		Closing balance	37,000
	38,000		38,000

2.

Equipment

	$		$
Opening balance	17,600	P & L account —	
Additions	36,400	depreciation	3,000
		Disposal	5,200
		Closing balance	45,800
	54,000		54,000

3.

Equipment disposal

	$		$
Equipment	5,200	Sale proceeds	5,630
P & L account — Profit	430		
	5,630		5,630

4.

Cars

	$		$
Opening balance	4,080	P & L account —	
Additions	19,860	depreciation	3,000
		Disposal	2,010
		Closing balance	18,930
	23,940		23,940

5.

Car disposal

	$		$
Cars	2,010	Sale proceeds	1,270
		P & L account — Loss	740
	2,010		2,010

(b) A substantial amount of capital expenditure during the current period, i.e., $64,260 on investments, equipment and cars, has led to a shortage of funds amounting to almost $50,000. This has been financed partly by stock and debtors but in the main by creditors and bank borrowings. Both of these have a cost, creditors in terms of a deteriorating relationship with suppliers if credit periods are being extended beyond reasonable limits, and the bank overdraft in terms of interest payable at a rate probably exceeding 15% per annum. A substantial amount of the resources are held in investments — $25,000 long-term and $4,800 short-term. Unless the return on these investments in terms of interest or dividend and capital growth is in excess of the cost of bank borrowing, consideration should be given to realisation and repayment of the overdraft. The existence of negative working capital is for most businesses an unhealthy sign and attempts should be made to correct this either by the action recommended above or by restriction of drawings over future periods.

3 LIGHT ENGINEERING COMPANY LTD

(a) Profit and loss account

	£		£
Capital redemption reserve fund	100,000	Opening balance	149,617
Dividend	20,000	Surplus on sale of plant	4,000
Tax	20,000	Trading profit	9,043
Deficit on sale of vehicles	1,345		
Closing balance	21,315		
	162,660		162,660

Taxation account

	£		£
ACT recoverable	10,286	Opening balance	31,460
Deferred tax	10,000	Provision	20,000
Tax paid	5,884		
Balance c/f	25,290		
	51,460		51,460

(b) Funds flow statement for the year ending 31 December 19X1

Funds from operations	£	£
Profit before tax	9,043	
Depreciation	39,531	
Goodwill	5,000	
Carried forward		53,574

	£	£
Brought forward		53,574
Funds from other sources		
Issue of ordinary shares + premium	130,000	
Issue of debenture less discount	68,250	
Sale of plant	11,000	
Sale of vehicles	2,800	
		212,050
		265,624
Application of funds		
Dividend paid plus ACT	20,286	
Tax paid	5,884	
Purchase of premises	100,000	
Purchase of plant	23,000	
Purchase of vehicles	16,418	
Purchase of fixtures and fittings	4,602	
Redemption of preference shates plus premium	101,000	
		271,190
		(5,566)
Reduction in working capital		
Stock decrease	9,915	
Debtors increase	(4,954)	
Creditors decrease	(18,523)	
		(13,562)
Decrease in liquid position (£18,612 + £516)		(19,128)

(c) The long term applications exceed the long term sources — the profits retained plus the funds injected are insufficient to finance long term expenditure. Stock reduction is not adequate to offset increased debtors and decreased creditors. Deficit financed by reduction of liquidity plus small overdraft. 14% preference shares redeemed but replaced by 16% loan stock.

4   GLS LTD

Statement of source and application of funds for the year ended 31 August 19X8

	£'000	£'000	£'000
Source of funds			
Profit before tax			100
Adjustments for items not involving the movement of funds			
Depreciation			71
Total generated from operations			171
Carried forward			171

	£'000	£'000	£'000
Brought forward			171
Funds from other sources			
Issue of ordinary shares for cash		100	
Issue of preference shares for cash		50	
Loan raised		50	
Debentures raised		100	
Sale of freehold land and buildings		200	
Sale of investments		80	
Government grants received		20	
			600
			771
Application of funds			
Tax paid		60	
Purchase of plant and machinery		900	
Purchase of leasehold land and buildings		50	
			1,010
			(239)
Increase/(decrease) in working capital			
Decrease in stocks		(100)	
Increase in creditors		(30)	
Acceptance credits		(5)	
Movement in net liquid funds		(135)	
Decrease in cash	(10)		
Increase in overdraft	(94)		
		(104)	
			(239)

14 Partnership accounts

The questions in this section cover the appropriation of profits of a partnership in all of the situations likely to be encountered in examinations at this level. As well as examples of standard trading situations with, possibly, changes in the partnership agreement, there are examples on the admission or retirement of a partner and the dissolution of a partnership.

QUESTIONS

1 CHISH & PHIPPS

Chish & Phipps commenced trading on 1 January 19X6 as wholesalers of frozen seafoods Their affairs were governed by a partnership agreement which provided amongst other things that they should share profits in the proportion Chish $\frac{2}{3}$, Phipps $\frac{1}{3}$, after allowing for interest on the capital introduced by the partners, at the rate of 10% per annum, and that Phipps should receive a salary of £1,000 per annum.

The accounting system used in the business is rudimentary and you have been asked by the partners to produce their annual accounts.

The following is a summary of the bank statements for the year:

Receipts Cash introduced as capital on 1 January 19X6: Chish £7,000, Phipps £4,000. Balance of receipts from customers £25,400.

Payments Motor van £2,000, freezer equipment £5,000, office furniture £750, factory rental £750, wages £3,544, salary of sales manager £2,400, goods purchased for resale £19,800, rates £400, repairs £125, insurance £110, motor expenses £373.

Note The following cash payments were made before banking the balance of the takings: motor expenses £258, wages £296, sundry expenses £50, drawings – Chish £15 per week, Phipps £12 per week.

You also ascertain the following information:

During the year to 31 December 19X6 discounts allowed to customers were £245 whilst discounts received from suppliers were £110. Goods were sold to Shark during the year for £400. At 31 December it was discovered that Shark had disappeared without payment of the amount due. The debt was therefore written off as bad.

The partners had taken goods for their own use as follows: Chish £100, Phipps £150 (selling prices).

At 31 December 19X6 the amounts owing to suppliers amounted to £1,500 and the amount owing by customers was £3,100. The prepayment of rates was £50 and insurance £10. Stock on hand at cost amounted to £2,410.

The factory had been occupied since 1 January 19X6 at an annual rental of £1,000 per annum.

Depreciation is to be provided on a straight line basis as follows: motor van 25% per annum, freezer equipment and office equipment at the rate of 10% per annum.

You are required to:

(a) write up the bank account, petty cash account, sales account and purchases account, and

(b) produce a trading, profit and loss and appropriation account for the year ended 31 December 19X6, and a balance sheet as at that date.

20 marks

2 BOON, MOON AND SOON

Boon, Moon and Soon are in partnership sharing profits and losses in the ratio of 2:2:1. The following balances have been extracted from the partnership books as at 31 August 19X1 after the preparation of the trading, profit and loss account for the year to 31 August 19X1, but before any partnership appropriations have been made:

	Dr. £	Cr. £
Net profit for the year to 31 August 19X1		49,000
Partners' capital accounts:		
Boon		10,000
Moon		10,000
Soon		5,000
Partners' current accounts:		
Boon		500
Moon	1,000	
Soon		500
Freehold premises, at cost	50,000	
Furniture and fixtures, at cost	10,000	
Depreciation – Furniture and fixtures		5,000
Stock	10,000	
Debtors	18,000	
Cash at bank and in hand	1,000	
Creditors		10,000
	90,000	90,000

According to the partnership agreement, Soon is entitled to an annual salary of £5,000, and interest at the rate of 10% per annum is payable on the partners' capital account balances as at the beginning of each financial year. Interest is not charged to or on the partners' current account balances. During the year, the partners' drawings were: Boon £8,000, Moon £7,000 and Soon £5,000, but Boon and Soon had also withdrawn goods estimated to be worth £500 each. Cash drawings had been debited to the partners' current accounts, but no entry had been made in the books to record any goods withdrawn by the partners for their personal use.

You are required to prepare the partnership appropriation account for the year to 31 August 19X1 and a balance sheet as at that date.

18 marks

3 MANLY AND BLANK

Manly and Blank are in partnership on the following terms:

1. Partners' capitals and Manly £12,000, Blank £5,000.
2. Interest at 5% per annum is to be allowed upon capital and current account balances at the beginning of the year.
3. Manly has guaranteed that Blank's total income from the firm shall not be less than £3,750 per annum.
4. Partners are entitled to salaries of, Manly £1,000 and Blank £700 per annum.
5. Profits and losses are shared in the ratio of Manly two-thirds and Blank one-third.
6. The partners are entitled to withdraw on the last day of March, June, September and December, the following quarterly amounts: Manly £700 and Blank £500, and these withdrawals have been made regularly.

In addition to the accounts arising out of the above the following balances were extracted from the books on 31 December 19X6.

	Dr. £	Cr. £
Capital accounts – January 19X6:		
Manly		12,000
Blank		5,000
Current accounts – January 19X6:		
Manly		3,000
Blank		1,000
Stock – 1 January 19X6	19,000	
Freehold warehouse – at cost	8,500	
Fixtures and fittings – at cost	3,200	
Additions and alterations to warehouse during year	1,500	
Sales		87,460
Purchases	62,140	
Rates (Warehouse £300 : Office £100)	400	
Heat and light (Warehouse £380 : Office £120)	500	
Bank overdraft		1,070
Sundry creditors		6,200
Sundry debtors	5,660	
Warehouse expenses	1,320	
Warehouse wages	4,700	
Insurance (Warehouse £240 : Office £60)	300	
Carriage outwards	960	
Bad debts	270	
Staff salaries	2,400	
Office expenses	600	
Provision for depreciation on fixtures and fittings at 1 January 19X6		750
Cash	230	
Drawings: Manly	2,800	
Blank	2,000	
	116,480	116,480

You are required to prepare the trading and profit and loss account for the year ended 31 December 19X6, and the balance sheet as at that date in vertical form taking the following additional information into consideration:

(a) Stock on 31 December 19X6 was valued at £15,600.

(b) The cost of additions and alterations to the warehouse is to be written off over three years, including the year in which the expenditure was incurred.

(c) The following amounts were owing at the close of the year:

| Warehouse wages | £90 |
| Staff salaries | £200 |

(d) £200 is to be carried forward as a provision for bad debts.

(e) Insurance paid in advance at the end of the year on the warehouse amounted to £40.

(f) Fixtures and fittings are to be depreciated at the rate of 10% per annum on cost.

(g) During the year goods were supplied to the partners from stock as follows:

| Manly | £150 |
| Blank | £590 |

No entries have been made in the books and it has been agreed that these should be charged to the partners at the above retail prices.

22 marks

4 DIXON AND KELK

Dixon and Kelk are partners in an old established trading business. Their partnership agreement provides for interest on partners' capital at a rate of 5% per annum, a salary of £3,900 per annum payable to Kelk, and interest to be charged on drawings at 5% per annum, on the total for the year. Net profit after these adjustments is to be divided in the ratio 4:1 to Dixon and Kelk respectively.

The agreement was varied as from 31 August 19X1, in that Kelk's salary was reduced to £3,000 per annum, and the profit sharing ratio became 3:2 to Dixon and Kelk respectively. The partners agreed to assume that profits and drawings accrued evenly over the year.

Dixon has guaranteed Kelk a net income of £6,500 from the partnership for the year.

The following trial balance has been extracted from the books of the partnership as at 31 December 19X1.

	£	£
Capital accounts: Dixon		30,000
Kelk		24,000
Current accounts at 31 December 19X0: Dixon		6,516
Kelk		3,264
Freehold property	20,000	
Fittings at cost	14,000	
Provision for depreciation of fittings as at 31 December 19X0		7,000
Vehicles at cost	8,000	
Provision for depreciation of vehicles as at 31 December 19X0		2,000
Stocks as at 31 December 19X0	21,814	
Purchases	183,212	
Sales		241,983
Staff salaries	23,458	
Drawings: Dixon	9,000	
Kelk	4,500	
Administration expenses	7,140	
Office expenses	5,826	
Bank	2,020	
Petty cash	114	
Debtors	28,000	
Creditor		12,321
	327,084	327,084

Additional information:

1. Dixon's drawings of £480 in cash had been debited in error to the salaries account.

2. Depreciation is to be provided on certain assets held at the end of each year.

   Fittings 5% on cost. Vehicles 25% on cost.

3. Land is included in the balance on the freehold property account at a cost of £5,000. The buildings are expected to have a useful life of thirty years from 31 December 19X0.

4. Accrued administrative expenses at 31 December 19X1 amounted to £567 whereas office expenses had been paid in advance in the sum of £214 on that date.

5. The partners have decided to create a provision for doubtful debts amounting to 5% of trade debtors at the year end.

6. Stock was valued at cost as £16,000 as at 31 December. It was considered to have a net realisable value of £17,946 on that date.

You are required to prepare:

(a) trading, profit and loss, and appropriation, accounts for Dixon and Kelk for the year ended 31 December 19X1, and a balance sheet as at that date; and

(b) partners' current accounts.

24 marks

5 X, Y AND Z

X, Y and Z are trading in partnership under an agreement which provides for interest on partners' capital accounts at the rate of 10% per annum, annual salaries of £8,000 and £5,000 for Y and Z respectively and the balance of the profit or loss divided between X, Y and Z in the proportions ½, 3/10ths and 1/5th respectively.

Partners' cash drawings for the year ended 30 April 19X4 were as follows:

	£
X	9,000
Y	6,000
Z	7,000

The draft balance sheet at 30 April 19X4 of X, Y and Z is as follows:

Capital accounts, at 30 April 19X3	£		Fixed assets:	£	
X		40,000	At cost		120,000
Y		30,000	Provision for		
Z		25,000	depreciation		45,000
		95,000			75,000
Current accounts:	£		Current assets:	£	
X	3,200		Stock in trade	18,000	
Y	2,800		Trade debtors	6,800	
Z	1,700		Balance at bank	7,900	
		7,700			32,700
		102,700			
Current liabilities:					
Trade creditors		5,000			
		107,700			107,700

After the preparation of the draft final accounts for the year ended 30 April 19X4, which disclosed a net loss of £12,000, it was discovered that:

1. The partners' cash drawings for the year under review have been debited to purchases.

2. On 1 November 19X3 it was agreed that Y should increase his partnership capital from £30,000 by the transfer to the partnership of a freehold property bought by Y ten years ago at a cost of £15,000 and currently valued at £35,000. Although the appropriate correct debit entry had been made in the fixed asset account, the corresponding credit entry appeared in the profit and loss appropriation account.

3. The partners' salaries for the year ended 30 April 19X4 have been debited to staff salaries and credited to the relevant partners' current accounts.

The partners have now decided that a provision for doubtful debts should be created of 5% of trade debtors at 30 April 19X4.

You are required to prepare:

(a) A computation of the corrected net profit or loss for the year ended 30 April 19X4 of the partnership.

(b) The corrected partners' current accounts for the year ended 30 April 19X4.

Note: The partners' current accounts should commence with the balances shown in the draft partnership balance sheet at 30 April 19X4.

(c) The corrected balance sheet at 30 April 19X4 of the partnership.   *18 marks*

(d) Outline the reasons for maintaining separate partners' capital and current accounts in partnership accounts.   *4 marks*

Total 22 marks

6 CHECKE AND TIKK

(a) For a number of years you have been employed in a senior position by a firm of certified accountants.

The two partners, Checke and Tikk, have now offered to take you into the firm as a junior partner with effect from 1 April 19X5.

Hitherto the partners have contributed capital thus:

	£
Checke	50,000
Tikk	30,000

on which they receive interest at 5% per annum. They have shared profits (and losses) in the ratio of 3:2 respectively.

After admission to the partnership you will be expected to continue managing the practice for which you will receive exactly half your present annual salary of £14,000 as a partnership salary. You will also be expected to contribute £20,000 as capital (on which you will receive interest at 5% per annum).

The profit sharing ratio will then be altered to give you a one-sixth share of the profits and losses, without disturbing the relative shares of the other two partners.

For the year ended 31 March 19X5, the total amount appropriated by the two partners was £34,000.

You are required to prepare a statement showing the details of the amounts appropriated by Checke and Tikk during year ended 31 March 19X5 together with details of the amounts which would have been appropriated if you had been taken into partnership on 1 April 19X4.   *12 marks*

(b) The financial arrangements between the members of a partnership are usually contained in an agreement.

You are required to state: the position where a partnership agreement contains financial arrangements which conflict with the requirements of the Partnership Act 1890; and the requirements of the Partnership Act 1890 regarding:

(i) interest on capital
(ii) interest on loans made by partners
(iii) remuneration of partners
(iv) sharing of profits and losses.   *6 marks*

Total 18 marks

7 RED, WHITE AND BLUE

Red and White are in partnership sharing profits and losses in the ratio of 3:2. The balance sheet of the partnership as at 30 April 19X2 is shown below:

Fixed assets	Cost £	Accumulated depreciation £	Net book value £
Office equipment, at cost	1,500	500	1,000
Motor vehicles, at cost	7,000	1,400	5,600
	8,500	1,900	6,600
Current assets			
Stocks		11,200	
Debtors		12,500	
Cash at bank and in hand		100	
		23,800	
Less: Current liabilities			
Creditors		11,800	12,000
			18,600
Financed by:			
Capital			
Red			12,000
White			6,600
			18,600

It has been decided to admit Blue to the partnership as from 1 May 19X2. He is to contribute £3,000 in cash immediately to the new partnership as his capital contribution; profits and losses are to be shared in the ratio of 6:3:1. The assets of the new partnership are to be revalued as follows:

	£
1. Office equipment	300
2. Motor vehicles	8,000
3. Stocks	12,000
4. Debtors	12,000
5. Goodwill	10,000

However, the partners do not intend to retain a goodwill account in the new partnership books, and goodwill is to be written off.

You are required to:

(a) prepare the partners' capital accounts to record the above transactions; and

(b) construct the partnership balance sheet of Red, White and Blue immediately after the admittance of Blue on 1 May 19X2.

15 marks

8   ALAN, BOB, CHARLES AND DON

Alan, Bob and Charles are in partnership sharing profits and losses in the ratio 3:2:1 respectively. The balance sheet for the partnership as at 30 June 19X2 is as follows:

Capital	£	£	Fixed assets	£	£
Alan		85,000	Premises		90,000
Bob		65,000	Plant		37,000
Charles		35,000	Vehicles		15,000
		———	Fixtures		2,000
		185,000			———
Current account					144,000
Alan	3,714		Current assets		
Bob	(2,509)		Stock	62,379	
Charles	4,678	5,883	Debtors	34,980	
	———		Cash	760	98,119
Loan – Charles		28,000			———
Current liabilities					
Creditors		19,036			
Bank overdraft		4,200			
		———			———
		242,119			242,119
		=====			=====

Charles decides to retire from the business on 30 June 19X2, and Don is admitted as a partner on that date. The following matters are agreed:

1. Certain assets were revalued — Premises £120,000
   — Plant   £ 35,000
   — Stock   £ 54,179

2. Provision is to be made for doubtful debts in the sum of £3,000.

283

3. Goodwill is to be recorded in the books on the day Charles retires in the sum of £42,000. The partners in the new firm do not wish to maintain a goodwill account so that amount is to be written back against the new partners' capital accounts.

4. Alan and Bob are to share profits in the same ratio as before, and Don is to have the same share of profits as Bob.

5. Charles is to take his car at its book value of £3,900 in part payment, and the balance of all he is owed by the firm in cash except £20,000 which he is willing to leave as a loan account.

6. The partners in the new firm are to start on an equal footing so far as capital and current accounts are concerned. Don is to contribute cash to bring his capital and current accounts to the same amount as the original partner from the old firm who has the lower investment in the business. The original partner in the old firm who has the higher investment will draw out cash so that his capital and current account balances equal those of his new partners.

You are required to:

(a) account for the above transactions, including goodwill and retiring partner's accounts; *20 marks*

(b) draft a balance sheet for the partnership of Alan, Bob and Don as at 30 June 19X2. *5 marks*

Total 25 marks

9 MYRES, WHYTE AND THOMAS

Myres, Whyte and Thomas are in partnership sharing profits and losses in the ratio 2:1:1. The balance sheet of the firm as at 31 May 19X9 was as follows:

Balance sheet of Myres, Whyte and Thomas

	£	£		£	£	£
				Cost	Depreciation	Net
Capital accounts			Fixed assets			
Myres	40,000		Premises	60,000	–	60,000
Whyte	20,000		Plant and			
Thomas	20,000		equip-			
		80,000	ment	10,000	3,440	6,560
				70,000	3,440	66,560
Current liabilities			Current assets			
Bank overdraft	1,300		Stock	16,000		
Trade creditors	5,500		Debtors	4,240		
		6,800				20,240
		86,800				86,800

On 31 May 19X9 it was agreed to dissolve the partnership and as Whyte is continuing in business on his own account he agrees to take over the stock, plant and debtors at valuations of £18,000, £5,500, and £4,100 respectively. He also agrees to acquire the premises at a cost of £105,000 and obtains a mortgage loan of £80,000 which is paid to the partnership. The balance owing by Whyte is charged against Myres's capital account as the two parties have agreed that Whyte will repay the loan to Myres over a period of three years. Realisation expenses amounting to £1,000 are paid in cash and the creditors of the firm are paid in full.

You are required to record the above transactions in the ledger accounts of the partnership.

20 marks

10   GAIN AND MAIN

The following trial balance has been extracted from the books of Gain and Main as at 31 March 19X2; Gain and Main are in partnership sharing profits and losses in the ratio 3 to 2:

	£	£
Capital accounts:		
Gain		10,000
Main		5,000
Cash at bank	1,550	
Creditors		500
Current accounts:		
Gain		1,000
Main	2,000	
Debtors	2,000	
Depreciation: Fixtures and fittings		1,000
Motor vehicles		1,300
Fixtures and fittings	2,000	
Land and buildings	30,000	
Motor vehicles	4,500	
Net profit (for the year to 31 March 19X2)		26,250
Stock, at cost	3,000	
	45,050	45,050

In appropriating the net profit for the year, it has been agreed that Main should be entitled to a salary of £9,750. Each partner is also entitled to interest on his opening capital account balance at the rate of 10% per annum.

Gain and Main have decided to convert the partnership into a limited company, Plain Ltd, as from 1 April 19X2. The company is to take over all the assets and liabilities of the partnership, except that Gain is to retain for his personal use one of the motor vehicles at an agreed transfer price of £1,000.

The purchase consideration will consist of 40,000 ordinary shares of £1 each in Plain Ltd, to be divided between the partners in profit sharing ratio. Any balance on the partners' current accounts is to be settled in cash.

You are required to prepare the main ledger accounts of the partnership in order to close off the books as at 31 March 19X2.

20 marks

11 LEEK AND BEAN

Leek and Bean were in partnership as lawn mower manufacturers, Leek being responsible for the factory and Bean for the warehouse. All completed lawn mowers were transferred from the factory to the warehouse at agreed prices. Profits are to be shared as follows:

	Factory	Trading
Leek	75%	25%
Bean	25%	75%

The following trial balance has been extracted from the books on 30 June 19X9:

	£	£
Capital accounts		
Leek		48,000
Bean		49,000
Drawings		
Leek	6,000	
Bean	5,000	
Freehold factory, at cost	42,150	
Factory plant, at cost	25,750	
Provision for depreciation to 30/6/X8		6,050
Delivery vans, at cost	8,050	
Provision for depreciation to 30/6/X8		3,450
Stocks at 30 June 19X8		
Raw materials	4,028	
Work in progress	3,400	
Lawn mowers completed (1,200 at £40)	48,000	
Sales (1,820 lawn mowers)		111,020
Purchase of raw materials	28,650	
Factory wages	15,020	
Warehouse wages	6,030	
Expenses:		
Factory	12,070	
Warehouse	10,020	
Provision for doubtful debts		1,600
Trade debtors and creditors	18,000	6,000
Bank overdraft		7,048
	232,168	232,168

1,520 lawn mowers at £45 each were transferred to the warehouse in 19X9; lawn mowers in stock at the end of the year were to be valued at £45 each. Stock of raw materials was £3,180 and work in progress was valued at prime cost of £5,050 at 30 June 19X9.

Accrued expenses outstanding on 30 June 19X9 were:

	Factory £	Warehouse £
Expenses	2,090	1,080
Factory wages	280	–

The general provision for bad debts was to be maintained at 10% of the trade debtors. Bad debts for the year to 30 June 19X9 have already been written off against last year's provision.

Provision for depreciation is to be made as follows:

Factory plant 10% p.a. on cost.
Motor vehicles 20% p.a. on cost.

You are required to prepare:

(a) manufacturing, trading and profit and loss accounts for the year ended 30 June 19X9; and

(b) a balance sheet as at that date.

24 marks

ANSWERS

1 CHISH & PHIPPS

(a)

Bank account

	£		£
Capital		Van	2,000
Chish	7,000	Freezer	5,000
Phipps	4,000	Furniture	750
		Rent	750
Sales	25,400	Wages	3,544
		Salary	2,400
		Purchases	19,800
		Rates	400
		Repairs	125
		Insurance	110
		Motor expenses	373
		Balance c/f	1,148
	36,400		36,400

Petty cash account

	£		£
Sales receipts	2,008	Motor expenses	258
		Wages	296
		Sundries	50
		Drawings:	
		Chish	780
		Phipps	624
	2,008		2,008

Sales account

	£		£
Trading account	31,403	Petty cash	2,008
		Bank	25,400
		Drawings:	
		Chish	100
		Phipps	150
		Discounts allowed	245
		Bad debt	400
		Debtors 31.12.X6	3,100
	31,403		31,403

Purchase account

	£		£
Bank	19,800	Trading account	21,410
Discounts received	110		
Creditors 31.12.X6	1,500		
	21,410		21,410

(b) **Trading and profit and loss account for year ending 31 December 19X6**

	£	£	£
Sales			31,403
Purchases	21,410		
Closing stock	2,410		
			19,000
Gross profit			12,403
Discounts received			110
			12,513
Expenses			
Wages		3,840	
Rent		1,000	
Rates		350	
Insurance		100	
Salary		2,400	
Motor expenses		631	
Bad debt		400	
Discount allowed		245	
Repairs		125	
Sundry		50	
Depn: Van	500		
Plant	500		
Furniture	75		
		1,075	
			10,216
			2,297
Appropriated			
Chish – Interest	700		
Phipps – Interest	400		
– Salary	1,000		
			2,100
			197
Balance divided: Chish (²⁄₃)		131	
Phipps (¹⁄₃)		66	
			197

289

Balance sheet at 31 December 19X6

	Cost £	Depreciation £	£
Fixed assets			
Freezer equipment	5,000	500	4,500
Office equipment	750	75	675
Motor vehicle	2,000	500	1,500
	7,750	1,075	6,675
Current assets			
Stock		2,410	
Debtors		3,160	
Cash		1,148	
		6,718	
Current liabilities			
Creditors		1,750	
			4,968
			11,643
Capital account			
Chish			7,000
Phipps			4,000
			11,000
Current account			
Chish		(49)	
Phipps		692	
			643
			11,643

2 BOON, MOON AND SOON

Profit and loss appropriation account for the year to 31 August 19X1

	£	£	£
Net profit for the year			49,000
Add: Partners' withdrawal of goods			1,000
			50,000
Less:			
Soon's salary		5,000	
Interest on capital:			
Boon	1,000		
Moon	1,000		
Soon	500		
		2,500	
			7,500
Carried forward			42,500

		£	£	£
Brought forward				42,500
Less: Balance of profit				
Boon (2/5)			17,000	
Moon (2/5)			17,000	
Soon (1/5)			8,500	
				42,500
				—

Balance sheet at 31 August 19X1

	£	£
Fixed assets		
Freehold premises, at cost		50,000
Fixtures and fittings, at cost	10,000	
Less: Depreciation to date	5,000	
		5,000
		55,000
Current assets		
Stock	10,000	
Debtors	18,000	
Cash at bank and in hand	1,000	
	29,000	
Less: Current liabilities		
Creditors	10,000	
		19,000
		74,000
Capital accounts		
Boon	10,000	
Moon	10,000	
Soon	5,000	
		25,000
Current accounts		
Boon	18,000	
Moon	17,000	
Soon	14,000	
		49,000
		74,000

Workings

Partners' current accounts

	Boon £	Moon £	Soon £
Balances as per trial balance	500	(1,000)	500
Less: Goods withdrawn	(500)	–	(500)
	–	(1,000)	–
Add: Salary	–	–	5,000
Interest on capital	1,000	1,000	500
Balance of profits	17,000	17,000	8,500
Balances at 31.8.X1	18,000	17,000	14,000

Note: The partners' cash drawings had already been debited to the partners' current accounts and so no further adjustment is necessary.

3 MANLY AND BLANK

Trading, profit and loss account for the year ending 31 December 19X6

	£	£	£
Sales (W1)			88,200
Opening stock		19,000	
Add: Purchases		62,140	
		81,140	
Less: Closing stock		15,600	
			65,540
Gross profit			22,660
Warehouse expenses			
Rates	300		
Heat and light	380		
General expenses	1,320		
Wages (4,700 + 90)	4,790		
Insurance (240 – 40)	200		
Carriage	960		
Depreciation	500		
		8,450	
Office expenses			
Rates	100		
Heat and light	120		
Insurance	60		
Staff salaries (2,400 + 200)	2,600		
General expenses	600		
Depreciation	320		
		3,800	
Selling expenses			
Bad debts	270		
Bad debts provision	200		
		470	
			12,720
Net profit			9,940

Appropriation account	£	£	£
Net profit			9,940
Interest Manly	750		
Blank	300		
		1,050	
Salary Manly	1,000		
Blank	700		
		1,700	
Profit Manly (W3)	4,440		
Blank	2,750		
		7,190	
			9,940

Balance sheet as at 31 December 19X6

Fixed assets		Cost £	Depreciation £	Net £
Buildings		10,000	500	9,500
Fixtures and fittings		3,200	1,070	2,130
		13,200	1,570	11,630

Current assets				
Stock		15,600		
Debtors	5,660			
Less: Bad debts provision	200			
		5,460		
Cash		230		
Prepaid expenses		40		
			21,330	
Less: Current liabilities				
Creditors		6,200		
Bank overdraft		1,070		
Accrued charges		290		
			7,560	
				13,770
				25,400

Capital accounts		
Manly		12,000
Blank		5,000
		17,000
Current accounts (W2)		
Manly	6,240	
Blank	2,160	
		8,400
		25,400

Workings

1. Sales

	£
Per trial balance	87,460
To partners — Manly	150
— Blank	590
	88,200

2. **Current accounts**

	Manly £	Blank £		Manly £	Blank £
Drawings	2,800	2,000	Balance b/d	3,000	1,000
Goods	150	590	Interest	750	300
			Salary	1,000	700
Balance c/d	6,240	2,160	Share of profit (W3)	4,440	2,750
	9,190	4,750		9,190	4,750

3. Share of profit

	£
Blank — Interest	300
Salary	700
Share of profit (1/3 × £7,190)	2,397
	3,397

As this is less than £3,750, Blank's share of profit should be £2,750 to give him a total income of £3,750. Manly therefore has balance of £4,440.

4 DIXON AND KELK

(a) **Trading and profit and loss account — year ended 31 December 19X1**

	£	£
Sales		241,983
Opening stock	21,814	
Add: Purchases	183,212	
	205,026	
Less: Closing stock	16,000	
Cost of sales		189,026
Gross profit carried forward		52,957

	£	£
Gross profit brought forward		52,957
Administrative expenses (7,140 + 567)	7,707	
Office expenses (5,826 − 214)	5,612	
Salaries (23,458 − 480)	22,978	
Depreciation — Buildings (15,000 ÷ 30)	500	
Fittings	700	
Vehicles	2,000	
Provision for doubtful debts	1,400	
		40,897
Net profit		12,060

Appropriation account

	Jan–Aug £	Sept–Dec £
Net profit	8,040	4,020
Add: Interest on drawings (W1) — Dixon	316	158
— Kelk	150	75
	8,506	4,253
Interest on capital (W2) — Dixon	(1,000)	(500)
— Kelk	(800)	(400)
Partner's salary — Kelk	(2,600)	(1,000)
Profit to be shared	4,106	2,353
Dixon	3,285	1,412
Kelk	821	941
	4,106	2,353

Note: Kelk's income is £6,337 after interest on drawings and therefore Dixon will have to pay him £163 to bring his net income to £6,500.

Balance sheet at 31 December 19X1

Fixed assets	Cost £	Depreciation £	£
Freehold property	20,000	500	19,500
Fittings	14,000	7,700	6,300
Vehicles	8,000	4,000	4,000
	42,000	12,200	29,800
Carried forward			29,800

		£	£	£
Brought forward				29,800
Current assets				
Stock			16,000	
Debtors		28,000		
Less: Provision		1,400		
			26,600	
Prepayments			214	
Bank			2,020	
Cash			114	
			44,948	
Less: Current liabilities				
Creditors		12,321		
Accruals		567	12,888	
				32,060
				61,860
Capital – Dixon				30,000
– Kelk				24,000
				54,000
Current accounts – Dixon			2,360	
– Kelk			5,500	
				7,860
				61,860

(b) **Current accounts**

	Dixon £	Kelk £		Dixon £	Kelk £
Interest on			Balances b/d	6,516	3,264
drawings	474	225	Salary	–	3,600
Drawings	9,480	4,500	Interest on		
Transfer	163	–	capital	1,500	1,200
Balance c/f	2,596	5,264	Share of profits	4,697	1,762
			Transfer (note above)		163
	12,713	9,989		12,713	9,989

Workings

1. **Drawings**

	Dixon £	Kelk £
Per T.B.	9,000	4,500
Transferred from salaries	480	—
	9,480	4,500
Interest on drawings	474	225
Jan–Aug	316	150
Sept–Dec	158	75
	474	225

2. **Interest on capital**

	Dixon	Kelk
	£1,500	£1,200
Jan–Aug	1,000	800
Sept–Dec	500	400
	1,500	1,200

5 X, Y AND Z

(a) **Corrected net profit**

		£	£
Net loss per draft accounts			(12,000)
Add: Partners' salaries incorrectly charged to staff salaries	X	—	
	Y	8,000	
	Z	5,000	
			13,000
			1,000
Add: Drawings incorrectly charged as purchases	X	9,000	
	Y	6,000	
	Z	7,000	
			22,000
			23,000
Less: Provision for doubtful debts (5% × £6,800)			340
Corrected net profit			22,660

(b) **Partners' current accounts**

	X £	Y £	Z £		X £	Y £	Z £
Reversal of				Balance b/d	3,200	2,800	1,700
Appropriation (W1)	6,750	4,050	1,700	Additional interest			
Drawings	9,000	6,000	7,000	on capital		1,750	
Balance of profit							
and loss (W2)	795	477	318	Balances c/d	13,345	5,977	8,318
	16,545	10,527	10,018		16,545	10,527	10,018
Balances b/d	13,345	5,977	8,318				

(c) **Balance sheet at 30 April 19X4**

	Cost £	Depreciation £	£
Fixed assets	120,000	45,000	75,000
Current assets			
Stocks		18,000	
Debtors		6,460	
Bank balance		7,900	
		32,360	
Current liabilities			
Trade creditors		5,000	
			27,360
			102,360
Capital accounts			
X			40,000
Y			65,000
Z			25,000
			130,000
Current accounts			
X		(13,345)	
Y		(5,977)	
Z		(8,318)	
			(27,640)
			102,360

(d) Separate partners' capital and current accounts are maintained:

    (i) to ensure that the fixed capital (per the partnership agreement) is not drawn out of the business;

(ii) to separate the long term investment from the short term investment;

(iii) to make the calculation of interest on capital more straightforward.

Workings

1. **Profit and loss appropriation using draft figures**

Appropriation account

	£	£		£
Loss		12,000	Additions to freehold	35,000
Interest on capital				
X	4,000			
Y	3,000			
Z	2,500			
		9,500		
∴ Balance was divided				
X (1/2)	6,750			
Y (3/10)	4,050			
Z (1/5)	2,700			
		13,500		
		35,000		35,000

2. **Profit and loss appropriation using corrected figures**

Appropriation account

	£	£		£	£
Interest on partners' capital			Net profit		22,660
X	4,000				
Y	4,750				
Z	2,500				
		11,250	∴ Balance is to be divided		
Partners' salaries			X (1/2)	795	
Y	8,000		Y (3/10)	477	
Z	5,000		Z (1/5)	318	
		13,000			1,590
		24,250			24,250

6 CHECKE AND TIKK

(a) **Appropriation account**

	£	£
Profit for the period		34,000
Interest on capital		
Checke: 50,000 × 5% =	2,500	
Tikk: 30,000 × 5% =	1,500	
		4,000
		30,000
Share of profit		
Checke: 3/5 × 30,000 =	18,000	
Tikk: 2/5 × 30,000 =	12,000	
		30,000

Appropriation account based on change at 1 April 19X4

	£	
Profit for the period, 34,000 + 14,000	48,000	
Salary — self		7,000
		41,000
Interest on capital		
Checke	2,500	
Tikk	1,500	
Self: 20,000 × 5%	1,000	
		5,000
		36,000
Share of profit		
Checke: 3/6 × 36,000 =	18,000	
Tikk: 2/6 × 36,000 =	12,000	
Self: 1/6 × 36,000 =	6,000	
		36,000

(b) The agreement dealt with in part (a) does not conflict with the Partnership Act 1890 as the provisions of the Act only apply in the absence of any agreement between the partners.

The requirements of the Act include:

(i) no interest on capital;
(ii) interest at 5% on loans by partners in excess of agreed capitals;
(iii) partners do not receive any salaries;
(iv) profits and losses to be shared equally.

7 RED, WHITE AND BLUE

(a) **Capital accounts**

	Red £	White £	Blue £		Red £	White £	Blue £
Balances c/d	19,200	11,400		Balances b/d	12,000	6,600	
				Goodwill (W1)	7,200	4,800	
	19,200	11,400			19,200	11,400	
Goodwill (W2)	6,000	3,000	1,000	Balances b/d	19,200	11,400	
Balances c/d	13,200	8,400	2,000	Cash introduced			3,000
	19,200	11,400	3,000		19,200	11,400	3,000

(b) **Balance sheet at 1 May 19X2**

	£	£
Fixed assets		
Office equipment, at cost		300
Motor vehicles, at cost		8,000
		8,300
Current assets		
Stocks	12,000	
Debtors	12,000	
Cash at bank and in hand	3,100	
	27,100	
Less: Current liabilities		
Creditors	11,800	15,300
		23,600
Capital		
Red		13,200
White		8,400
Blue		2,000
		23,600

Workings

1. Revaluation (including goodwill)

	£
Revalued assets	42,300
Original value	30,300
Excess	12,000

   To be split 3:2.
   i.e., £7,200:£4,800

2. Goodwill written back is £10,000.
   To be split 6:3:1.
   i.e., £6,000:£3,000:£1,000.

8 ALAN, BOB, CHARLES AND DON

(a)

Revaluation account

	£	£		£
Premises		90,000	Premises	120,000
Plant		37,000	Plant	35,000
Stock		62,379	Stock	54,179
Doubtful debts		3,000		
Profit on revaluation:				
Alan	8,400			
Bob	5,600			
Charles	2,800			
		16,800		
		209,179		209,179

Goodwill account

	£		£
Goodwill raised – to Capital account (3:2:1)		Goodwill written back to Capital account (3:2:2)	
Alan	21,000	Alan	18,000
Bob	14,000	Bob	12,000
Charles	7,000	Don	12,000
	42,000		42,000

Capital account

	A £	B £	C £	D £		A £	B £	C £	D £
Goodwill	18,000	12,000	–	12,000	Balance b/d	85,000	65,000	35,000	–
Retiring partner's account	–	–	42,000	–	Goodwill	21,000	14,000	7,000	–
Cash	21,000	–	–	–	Cash	–	–	–	79,000
Balance c/f	67,000	67,000	–	67,000					
	106,000	79,000	42,000	79,000		106,000	79,000	42,000	79,000
					Balance b/d	67,000	67,000	–	67,000

302

Current account

	A £	B £	C £	D £		A £	B £	C £	D £
Balance b/d	–	2,509	–	–	Balance b/d	3,714	–	4,678	–
Retiring partner's account	–	–	7,478	–	Profit on revaluation	8,400	5,600	2,800	–
Cash	9,023	–	–	–	Cash	–	–	–	3,091
Balance c/f	3,091	3,091	–	3,091					
	12,114	5,600	7,478	3,091		12,114	5,600	7,478	3,091
					Balance b/d	3,091	3,091		3,091

Retiring partner's account

	£		£
Car	3,900	Capital account	42,000
Cash	53,578	Current account	7,478
Balance c/f	20,000	Loan account	28,000
	77,478		77,478
		Balance b/d	20,000

Bank account

	£		£
Don – Capital	79,000	Balance b/d	4,200
– Current	3,091	Retiring partner's account	53,578
Balance c/f	5,710	Repaid to Alan – Capital	21,000
		– Current	9,023
	87,801		87,801
		Balance b/d	5,710

(b) **Balance sheet at 30 June 19X2**

	£	£	£
Fixed assets			
Premises			120,000
Plant			35,000
Vehicles			11,100
Fittings			2,000
			168,100
Current assets			
Stock		54,179	
Debtors less provision		31,980	
Cash		760	
Carried forward		86,919	168,100

		£	£	£
	Brought forward		86,919	168,100
	Current liabilities			
	Creditors	19,036		
	Overdraft	5,710		
			24,746	
				62,173
				230,273
	Loan – Charles			20,000
				210,273
	Capital accounts			
	Alan			67,000
	Bob			67,000
	Don			67,000
				201,000
	Current accounts			
	Alan		3,091	
	Bob		3,091	
	Don		3,091	
				9,273
				210,273

9 MYRES, WHYTE AND THOMAS

Realisation account

19X9		£	19X9		£
31 May	Premises	60,000	31 May	Assets taken over by Whyte:	
	Plant and equipment	6,560		Stock	18,000
	Stock	16,000		Plant and equipment	5,500
	Debtors	4,240		Debtors	4,100
	Realisation expenses	1,000		Premises	105,000
	Gain on realisation:				
	Myres 22,400				
	Whyte 11,200				
	Thomas 11,200				
		44,800			
		132,600			132,600

Bank account

19X9		£	19X9		£
31 May	Whyte –		31 May	Balance	1,300
	on account	80,000		Creditors	5,500
				Realisation	
				expenses	1,000
				Myres capital	41,000
				Thomas capital	31,200
		80,000			80,000

Myres capital account

19X9		£	19X9		£
31 May	Loan to Whyte	21,400	31 May	Balance	40,000
	Cash (balance)	41,000		Gain on realisation	22,400
		62,400			62,400

Whyte capital account

19X9		£	19X9		£
31 May	Assets taken over	132,600	31 May	Balance	20,000
				Gain on realisation	11,200
				Cash	80,000
				Loan from Myres	
				(balance)	21,400
		132,600			132,600

Thomas capital account

19X9		£	19X9		£
31 May	Cash	31,200	31 May	Balance	20,000
				Gain on realisation	11,200
		31,200			31,200

10 GAIN AND MAIN

Profit and loss appropriation account

19X2			£	19X2		£
31.3	Salary – Main		9,750	31.3	Balance b/d	26,250
	Interest on capital –					
	Gain	1,000				
	Main	500	1,500			
	Balance of profit					
	Gain	9,000				
	Main	6,000				
			15,000			
			26,250			26,250

Current accounts

		Gain £	Main £			Gain £	Main £
19X1				19X1			
1.4	Balance b/d	–	2,000	1.4	Balance b/d	1,000	–
				19X2			
				31.3	Capital accounts – transfer of balances	10,000	5,000
					Profit and loss appropriation account		
					Salary	–	9,750
					Interest on capital	1,000	500
19X2					Balance of profit	9,000	6,000
31.3	Balances c/d	21,000	19,250				
		21,000	21,250			21,000	21,250
31.3	Realisation account – car taken over	1,000	–	31.3	Balances b/d	21,000	19,250
	Plain Limited – allocation of shares	24,000	16,000		Profit on realisation	1,380	920
	Cash – owing to Main	–	4,170		Cash – amount paid in by Gain	2,620	–
		25,000	20,170			25,000	20,170

Realisation account

19X2		£	19X2		£
31.3	Debtors	2,000	31.3	Creditors	500
	Fixtures and fittings	2,000		Provision for depreciation –	
	Land and buildings	30,000		Fixtures and fittings	1,000
	Motor vehicles	4,500		Motor vehicles	1,300
	Stock	3,000		Current account –	
	Current accounts – balance written off (3:2) –			Gain (motor vehicle)	1,000
				Plain Ltd – purchase consideration	40,000
	Gain	1,380			
	Main	920			
		43,800			43,800

Cash at bank account

19X2		£	19X2		£
31.3	Balance b/d	1,550	31.3	Current account –	
	Current account – Gain	2,620		Main	4,170
		4,170			4,170

Plain Ltd account

19X2		£	19X2		£
31.3	Realisation account –			Current accounts –	
	purchase consideration	40,000		Gain	24,000
				Main	16,000
		40,000			40,000

11 LEEK AND BEAN

Manufacturing, trading and profit and loss accounts for the year ended 30 June 19X9

	£	£
Raw materials consumed		
Stocks 1 July 19X8		4,028
Purchases		28,650
		32,678
Less: Stocks 30 June 19X9		3,180
		29,498
Productive wages		15,300
		44,798
Add: Work in progress 1 July 19X8		3,400
		48,198
Less: Work in progress 30 June 19X9		5,050
Prime cost of goods produced		43,148
Works expenses		
Factory expenses	14,160	
Depreciation of plant	2,575	16,735
Works cost of goods produced		59,883
Factory profit		8,517
Value of goods transferred to warehouse (1,520 @ £45)		68,400
Stock of finished goods 1 July 19X8		48,000
Carried forward		116,400

	£	£
Brought forward		116,400
Stock of finished goods 30 June 19X9		40,500
Cost of goods sold		75,900
Sales		111,020
Gross profit		35,120
General expenses		
Warehouse wages	6,030	
Warehouse expenses	11,100	
Depreciation of vans	1,610	
Provision for doubtful debts	200	18,940
Net profit on trading		16,180
Add: Profit earned by factory		8,517
Net profit for the year		24,697

Appropriation account

	Leek £	Bean £	
Factory profit	6,388	2,129	
Selling profit	4,045	12,135	
	10,433	14,264	24,697

(b) **Balance sheet as at 30 June 19X9**

Fixed assets

	Cost £	Depreciation £	£
Freehold factory	42,150	—	42,150
Plant	25,750	8,625	17,125
Vans	8,050	5,060	2,990
	75,950	13,685	62,265

Current assets

Stocks and work in progress		48,730	
Debtors	18,000		
Less: Provision for doubtful debts	1,800		
		16,200	
		64,930	

Less: Current liabilities

Sundry creditors	9,450		
Bank overdraft	7,048		
		16,498	
			48,432
			110,697

	Leek	Bean	
Capital accounts	£	£	£
Balance 1 July 19X8	48,000	49,000	
Add: Profit for the year	10,433	14,264	
	58,433	63,264	
Less: Drawings	6,000	5,000	
	52,433	58,264	110,697

Workings

1. Lawn mowers

Stock of completed items 19X8		1,200
Produced (to warehouse 1,520 × £45 = £68,400)		1,520
		2,720
Less: Sold		1,820
Stock at 30/6/X9		900
Stock to be valued at £45		£40,500

2. Overheads

	Trial balance £	Creditors £	Total P & L £	Man. account £
Factory overheads	12,070	2,090		14,160
Warehouse overheads	10,020	1,080	11,100	
Factory wages	15,020	280		15,300
		3,450		
Creditors from trial balance		6,000		
Creditors for balance sheet		9,450		

3. Depreciation

	Cost £		Depn. for year £	Depn. to 30/6/X8 £	Balance sheet £
Plant	25,750	10%	2,575	6,050	8,625
Vans	8,050	20%	1,610	3,450	5,060

4. Provision for doubtful debts

			£
Debtors	£18,000	10% required	1,800
		At 30/6/X8	1,600
Charge to P & L			200

15 Departmental accounts

The questions in this section cover departmental profit and loss accounts as well as the recording of transactions between branches (sometimes known as departmental branch accounts). As departmental accounts are for internal use only, there are no standard formats and the style of the answer will depend a great deal on the information given in the question.

QUESTIONS

1 PZT LTD

The managing director of PZT Ltd, a company owning three cinemas, has complained that the form of presentation of the company's profit and loss account for the year ended 31 December 19X3, given below, does not tell him where the loss has been incurred and is of little use for management purposes.

You are required to redesign the profit and loss account so that his objections will be overcome.

	£	£
Sales of tickets		539,800
Sale of ice creams, etc.		37,000
		576,800
Less: Hire of films	107,960	
Salaries: Managers	36,000	
Projectionists	30,000	
Ticket salesgirls	12,000	
Usherettes	36,000	
Ice-cream salesgirls	12,000	
General cinema costs	180,000	
Cost of ice-cream	18,500	
Head office costs	160,000	
		592,460
Trading loss		(15,660)

You are given the following information:

1. The three cinemas are the Astoria, Plaza and Regal. Each is a large old cinema which has now been subdivided into three smaller units, called studios, showing different films.

2. Each cinema employs:

   A manager.
   A projectionist who is responsible for the showing of the films in all three studios.
   A ticket salesgirl, who sells tickets for all three studios.
   An usherette for each of the studios.
   An ice-cream etc. salesgirl covering all studios. It is not possible to record the sales made in any one studio.

3. Films are hired at a cost of 20% of the takings for that film.

4. Sales of tickets for the year were as follows:

Cinema	Studio	£
Astoria	1	50,000
	2	4,800
	3	25,000
Plaza	1	60,000
	2	40,000
	3	30,000
Regal	1	150,000
	2	100,000
	3	80,000

5. Individual annual salaries are as follows:

	£
Cinema manager	12,000
Projectionist	10,000
Ticket salesgirl	4,000
Usherette	4,000
Ice-cream salesgirl	4,000

6. Sales of ice-cream etc. were as follows:

	£
Astoria	7,000
Plaza	10,000
Regal	20,000

These items are sold in all cinemas at a mark-up of 100% on cost.

7. General cinema costs were as follows:

	£
Astoria	30,000
Plaza	50,000
Regal	100,000

20 marks

2 LAYA EMPORIUMS LTD

The following information relates to two departments of Coleman Ltd a branch of Laya Emporiums Ltd. The parent organisation supplies all goods to the departments at selling price and department X operates at cost plus 20 per cent, whereas department Z operates at cost plus $33\frac{1}{3}$ per cent. All credit accounts are controlled by head office, to which cash is remitted, and wages and expenses are also paid by head office.

	X	Z
	£	£
Sales — Cash	220,032	276,640
— Credit	28,128	—
Stock at beginning at selling price	2,640	1,888
Stock at end at selling price	36,120	47,360
Goods sent to departments at selling price	288,288	324,080
Returns from departments at selling price	6,408	960
Mark down of 10% on the selling price of goods which cost	400	1,920
Wages and expenses	15,008	15,688

	£
Cash collected from debtors	28,492
Cash received from Coleman Ltd	514,688
Opening cash balance	18,816
Debtors outstanding at beginning	2,732
Closing cash balance	800

You are required to show the appropriate entries in the ledger at head office; and prepare a statement showing the trading profit earned by each department.

16 marks

3 MURCHIE LTD

The following information relates to Murchie Ltd which has a head office in Abindon and operates a branch in Bexley. All purchases are made by the head office and supplied to the branch at selling price, which is cost plus 20 per cent. All branch transactions are recorded in the books at head office, which also pays branch expenses. All cash received by the branch is sent to head office, and branch sales are on credit terms.

On 1 November 19X2 the stocks of goods held by the branch at invoice price amounted to £10,800 and the debtors were £7,725. At the same date the credit balance of the branch adjustment account amounted to £1,800.

During the financial year to 31 October 19X3, the following transactions took place at the branch:

	£
Goods forwarded by head office (at invoice price)	97,380
Goods returned by branch (at invoice price)	1,926
Discount allowed	4,245
Sales	101,340
Sales returns	1,062
Expenses	12,081
Cash collected from debtors	98,544

On 31 October 19X3 the stock of goods held by the branch at invoice price amounted to £5,886 and the expenses figure was that for the year.

You are required to show the appropriate entries in the ledger at head office, and show the profit earned by the Bexley branch.

15 marks

4 JOHN DELL

John Dell commenced trading on 1 April 19X8 as Highway Stores, retail stationers and confectioners, with an initial capital of £3,000 which was utilised in the opening of a business bank account.

All receipts and payments are passed through the bank account. The following is a summary of the items credited in the business cash book during the year ended 31 March 19X9:

	£
Purchase of fixtures and fittings:	
Stationery department	2,600
Confectionery department	1,500
Staff wages:	
Stationery department	2,200
Confectionery department	1,540
Rent for the period 1 April 19X8 to 30 April 19X9	1,300
Rates for the year ended 31 March 19X9	570
Electricity	370
Advertising	1,100
Payments to suppliers	53,550
Drawings	5,000

The purchases during the year under review were:

	£
Stationery department	26,000
Confectionery department	29,250

The above purchases do not include goods costing £500 bought by the business and then taken by Mr Dell for his own domestic use. The figure of £500 is included in payments to suppliers.

The gross profit in the stationery department is at the rate of 20 per cent of sales whilst in the confectionery department it is 25 per cent of sales. In both departments, sales each month are always at a uniform level. The policy of Mr Dell is to have the month end stocks in each department just sufficient for the following month's sales. The prices of all goods bought by Highway Stores have not changed since the business began.

Total trade debtors at 31 March 19X9 amounted to £9,000.

In August 19X8 Mr Dell and his sister, Mrs Beck, benefited from legacies from their late mother's estate of £5,000 and £4,000 respectively. Both legacies were paid into the bank account of Highway Stores; Mrs Beck has agreed that her legacy should be an interest free loan to the business.

At 31 March 19X9 electricity charges accrued due, amounted to £110.

Mr Dell has decided that expenses not incurred by a specific department should be apportioned to departments as follows:

rent and rates — according to floor area occupied,
electricity — according to consumption,
advertising — according to turnover.

Two-thirds of the business floor space is occupied by the stationery department whilst three-quarters of the electricity is consumed by that department. All the floor space of the business is allocated to a department.

It has been decided that depreciation on fixtures and fittings should be provided at the rate of 10 per cent of the cost of assets held at the year end.

You are required to produce:

(a) a trading and profit and loss account for the year ended 31 March 19X9 for:

   (i) the stationery department, and
   (ii) the confectionery department;

(b) a balance sheet at 31 March 19X9.

22 marks

5 BRIAN AND TREVOR

Brian and Trevor are in partnership managing a small retail store which specialises in sweets and confectionery (managed by Brian), and newspapers and periodicals (managed by Trevor). The partnership agreement provides for Brian to receive 3/5 of the profit, and Trevor 2/5, each partner to be allowed 8 per cent interest on capital, and each to receive a commission of 10 per cent of the profit of their respective sections prior to any other appropriation of profit.

During the year to 31 March 19X8, a trial balance extracted at that date revealed the following financial features.

	£	£
Capital — Brian		14,000
— Trevor		8,000
Current accounts — Brian		2,020
— Trevor	250	
Drawings — Brian	1,100	
— Trevor	900	
Freehold shop premises	10,000	
Equipment (at written down value)		
— Confectionery section	4,500	
— Periodical section	3,500	
Purchases — Confectionery section	15,900	
— Periodical section	17,700	
Stock at 1 April 19X7 — Confectionery section	2,300	
— Periodical section	3,100	
Sales — Confectionery section		18,500
— Periodical section		21,500

	£	£
Wages — Confectionery section	1,175	
— Periodical section	1,470	
Miscellaneous expenses	230	
Rates	500	
Light and heat	400	
Advertising	250	
Debtors and creditors	1,800	2,100
Bad debts — Periodical section	95	
Cash in hand	950	
Cash at bank	50	
Provision for doubtful debts — periodical section		50
	66,170	66,170

Additional information available.

1. Stock at 31 March 19X8 was £3,600 in the Confectionery Section, and £4,400 in the Periodical Section.

2. The partners have agreed that, rates should be apportioned between the Confectionery and Periodical sections on a 3:2 ratio, advertising on a 1:1 ratio, lighting and heating on a 2:3 ratio, and miscellaneous expenses on a 1:1 ratio.

3. Wages owing at 31 March 19X8 amounted to £25 for the Confectionery section and £30 for the Periodical section.

4. Advertising prepaid at 31 March 19X8 amounted to £100.

5. The provision for doubtful debts is to be increased to 5% of the debtors of the Periodical section, which amount to £1,500 at 31 March 19X8.

6. Equipment of both sections is to be depreciated at 10% of the written down value at 1 April 19X7.

You are required to:

(a) prepare a trading, and profit and loss account for the Confectionery and the Periodical sections, and also for the business as a whole, for the year ended 31 March 19X8. (**Note**: A balance sheet is not required.)   *14 marks*

(b) prepare an appropriation account for the year ended 31 March 19X8; *4 marks*

(c) prepare the partners' current accounts for the year ended 31 March 19X8.
4 marks
Total 22 marks

ANSWERS

1 PZT LTD

Analysed profit and loss account for the year ended 31 December 19X3

	Astoria 1 £	Astoria 2 £	Astoria 3 £	Total £	Plaza 1 £	Plaza 2 £	Plaza 3 £	Total £	Regal 1 £	Regal 2 £	Regal 3 £	Total £	Total £
Sale of tickets	50,000	4,800	25,000	79,800	60,000	40,000	30,000	130,000	150,000	100,000	80,000	330,000	539,800
Deduct:													
Film hire	(10,000)	(960)	(5,000)	(15,960)	(12,000)	(8,000)	(6,000)	(26,000)	(30,000)	(20,000)	(16,000)	(66,000)	(107,960)
Usherettes	(4,000)	(4,000)	(4,000)	(12,000)	(4,000)	(4,000)	(4,000)	(12,000)	(4,000)	(4,000)	(4,000)	(12,000)	(36,000)
Contribution to cinema costs	36,000	(160)	16,000	51,840	44,000	28,000	20,000	92,000	116,000	76,000	60,000	252,000	395,840
Add: Ice-cream Sales			7,000				10,000				20,000		37,000
Deduct: Ice-cream cost			(3,500)				(5,000)				(10,000)		(18,500)
Sales girls			(4,000)				(4,000)				(4,000)		(12,000)
Contribution from ice-cream				(500)				1,000				6,000	6,500
Total contribution				51,340				93,000				258,000	402,340
Deduct: Cinema costs													
Salaries				(26,000)				(26,000)				(26,000)	(78,000)
General costs				(30,000)				(50,000)				(100,000)	(180,000)
Contribution per cinema				(4,660)				17,000				132,000	144,340
Head office costs													(160,000)
Loss for the year													(15,660)

2 LAYA EMPORIUMS LTD

Branch stock account

	X £	Z £		X £	Z £
Balance b/d	2,640	1,888	Returns to head office	6,408	960
Goods from head office	288,288	324,080	Debtors (sales)	28,128	—
			Cash sales	220,032	276,640
			Mark down	48	256
			Deficiency	192	752
			Balance c/d	36,120	47,360
	290,928	325,968		290,928	325,968

Branch adjustment account

	X £	Z £		X £	Z £
Stock	1,068	240	Balance b/d	440	472
Deficiency	192	752	Stock	48,048	81,020
Balance c/d	6,020	11,840			
Gross profit	41,208				
	48,488	81,492		48,488	81,492

Branch profit and loss account

	X £	Z £		X £	Z £
Wages and expenses	15,008	15,688	Gross profit	41,208	68,660
Mark down	48	256			
Net profit	26,152	52,716			
	41,208	68,660		41,208	68,660

Branch debtors

	£		£
Balance b/d	2,732	Cash	28,492
Stock (sales)	28,128	Balance c/d	2,368
	30,860		30,860

318

Branch cash

	£		£
Balance b/d	18,816	To head office	514,688
Cash sales – X	220,032		
– Z	276,640	Balance c/d	800
	515,488		515,488

3 MURCHIE LTD

Branch stock account

	£		£
Balance b/d	10,800	Returns	1,926
Goods from head office	97,380	Debtors (sales)	101,340
Debtors (returns)	1,062	Deficiency	90
		Balance c/d	5,886
	109,242		109,242

Branch adjustment account (mark-up)

	£		£
Stock ($\frac{20}{120}$ × 1,926)	321	Balance b/d	1,800
Deficiency	90	Stock ($\frac{20}{120}$ × 97,380)	16,230
Balance c/d ($\frac{20}{120}$ × 5,886)	981		
Gross profit	16,638		
	18,030		18,030

Branch debtors account

	£		£
Balance b/d	7,725	Stock (returns)	1,062
Stock (sales)	101,340	Cash	98,544
		Discount	4,245
		Balance c/d	5,214
	109,065		109,065

Branch profit & loss account

	£		£
Expenses	12,081	Gross profit	16,638
Discount	4,245		
Profit	312		
	16,638		16,638

4 JOHN DELL

(a) **Trading and profit and loss accounts for the year ended 31 March 19X9**

		Stationery		Confectionery	
	£	£	£	£
Sales (W1)		30,000		36,000
Less: Cost of goods sold				
Purchases	26,000		29,250	
Closing stock	2,000		2,250	
		24,000		27,000
Gross profit		6,000		9,000
Less:				
Wages	2,200		1,540	
Rent (W2)	800		400	
Rates (W2)	380		190	
Electricity (W2)	360		120	
Advertising (split 30:36)	500		600	
Depreciation (10%)	260		150	
		4,500		3,000
Net profit		1,500		6,000

(b) **Balance sheet at 31 March 19X9**

	£	£	£
Fixed assets – Cost			4,100
– Depreciation			410
			3,690
Current assets			
Stock (W1)		4,250	
Debtors		9,000	
Prepayments (W2)		100	
Carried forward		13,350	3,690

	£	£	£
Brought forward		13,350	3,690
Current liabilities			
Creditors (W3)	2,200		
Bank overdraft	730		
Accruals (W2)	110		
		3,040	
			10,310
			14,000
Loan – Mrs Beck			4,000
			10,000
Capital – At 1 April 19X8			3,000
Introduced during year			5,000
Profit for year			7,500
			15,500
Less: Drawings (W5)			5,500
			10,000

Workings

1. **Sales**

	Stationery £	Confectionery £
Purchases	26,000	29,250
Less: Closing stock (1/13th of purchases)	2,000	2,250
Cost of goods sold	24,000	27,000
Sales: Stationery ($\frac{100}{80}$ × Cost)	30,000	
Confectionery ($\frac{100}{75}$ × Cost)		36,000

2.

	£
Rent for 13 months	1,300
Less: Prepayment	100
	1,200
Split: Stationery (2/3)	800
Confectionery (1/3)	400
	1,200

		£
Rates		
Split: Stationery (2/3)		380
Confectionery (1/3)		190
		570
Electricity paid to date		370
Accrued		110
		480
Split: Stationery (3/4)		360
Confectionery (1/4)		120
		480

3. Creditors £
Purchases: Stationery 26,000
 Confectionery 29,250
 For Mr Dell 500
           55,750
Less: Payments 53,550
           2,200

4.   **Bank account**

	£	£		£
Capital		3,000	Payments (per question)	69,730
Legacies: Mr Dell (capital)		5,000		
Mrs Beck (loan)		4,000		
Sales receipts				
Sales	66,000			
Debtors	9,000	57,000		
Balance c/d		730		
		69,730		69,730

5. Drawings £
 Per question 5,000
 Goods 500
           5,500

5 BRIAN AND TREVOR

(a) **Trading and profit and loss account for the year ended 31 March 19X8**

	Confectionery		Periodical		Total	
	£	£	£	£	£	£
Sales		18,500		21,500		40,000
Less: Cost of sales						
Stock at 1 April 19X7	2,300		3,100		5,400	
Purchases	15,900		17,700		33,600	
	18,200		20,800		39,000	
Stock at 31 March 19X8	3,600		4,400		8,000	
		14,600		16,400		31,000
Gross profit		3,900		5,100		9,000
Less: Wages	1,200		1,500		2,700	
Miscellaneous expenses	115		115		230	
Rates	300		200		500	
Advertising	75		75		150	
Lighting and heating	160		240		400	
Bad and doubtful debts	–		120		120	
Depreciation	450		350		800	
		2,300		2,600		4,900
Net profit		1,600		2,500		4,100

(b) **Appropriation account for the year ended 31 March 19X8**

	£		£
Commission – Brian	160	Profit – Confectionery	1,600
– Trevor	250	– Periodicals	2,500
Interest on capital – Brian	1,120		
– Trevor	640		
Balance split 3:2			
Brian	1,158		
Trevor	772		
	4,100		4,100

(c) **Current accounts**

	Brian £	Trevor £		Brian £	Trevor £
Balance at 1 April	–	250	Balance at 1 April	2,020	–
Drawings	1,100	900	Commission	160	250
	3,358	512	Interest on capital	1,120	640
			Share of profit	1,158	772
	4,458	1,662		4,458	1,662

16 Written questions

Students will have observed that a large number of questions in other sections have a final part which requires a written answer. However, about 20 per cent of the questions in examinations at this level are entirely written and this section illustrates questions of that nature. The student will notice that the range of topics covered is not very wide and that the questions are mainly concerned with the understanding of basic accounting principles.

For many students, these are possibly the most difficult questions to answer *well*. This is because no time is spent planning the answer and ensuring that it does answer the specific question posed. Instead, students have a tendency to grasp one word or phrase from the question and then to pour onto paper all of their knowledge of that topic. This means that the answer is verbose, contains many irrelevancies and does not answer the question.

The format of the answer is also important as many questions have instructions such as 'write brief notes on', 'discuss', 'write concisely about' or 'compare the advantages and disadvantages of'. Where possible students are advised to itemise the points made, as this form of answer is easier for the examiner to mark.

QUESTIONS

1   Statement of Standard Accounting Practice Number 2 'Disclosure of Accounting Policies' distinguishes between three basic accounting terms.

What are these terms and how are they defined? For each of these terms give **three** different examples to illustrate it.
14 marks

2   'Those who use accounting information may be classified under many different headings, each type of user requiring slightly different information from the basic financial data produced by the accountant. The accountant must design his reports for users, ensuring that what interests them is visible and understandable.'

You are required to classify the users of accounting statements under six main headings and explain the particular information needs of each group.
17 marks

3   Distinguish carefully between each of the following terms:

(a)   Revenue and receipts   *4 marks*
(b)   Capital expenditure and revenue expenditure   *4 marks*
(c)   Accrual and prepayment   *4 marks*
(d)   Debit and credit   *2 marks*
Total 14 marks

4   Explain briefly but concisely what you understand by the following terms:

(a)   Materiality   *4 marks*
(b)   Asset   *3 marks*
(c)   Profit   *3 marks*
(d)   Objectivity   *4 marks*
Total 14 marks

5   Describe briefly the following terms in order to show the difference between:

(a)   provisions and reserves;
(b)   capital reserves and revenue reserves;
(c)   fixed assets and current assets;
(d)   single entry and double entry book-keeping.
14 marks

6   (a)   Distinguish between the nature and functions of a trial balance and a balance sheet.
8 marks

(b)   Give three distinct reasons why, in the case of limited companies, the earning of accounting profits may be accompanied by a shortage of liquid resources.
9 marks
Total 17 marks

7 (a) Explain the functions of books of prime entry and outline modern developments of such books. *9 marks*

(b) What is meant by the terms revenue expenditure and capital expenditure. Explain why it is important to distinguish revenue expenditure from capital expenditure. *8 marks*
Total 17 marks

8 (a) Why does any accountant provide for depreciation when he measures profit? *12 marks*

(b) A company bought a moulding machine five years ago for £10,000. It is now fully written down, since straight line depreciation has been applied based on a five year life.

The company do not however intend to scrap the machine, and propose to work on with it into the future.

How would you account for this situation? *7 marks*
Total 19 marks

9 If asked to point out one major weakness in the knowledge of accounting students, many teachers of the subject would say that students do not understand the framework of ideas which surrounds the practice of accounting, and which is so basic to its proper appreciation.

You are required to:

(a) list eight concepts which you consider to be part of this framework; and
6 marks

(b) explain two concepts with an appropriate example in each case. *13 marks*
Total 19 marks

10 'Accounting is concerned with the quantification of economic events in money terms in order to collect, record, evaluate, and communicate the results of past events and to aid in decision-making'. Explain. *20 marks*

11 State the general rule for the recognition of revenue and discuss the exceptions to the rule. *18 marks*

12 In preparing the accounts of your company, you are faced with a number of problems. These are summarised below:

1. The managing director wishes the company's good industrial relations to be reflected in the accounts.

2. The long-term future success of the company is extremely uncertain.

3. Although the sales have not yet actually taken place, some reliable customers of the company have placed several large orders that are likely to be extremely profitable.

4. One of the owners of the company has invested his drawings in some stocks and shares.

5. At the year-end, an amount is outstanding for electricity that has been consumed during the accounting period.

6. All the fixed assets of the company would now cost a great deal more than they did when they were originally purchased.

7. During the year, the company purchased £10 worth of pencils; these had all been issued from stock and were still in use at the end of the year.

8. The company has had a poor trading year, and the owners believe that a more balanced result could be presented if a LIFO (last-in, first-out) stock valuation method was adopted, instead of the present FIFO (first-in, first-out) method.

9. A debtor who owes a large amount to the company is rumoured to be going into liquidation.

10. The company owns some shares in a quoted company which the accountant thinks are worthless.

You are required to:

(a) state which accounting rule the accountant should follow in dealing with each of the above problems; and
5 marks

(b) explain briefly what each rule means.
15 marks
Total 20 marks

13 What is a control account?

Explain with an example how such an account operates.

What advantages are derived from control accounts?
19 marks

14 Discuss with an example of each, the significance for the profit calculation of provisions and reserves. Explain what it is that reserves represent in the balance sheet.
19 marks

15 Chris is the proprietor of a small garage where vehicle testing is undertaken. He has recently purchased for £4,000 some new equipment. He confides in you that he does not know how to treat this item in the books of the business and remarks 'I cannot see why I need to worry about depreciation. The plant will last me five years, but by that time it will be only worth £500, and in any case the money is sunk and gone'.

You are required to:

(a) explain to Chris why he needs to depreciate the machinery;   *8 marks*

(b) account for the asset in the books for the first year, and show the balance sheet position at the end of that year;   *5 marks*

(c) discuss briefly the impact of inflation on depreciation.   *6 marks*

Total 19 marks

16 (a) What is goodwill?

(b) In what circumstances can goodwill be recorded in a company's books?

(c) In what ways can goodwill be treated in preparing a company's profit and loss account and balance sheet?

(d) What methods can be used to place a value on goodwill?

20 marks

17 'Users of corporate reports we define as those having a reasonable right to information concerning the reporting Entity. We consider such rights arise from the public accountability of the Entity whether or not supported by legally enforceable powers to demand information. A reasonable right to information exists where the activities of an organisation impinge or may impinge on the activities of the user group.' *The Corporate Report paragraph 1.8.*

'Users of accounts may be classified into certain groups but their requirements for information may not be the same, nor are they likely to regard certain types of information as equally important.' *The Sandilands Report paragraph 57.*

You are required to list the groups into which you would analyse the users of accounts and comment briefly on the various requirements of the groups in your analysis.

18 marks

18 Discuss major legal differences between a limited liability company and a partnership.

15 marks

19 The assets employed by limited companies are financed by loans of various sorts and/or by shares.

All limited companies, apart from those limited by guarantee, must have a share capital. The two most common types of share are preference and ordinary (equity).

The authorised share capital is stated in each company's memorandum of association and appears in the balance sheet, together with the issued share capital, which may, or may not, be fully called up. Some of the share capital may be redeemable.

Answer the following questions which relate to the above statements.

(a) In what respect are the rights of preference shareholders preferential over the rights of ordinary shareholders? *6 marks*

(b) For what main reason may a company issue preference shares rather than ordinary shares? *3 marks*

(c) For what main reason may a company issue redeemable shares rather than those which are irredeemable? *1 mark*

(d) What form of remuneration do shareholders receive on their holdings? *1 mark*

(e) How is the remuneration in (d) accounted for in a company's profit and loss account? *1 mark*

(f) Under what main circumstance may a company's share capital be only partly called up? *2 marks*

(g) What is the main effect of a preference share issue on the capital structure of a company? *2 marks*

Total 18 marks

20 In preparing the accounts of the Blake Manufacturing Company, the accountant has had to decide how to deal with a number of problems which have arisen during the year. These are as follows:

1. The proprietor wishes to include his private dwelling as part of the fixed assets of the company, since the company bank overdraft is secured on the dwelling.

2. The company has capitalised some significant expenditure on research being undertaken on a new and highly speculative product.

3. The results for the year have not been good, and a change to a different method of valuing closing stocks has been suggested.

4. The company has a stable and loyal work-force which is considered to be a great asset to the company.

5. The company's net profit for the year would be improved if the provision for bad debts was reduced to only a small proportion of bad debts, even though most of the debts are long outstanding.

6. Small stocks of stationery have not been included in the closing stock.

You are required to:

(a) state which rule the accountant would normally follow in dealing with each of the above problems; and *6 marks*

(b) explain briefly what each rule means, and how each should be applied in the case of the Blake Manufacturing Company.
12 marks
Total 18 marks

21 Explain how the double entry system works and attempt to formalise the basic rules which apply in double entry book-keeping. Illustrate your answer with a short simple example with specific reference to the way in which an account is balanced.
19 marks

ANSWERS

1 The three basic accounting terms distinguished in Statement of Standard Accounting Practice Number 2 are as follows:

Fundamental accounting concepts.

These are the broad basic assumptions underlying the periodic financial accounts of a business.

(a) The 'going concern concept' – the assumption that the business will continue to operate in the foreseeable future.

(b) The 'accruals concept' – taking revenue and costs into account in the period when they are earned or incurred (not when money is received or paid) and matched as well as is practicable.

(c) The 'consistency concept' – like items are to be treated on a consistent basis in following accounting periods.

(d) The concept of 'prudence' – revenue and profits are not anticipated but are included in the profit and loss account only when realised. On the other hand, provision is made for known liabilities and losses even if an estimate has to be made of the amount.

Accounting bases.

These are the methods used to give effect to fundamental concepts. There are alternative bases for:

(a) The depreciation of fixed assets.
(b) Taking profit on uncompleted contracts.
(c) The treatment of research and development expenditure.
(d) The conversion of foreign currencies, etc.

Accounting policies.

These are the specific bases chosen and followed consistently by management as most appropriate to the business. For example.

(a) Fixed assets might be depreciated on a straight line or other suitable basis.

(b) As a matter of prudence, research and development costs might be written off as incurred, not as they benefit the business.

(c) Fixed assets of foreign branches and subsidiaries might be converted into sterling at the rate of exchange ruling at the date of purchase or the year-end rate when consolidated accounts are being produced.

2 Users of accounting statements may be grouped under the following major heads:

(a) **Investors,** including present and prospective shareholders, debenture and loan stock holders.

Shareholders, or more particularly, equity shareholders are concerned to learn about future dividends and future prices or values of their shares. Of necessity, published historic accounts can be of only limited value as a basis for inferring what will happen in the future; and balance sheet figures can, at best, give only an approximate 'break-up value' of the business and a rough idea of the true asset backing for shares. In so far as published accounts give an account of the directors' stewardship, particularly when accounts are adjusted to a current cost basis, they satisfy reasonable requirements.

Long-term lenders (and preference share holders are similar) seek information about the ability of the business to continue paying their interest and, eventually, to repay the capital sum. Again, they must rely on information, even the most recent of which is still about the past. As they have first call on earnings and return of capital in the event of liquidation, they have only to be reassured that there will be enough for them, and reliable records of past performance satisfy their requirements as well as can be expected. New lenders would, of course, need security and a forecast of the business's future.

Any investor subscribing new capital (as distinct from purchasing shares from an existing holder) could expect forecast information. With a public issue, it would be published in the prospectus.

(b) **Short-term lenders** e.g., banks and trade creditors.

These are interested in the liquid position of a business and its short-term cash flow. Published accounts disclose this information but, generally, too seldom and too late to be completely useful. Apart from accounts, other information will be sought about creditworthiness beforehand and, subsequently. account balances kept by the bank or creditors will serve their purpose.

(c) **Management** communicates with and, in no small manner, is judged by the outside world through published financial information. It must be concerned with this published financial information but requires supplementary management accountant information for the purpose of managing.

(d) **The Inland Revenue** normally requires supplementary information and has to make adjustments to accounting profit for the purposes of assessing tax.

(e) **Employees.** It is often held that, if understood, financial information disseminated to employees would improve industrial relations. Some companies do publish simplified accounts and 'Value Added Statements' to this end. The idea is very attractive but there is no published evidence, one way or the other, that requirements are being satisfied.

(f) **Long-term lenders.** This group will be concerned that interest payments are made regularly and promptly and that the principal is secure.

3   (a)   Revenue is the aggregate exchange value received in exchange for the supply of goods or services marked by the increase of an asset — normally debtors or cash. A receipt is the inflow of cash into a business.

(b)   Capital expenditure is the outflow of funds to acquire an asset which will yield future benefits to the business for a period longer than one year. Revenue expenditure is the outflow of funds to meet the running expenses of the business, the benefit from which is consumed in the accounting period in which it is spent.

(c)   An accrual represents a benefit consumed during a period for which no payment has yet been made, e.g., the consumption of electricity for which no account has yet been received and paid. A prepayment represents that proportion of an expenditure which will provide a benefit in a future accounting period, e.g., the payment of rent in advance, part of which will be consumed during an accounting period, but part of which will provide a benefit for a future accounting period.

(d)   A debit represents an increase in an asset account or in an expense account or a decrease in a liability or revenue account. A credit represents an increase in a liability or revenue, or a decrease in an asset or expense.

4   (a)   **Materiality**

All of the Statements of Standard Accounting Practice deal only with *material* items (i.e., those which can distort the picture given by the accounts) and judgement can be used in dealing with small items of expenditure. For example, in a company with a turnover of three million pounds the true picture would not be distorted if five pounds of capital expenditure was treated as revenue expenditure. However what is material will depend upon the size of the business and this is usually measured in terms of turnover rather than profit. Once a rule of thumb has been established it is most important that consistency is maintained from year to year.

(b)   **Asset**

An asset can be defined as being of future use to the business. The two main categories of assets are fixed and current: fixed assets are acquired for use within the business and are not intended for resale; current assets are for conversion into cash in the normal course of business.

(c)   **Profit**

This can be defined as the excess of revenue over expenses. However in calculating revenue and expenses, care must be taken to apply the accrual concept, i.e., to include all income and expenditure which relate to the period concerned and not to consider only receipts and payments.

(d)   **Objectivity**

The accounts are purported to give a 'true and fair view' and it is considered that this means that they must be prepared objectively with independent evidence of the values assigned to assets and transactions, where possible. The main purpose of the SSAPs is to establish standard treatments for certain items in the accounts and hence to reduce the possibility of a subjective treatment.

5 (a) A **provision** is an amount written off or retained to provide for an asset diminishing in value (e.g., depreciation) or to provide for a known liability the amount of which cannot be determined with great accuracy (e.g., provision for doubtful debts). A **reserve**, on the other hand, is essentially undistributed profit whether it has arisen from trading, issuing shares at a premium or from a surplus on the sale or revaluation of assets.

(b) **Capital reserves** are those not available for distribution as dividends. There may be a legal capital reserve (e.g., share premium) or a reserve designated as capital by the directors. **Revenue reserves** are those which may be available for distribution (e.g., balance of profit and loss account).

(c) **Fixed assets** are those that are held in the business for use over a long period of time. Examples are buildings, plant and motor vehicles. **Current assets** are those which are constantly being turned over, such as stocks or debtors.

(d) **Single entry** book-keeping is a system where only one aspect of a business transaction is recorded in the books of account. Most often, this is only the receipt or payment of cash. In **double entry** book-keeping, two aspects of every transaction are recorded. For instance, a cash sale will entail recording the receipt of cash and the value of the sale made; payment by a debtor will occasion recording the increase in cash and the corresponding reduction of debtors.

6 (a) A trial balance is a list of the balances on all of the ledger accounts of a business. It can be extracted at any time and is used primarily to establish the accuracy of the records: if the trial balance does agree then this means that there cannot be any of certain kinds of posting or addition errors. It does not, however, reveal all errors and is not, therefore, a guarantee of 100 per cent accuracy.

A balance sheet is an accounting statement prepared from accounting balances at a given date and is usually prepared from an initial trial balance. It shows the financial position of the business by detailing the sources of funds and how they are used. There are recognised formats for the balance sheet and these formats are compulsory for companies, under the various Companies Acts. They will show the assets and liabilities grouped, classified and ordered in a specific manner. Unlike the trial balance, the balance sheet will show items after making such year-end adjustments as accruals, prepayments and depreciation.

(b) It is a common misconception that a company which is earning profits must necessarily have no cash problems. However a company which is earning a net profit may have liquidity problems because of:

(i) the payment of high dividends;

(ii) the purchase of fixed assets;
(iii) the investment in current assets such as stock or debtors.

In inflationary times, a company will have to spend cash on fixed and current assets merely to **maintain** its operational capacity.

7 (a) Books of prime entry provide chronological records of a business's transactions. This is the stage at which data evidencing a transaction enter the accounting system.

In particular, the record of each transaction will include:

(i) date;
(ii) name of account(s) to be debited and the amount(s);
(iii) name of account(s) to be credited and the amount(s);
(iv) a description or explanation of the transaction.

Wherever there are a large number of transactions of a similar nature, e.g., credit sales or credit purchases, a specialised book of prime entry will be used, e.g., sales day book.

The prime entries for cash (and bank) receipts and payments are recorded in the cash book which is incidentally also part of the ledger.

Where there is not an appropriate book of prime entry, the journal is used; the journal is very important for end of year adjustments and closing entries.

From the journal or other book of prime entry, each transaction is posted to the appropriate ledger (T) accounts. It is at this stage that an analysis of transactions within a columnar day book, permits their posting to the appropriate cost or revenue account.

The physical form of the book of prime entry is not of critical importance, in fact, files of suppliers' invoices or files of copy sales invoices may be quite adequate as purchases day books and sales day books respectively.

The actual form of the book of prime entry has undergone further changes in modern accounting systems.

In mechanised accounting systems, the prime entry and the ledger postings will be completed in one operation thus enhancing the possibility of accuracy. The 'book of prime entry' will be a copy of the ledger postings of a particular classification. The prime entry record remains of importance in computer based accounting systems where within the storage unit there will be appropriate files for various classified prime entries.

In all accounting systems information obtained from the prime entry records is important for accounting control purposes.

(b) Revenue expenditure results from the acquisition of goods and services which will be used fully in the accounting period of purchase or result in a current asset, e.g., stock in trade. A revenue expenditure item is one made to carry on the normal course of the business, or maintain the capital assets in a state of efficiency.

On the other hand, capital expenditure arises from the acquisition or improvement of fixed assets, that is assets which are expected to provide benefits to the business in more than one accounting period and have not been acquired with a view to resale in the normal course of trade.

The correct and consistent determination of accounting profit as well as the recognition of business assets is dependent upon an accurate and consistent distinction being made between revenue expenditure and capital expenditure.

Revenue expenditure is chargeable to the income statement, but expenditure classed as capital expenditure will be carried forward as an asset, and not written off immediately against income. The distinction therefore affects the measurement of profit in a number of accounting periods.

8 (a) The measurement of profit implies that the cost of goods sold, or service provided, will be accurately determined and set against revenue from the sale. Fixed assets will be purchased in one accounting period, and used to make goods for sale during a number of periods. It is necessary therefore to capitalise a long lived asset and spread its cost over all the periods in which it works. Unless this is done the entire cost will be written off in the year of acquisition, and later years will bear none of the cost, so that profit is distorted. Thus an accountant spreads the capital cost over the years of the useful life of an asset by means of depreciation.

Another view of depreciation holds that the earning power or physical efficiency of a fixed asset is reduced during each accounting period because of physical wear and tear and/or obsolescence. The fall in value of the fixed asset during an accounting period is seen as the cost of holding it or using it during the period. This cost (depreciation) must be measured and set against revenue when profit for the period is computed.

An alternative view holds that funds are invested in an asset when it is purchased, and that an amount should be set aside out of profit each year to replace that part of the original investment used up during the year. This amount is not to replace the asset but to replace the funds so that at the end of the life of the asset, the proprietor can decide how to reinvest those funds, and will have those funds at his disposal within the firm.

Without depreciation profit is overstated, and if those overstated profits are withdrawn, capital depletion will take place.

(b) The estimate of useful life from the machine was wrong when made at the beginning of its life. Depreciation has been too high for the last five years so profit has been understated.

The accountant must establish a current value for the machine and write it up to that amount, creating a revaluation reserve to balance the new asset value. The reserve represents the past understated profits and is part of the ownership interest in the business.

Next a reliable estimate of the remaining useful life of the asset must be established so that the new value can be spread over this period on a straight line basis. Thus the depreciation charge for the future use of the machine is computed.

9 (a) Monetary measurement
Going concern
Realisation
Business entity
Objectivity
Fairness
Consistency
Disclosure
Materiality
Conservatism or prudence
Matching
Cost
Dual aspect

(b) **Consistency**

In some cases there may be more than one way in which an item can be treated in the accounts, yet still conform to good accounting practice. The concept of consistency holds that when a company selects a method to use, it should continue using that method in subsequent periods. A change to a different method can take place if conditions warrant the change, but a note in the accounts should indicate the impact of the change to a different method on the profit, or balance sheet figures.

The object of this concept is to stop firms using whichever method suits their best interests in a particular period. Consistency makes possible a comparison of accounting figures over a period of time.

For example, a company which has consistently shown stocks of work in progress at prime cost, would need to note the impact on profit in a year when it changed to including a share of overheads in this valuation. A subsequent reversal to prime cost would be criticised as an inconsistent use of accounting policy.

Monetary measurement

Money acts as a common denominator to express the many different facets of an organisation, e.g., costs, sales, stocks, plant, investments, debts. The relative cost or value of the many different items shown in an accounting statement can be expressed, and their aggregate cost or value determined.

For example, a business with office premises, three vans, some machinery, stocks, debtors and investments, can not only list these items on the asset side of the balance sheet but show how much of the firm's funds have been invested in each one. Thus their relative importance is disclosed. Some business assets cannot be expressed in money terms, so they are perforce omitted from an accounting statement. This is unfortunate but perhaps wise since any method whereby such assets, e.g., morale of employees, could be valued would be imprecise.

10 The quotation refers to 'the quantification of economic events in money terms' which means that accounting is concerned with all economic activities which are capable of being expressed in money terms, hence, not only is accounting applicable to business operations but to national and local government activities, not-for-profit organisations, personal affairs and supra-national organisations.

The first requirement of accounting is the collection of data. For example, the accountant in a business organisation will make arrangements for the collection of data on all aspects of its financial operations — copies of invoices representing sales to customers, invoices for goods purchased, cheque counterfoils representing payments, and so on.

These data need to be recorded, hence we have records of sales, of purchases, of cash receipts, of cash payments, etc. In their simplest form these are the so-called 'subsidiary books'. Increasingly, more sophisticated techniques are used to record business transactions according to their nature and the use of computers for this task is now commonplace.

The recording of accounting data should not be regarded as an unproductive activity rendered necessary in order, for example, merely to satisfy audit or taxation requirements. A sensibly designed accounting system can provide much benefit in the evaluation of the results of business operations. The business proprietor needs to know the bank balance, how much is owing by customers, how much he owes to his suppliers, what the costs of running the business are, and so on.

Running a business means making decisions. For instance, the businessman will evaluate his debtor balances with a view to deciding which debtors need reminding that their debts are overdue. He will evaluate his cash position in order to decide whether he needs to arrange a loan or an overdraft or to seek additional long-term capital, or indeed to invest funds temporarily in excess of requirements. He will evaluate the profitability of the business and decide whether it could be made more profitable; purposeful accounting could well point to the action necessary to achieve this objective.

11 The revenue of a business is its income, and this must not be confused with revenue expenditure which is the cost incurred in earning that income. The general rule for the recognition of revenue is governed by the concept of conservatism, which states that no profit can be taken to the credit of the profit and loss account unless it is certain that it has been earned, but that provision must be made for all possible losses which could arise from transactions within a period. The recognition of revenue determines when profit from a transaction can be safely considered to be earned. The general rule in the United Kingdom and Ireland is that when a sale is made, one asset, stock, is exchanged for another asset, a debt, and the difference in value between these two assets is a profit. The point at which a sale is made depends on the terms of the contract between the parties, but once goods delivered have been accepted by the buyer, the sale is certain, and there is no need to wait until the price is paid in cash before recognising the revenue.

There are several exceptions to this general rule:

(a) Long-term building contracts. In this case profit is taken before completion of the job, on the basis of an architect's certificate for work completed to date. It would be wrong to take all the profit of a five-year job to the income statement for the one year when the job was completed.

(b) Hire purchase transactions. In this case profit is taken in proportion to the payment of the instalments of the price over the period of the contract.

(c) Cash basis. If payment of the price is so doubtful as to be considered a critical event in the completion of the sale, then revenue can only be recognised at this point.

(d) Accretion during production. The value of some items increases slowly during the production process, e.g., growth of woodlands and maturing of brandy. A profit of this type should be recognised but it cannot be distributed.

12 1. **Money measurement.** Only those transactions which are capable of being measured in monetary terms are recorded in the books of account. Since it is unlikely that any money has been exchanged specifically to purchase good industrial relations, this item will not be shown in the accounts, but it could be included in the directors' report.

2. **Going concern.** The accountant normally prepares the accounts on the assumption that the life of the business is long-term. If it is highly likely that the company is to be liquidated in the near future, he will prepare the accounts on the expected value of the assets at the time of dissolution. This must be included in its statement of accounting policies.

3. **Realisation.** Sales would only be included in the accounts when it was reasonably certain that they would materialise. Orders placed are not usually regarded as the same as sales, and they should not, therefore, be included in the sales revenue for that period.

4. **Business entity.** This is a matter which concerns the proprietor in his private capacity. As it is of no interest to the business, such an investment would not be recorded in the books of account.

5. **Matching (or accruals principle).** Since the business has had the benefit of the electricity, this item would normally be included in the accounts of that period, even though the amount has not actually been paid.

6. **Historic cost.** Fixed assets are usually recorded and retained at their original cost. Some assets may be revalued however, e.g., property, and restated in the balance sheet at the revalued amount. Sometimes also, a special reserve is created in order to allow for the replacement of assets at what is expected to be a greater cost. Nonetheless, the historic cost concept is still widely adopted.

7. **Materiality.** Although the pencils were still in use at the end of the year, their original value was so small that it would normally be considered quite unnecessary to value them and include them in closing stock. Instead, they should be written off to the profit and loss account in the period during which they were purchased.

8. **Consistency.** Accountants adhere to the rules that have been consistently applied over the years unless there are good reasons for change. Poor trading results would not be considered an adequate enough reason for wanting to change the company's stock valuation method, unless there were other reasons which made the old method out of date.

9. **Prudence (or conservatism).** The rumour should be carefully checked and if there is a strong possibility that the debt may not be cleared, a specific amount should be set aside as a provision for a doubtful debt and charged to the profit and loss account accordingly. Unless the debtor has actually gone into bankruptcy or liquidation, it would be premature to write-off the whole of the debt as being bad in the current period.

10. **Objectivity.** The investment would be shown on the balance sheet at cost with a note attached as to its market value. Only if there was likely to be a permanent difference between its original cost and the market value would a transfer be made to the profit and loss account. The accountant's own prejudices should not influence the compilation of the accounts.

13 A control account, or total account, maintains a summary of many transactions recorded in detailed or personal accounts comprising a subsidiary ledger. The balance on the control account must equal the aggregate of balances in the subsidiary ledger, if the book keeping is correct. As such the control account acts as part of the system of internal check.

Example

A company buys raw materials from fifty suppliers, and thus will maintain fifty personal accounts in its creditors ledger. Items in the purchases day book will be posted to the credit of individual creditors' accounts, but the total figure will be posted to the credit of the control account. Cash paid to creditors will be debited to individual creditors, and the total of such payments will be posted to the debit of the control account. Thus one account summarises many transactions, and is said to control the creditors ledger in that the control account balance must equal the aggregate of balances in the ledger concerned.

Creditors ledger control account

	£		£
Payments (Cash book)	x	Opening balance (Creditors	
Discounts rec'd (Cash book)	x	in balance sheet)	x
Returns outwards (Day book)	x	Purchases (Day book)	x
Closing balance	x		
(equals aggregate of Creditors'			
ledger balances)			
	xx		xx

Advantages

1. Shows up book-keeping errors – internal check.

2. Allows completion of accounts before small errors are located – speeds up interim reports.

3. Isolates errors to one section of the ledger.

4. Fraud within subsidiary ledger is made more difficult if the control account is written up independently.

14 A provision is an amount set aside out of profit to provide for any known expense, the exact amount of which cannot be accurately determined. If a true profit is to be derived by matching cost against revenue for a period, those costs of the period which have not yet been recorded must be recognised and estimated. Failure to charge accrued expenses in a period will overstate profit for that period, and if the accrued expenses are charged in a later period this will distort the profit figure for that period.

Example

Provision for doubtful debts. At the year-end the amount of debtor balances which will not be paid, is a matter of estimate, but a provision for doubtful debts is raised as a charge against profit. This amount is carried forward as a credit balance to offset the debit as debtors are written off to bad debts in the next accounting period.

A reserve is an amount set aside after the profit figure is struck; it is an appropriation of profit, not a charge against profit. As a broad classification profits are appropriated in three directions; for taxation, for dividend, and for re-investment in the business. Amounts appropriated to reserves, represent that part of the profit which the management intend to plough back into the business. Such profits belong to the shareholders, and the balance sheet item reserves shows the total of profits retained from past years. Reserves form part of the ownership interest in the balance sheet, and are increased each year by the amount of profits not paid out in tax or dividend. The funds thus retained in the business are invested in the general assets of the business, and by making the appropriation the management are implying that they do not intend to distribute this part of the profit. Reserves may be appropriated for specific purposes, e.g., a reserve fund to meet the post inflation replacement cost of assets. Some reserves are not available for distribution, e.g., those created by the upward revaluation of the assets (a book profit not realised in cash) or by the issue of shares at amounts in excess of face value which results in the creation of a share premium account.

15 (a) Depreciation is the way in which an accountant spreads the capital cost of a machine over the years of its useful life. In this way the cost of using the machine is matched to the revenue it earns and a true profit figure is disclosed. If £4,000 is written off in the first year and nothing in the later years a loss may be disclosed in the first year and exorbitant profits shown for the other four years. This fluctuating amount will not give a clear idea of the success of the operation year by year.

If no depreciation is charged, profit is overstated, and the asset will appear in the books at £4,000 in five years time when it is worth only £500. If the overstated profit is withdrawn from the business, capital will be depleted. No doubt the money is sunk and gone but even plant of such a degree of specificity can be resold during its lifetime, so that some of the funds sunk in the plant can be viewed as the fall in the value of the plant experienced during the year, and this fall in value is the cost of using the plant for that year which must be set against revenue from its use. If depreciation to date is subtracted in the balance sheet from the cost of the asset, the unexpired portion of the capital cost will be revealed.

(b)

Cash

	£		£
		Cash paid for machinery	4,000

Machinery

	£		£
Purchase of machinery for cash	4,000		

Profit and loss

	£		£
Depreciation on testing machinery	700		

Depreciation provision

	£		£
		Provision per profit and loss account	700

Assume straight line depreciation.

$$\frac{\text{Cost} - \text{Scrap}}{\text{Life}} = \text{Annual charge} \qquad \frac{4{,}000 - 500}{5} = £700$$

Balance sheet

Fixed assets	Cost	Depreciation	Net
	£	£	£
Machinery	4,000	700	3,300

(c) Inflation reduces the value of money in terms of goods and services. If depreciation is computed on the basis of historic cost, the charge for the use of the plant will not match the revenue from its production which has been sold at current and not historic prices. Thus profit will be overstated. At the same time the funds set aside by depreciation will build up over the life of the asset to the historic cost, but this amount will not command the same quantity of goods and services at the end, that it could have bought when it was invested in the machine. The historic cost of the asset set aside out of profits will not be enough to buy a new asset to replace the old one, so that the business has not depreciated sufficiently to maintain the assets, or earning capacity of the business. This is termed capital depletion.

16 (a) The value of a business as a whole usually differs from the value of the separable assets: the difference is described by accountants as goodwill. Positive goodwill will arise from circumstances such as an effective management team or weakness of competitors. Such circumstances will affect the profitability of a business which in turn will be reflected in the value of the business as a whole.

Goodwill is an intangible asset, intrinsic to the business and incapable of realisation separate from the business.

(b) Purchased goodwill arises when one business acquires another and the purchase price is greater than the value of the net tangible assets acquired. Most businesses have non-purchased goodwill in that they are worth more than the tangible assets. However, it is accepted practice to recognise only purchased goodwill and thus goodwill will be recorded at the time of acquiring a business.

(c) The principal possible methods for accounting for purchased goodwill are as follows:

(i) carry it as an asset and amortise it over its estimated useful life by writing it off through the profit and loss account or against reserves;

(ii) eliminate it against reserves on acquisition;

(iii) retain it in the accounts indefinitely;

(iv) charge it as an expense against profits when it is acquired;

(v) show it as a deduction from shareholders' equity (and either amortise it or carry it indefinitely).

(d) Purchased goodwill is the difference between fair value of the separable net assets acquired and the fair value of the consideration given.

It may well be necessary to place a value on goodwill in a partnership when there is no purchase involved. In such a case, the value given is often calculated as a number of years purchase of profits or as a number of years of purchase of super profits.

17 Groups of users of accounts and their special requirements.

(a) Owners, partners and shareholders need a statement of position and profit for the period, to see how their funds have been invested, and to assess the safety of and return on their investment.

(b) Managers (owners and partners are also in this category), require an analysis of costs and expense to help formulate plans, make decisions and monitor performance.

(c) Potential investors, and those advising them, are interested in future performance and potential, and they use the accounts based on the past to help predict the future.

(d) Creditors, banks and other lenders. This group is interested in the liquidity of the business, the security which its assets provide for repayment and the ability of the firm to generate enough income to meet interest requirements.

(e) The Inland Revenue need information on which to make a tax assessment. A statement of profit, and a position statement will reveal changes in capital assets, as well as income subject to tax.

(f) The government and its agencies use accounts as a source of statistics on which to base economic policy. They are interested in capital investment, price controls and the returns from monopolistic practices.

(g) Employees and their representatives use accounts to assess the future of the business and its prospects for expansion, and to establish whether they are getting a fair share of the profits.

(h) Customers and competitors. Other companies will use accounts to check the creditworthiness of customers and suppliers, for comparison, and to monitor competition.

18 In England a company has a separate legal personality quite distinct from its members whereas a partnership is an unincorporated association. As a result the property of a company belongs to the company itself, whereas in a partnership the property remains that of the partners.

The debts of a company are not enforceable against the members, whereas in a partnership the partner is jointly liable for the partnership debts. Members of a company have their liability for debts limited to the amount paid for shares, whereas the liability of partners for the partnership debts is unlimited, except of course in the case of a limited partner.

A company's existence is unaffected by the changes in its membership whereas a partnership is dissolved in cases of death or bankruptcy of partners. There is no maximum limit to the number of shareholders of a company although there is a minimum membership of two required. In the case of a partnership there must be at least two but no more than twenty except in certain cases. Other major differences concern such items as registration and incorporation, agency and transfer of shares.

19
(a) Preference shares are normally entitled to a fixed dividend out of profits available for distribution, prior to any dividend being paid to ordinary shareholders. This right to dividend is normally cumulative, that is, any dividend not paid in one year is payable in a subsequent period when divisible profits are available. Preference shares are also normally entitled to prior repayment of capital in the event of a winding-up (prior to ordinary shares).

(b) Companies issue preference shares for two major reasons. Firstly, preference shares meet the needs of certain investors for a fixed return. Secondly, the company is able to raise capital which requires only a fixed dividend which in extreme circumstances need not be met as would normally be the case with fixed interest capital such as loan stocks and debentures.

(c) A company may issue redeemable shares rather than those which are irredeemable for two main reasons:
  (i) Its need for capital may be comparatively short-term, e.g., where a company is just starting. Once the company has generated internal capital by retention of profits the shares can be redeemed.
  (ii) Certain investors prefer investments in unquoted companies but are penalised by the lack of market for their shares. For this reason a fixed redemption date limits the period of time over which their investment must be made.

(d) Shareholders receive remuneration on the shareholdings by way of dividends declared and paid by the company.

(e) Dividends are shown in the profit and loss account as an appropriation out of profits after taxation.

(f) A company's share capital is often only partly called up shortly after its issue. This enables the company to call in further sums as its capital needs increase.

(g) The main effect of a preference share issue on the capital structure of a company is to create gearing, that is, an element of capital on which a fixed return must be met.

20 1. **Business entity.**

The private affairs of the proprietor are not normally recorded in the business books, apart from those that record a state of mutual indebtedness. Although the dwelling provides additional security for a business debt, it is not in the ownership of the company, and as it would appear to be for the exclusive private use of the proprietor, it should not be brought into the accounts.

2. **Prudence.**

Accountants tend to adopt a cautious approach in assessing profitability. Since the product is highly speculative and future revenue presumably quite uncertain, such expenditure should be written off in the period in which it was incurred. This would meet the requirements of SSAP 13, *Accounting for Research and Development*, as well as those of SSAP 2, *Disclosure of Accounting Policies*.

3. **Consistency.**

As it is possible to adopt alternative accounting rules which may have conflicting results, a consistent approach should be followed. Unless there are sound reasons for adopting a different closing stock valuation method (and an unprofitable period would not normally be a sound reason), the old method should be retained. This would be in accordance with SSAP 2, *Disclosure of Accounting Policies.*

4. **Money measurement.**

    Only those items which it is easy to cost in monetary terms are normally included in the accounts. A loyal and stable work-force is beneficial but the benefit would be difficult to cost and hence to include in the accounts.

5. **Objectivity.**

    Accounts should be prepared as objectively as possible, and the methods adopted in their compilation should not be biased by the result that the proprietors would like to see. The bad debts provision should be calculated as carefully as possible, based on an objective assessment of the future bad debts of the company, unobscured by other considerations.

6. **Materiality.**

    Even though all stocks ought to be physically checked and assessed, the impact of small amounts of stock may be so insignificant that it would be a waste of time to assess such stocks. Provided that the stationery stock is immaterial (and that depends on the circumstances), the total cost of purchase may be written off to revenue.

21 The principle of duality underlies the double entry system. Every transaction has a dual effect on the business, and thus should be recorded twice to reveal this effect. The books are divided into accounts or pages in the ledger, an account being opened not for each transaction but to summarise transactions of a similar nature on the same page, e.g., a page for repair costs, another for factory wages, another for sales revenue, and another for cash. If there are many transactions of one type, then a separate book or ledger will be opened just for them, e.g., the cash book to record the cash part of transactions, payments or receipts, and the debtors ledger to maintain a detailed record of amounts owed to the business by customers who have bought goods on credit. In this latter case each debtor will have an account or page of his own in the debtors ledger.

Each page acts as a T account, having two sides, one for debits and one for credits. The debits are always on the lefthand side and the credits on the righthand side. When the two sides are added up, if the entries on the debit side are more than those on the credit side then the account is said to have a debit balance, and vice versa.

Dr.		Vehicles account		Cr.
	£			£
Purchased for cash	4,000	Sold to Brown		2,000
		Balance c/f		2,000
	4,000			4,000
Balance b/d	2,000			

Dr.		Cash		Cr.
	£			£
		Paid for vehicles		4,000

Dr.		Brown		Cr.
	£			£
Owed for vehicles	2,000			

In this example, the fixed asset account has been debited with the purchase price of the asset (the corresponding credit will occur in the cash book — reducing the asset cash), and credited with its sale. At the end of the accounting period when the account is closed the debit side is heavier than the credit side, and to balance the account to the total of the heaviest side, the difference between the two sides must be added to the lightest side. Thus the account has been credited with its balance, and a corresponding debit is required. This is supplied by carrying the balance down below the line to start the next accounting period on the opposite side. Thus the preponderance of debit over credit of this account is shown in the balance brought down.

Note that the amount for vehicles sold has not been taken away from the debit side, but has been posted to the credit side. This has the same effect since it reduces the amount of the debit balance carried forward, but it also allows the duality of transactions to be recorded via the double entry system.

This system has four basic rules:

1. Every debit must have a credit and every credit must have a debit. Each transaction is recorded twice, once on each side of the books, with the debits traditionally on the lefthand side.

2. The assets and expenses are debit balances and the liabilities and sales revenue are credit balances. Thus claims equal assets in the balance sheet, and when in the income statement sales exceed costs and a profit is made, this profit is added to the balance sheet claims on the credit side to balance the increase in assets represented by the profit.

3. When an asset or cost account is to be increased the entry is on the debit side and when a liability or sales revenue account is to be increased, the amount is credited. When however an account is to be decreased, the amount is not deducted from the side on which the balance is shown, but is instead posted to the opposite side, so that the balance is reduced in this way, e.g., an asset or cost account is decreased by crediting the account and a liability or sales revenue account is decreased by debiting the account.

4. This rule is more a mnemonic, than a rule. Briefly stated it is that the giving account is credited whilst the receiving account is debited. For example when wages are paid, the wages account receives and is debited whilst cash is given out so that this account is credited, and when a debtor pays what he owes, cash receives and is debited whilst the debtor gives and his account is credited (thus reducing his debit balance). This is a rather rough and ready rule which does not have a logical application in all cases.

Index

Page numbers in roman type refer to questions and those in *italics* to answers.

Accounting
  bases   326, *332*
  data collection   327, *339*
  framework concepts   327, *338-9*
  policies   326, *332*
  rules   327-8, 330-1, *340-1, 346-7*
Accounting records, advantages of full set   150, *169*
Accounting statements, users   326, *332-3*
  special requirements   329, *344-5*
Accrual, distinguished from prepayment   326, *334*
Accruals concept   *332, 340*
Acid test ratio   246-7, *253-4, 255*
Appropriation accounts   230-1, *242*
  partnerships   275-6, 277-82, 285-6, *289, 290-1, 293, 295, 299, 300, 305*
  departmental   315-16, *323*
Assets
  definition   326, *334*
  disposal accounts   43, *60-1*
  expenditure subsequent to purchase   44-5, *66*
  fixed and current defined   326, *339*
  historic cost   *340*
  ratio of current to total   246-7, *253-4*
  value in accounts, by reducing balance and straight line depreciation   42-3, *58*

Bad debts   47-50, 52-3, *71-6, 83*, 98-100, *105, 108*
  recovery after being written off   50, *77*
Balance sheets   3, 4-5, *8-9, 12-14*, 20-2, *32-4, 37*, 125-7, *136-7, 139-40*, 211-12, *220-2*
  adjusted   208-9, *215-16*
  adjusted profits   123-5, *133*
  compared with trial balance   326, *335*
  corrected   119-22, *129, 131*
  departmental   314-15, *320-2*
  estimated   3, *9*
  extract for fixed assets   44, *64*
  extract showing purchases and sales ledger control accounts   98, *104*
  from incomplete records   143-50, *156-9, 160-1, 162-3, 165-6, 168-70, 171*, 249, *256-8*
  in manufacturing accounts   224-31, *233-5, 237-8, 240, 241-2*
  motor vehicle account   46, *69*
  of charitable trusts   180-2, *195-203*
  partnerships   275-6, 277-81, 286-7, *290, 291-2, 293-4, 295-6, 298, 301, 308-9*
  summarised   209-11, *217-19*

Bank accounts
  from incomplete records   147, *164*
  partnerships   275-6, *283-6, 280, 303, 305, 307*
Bank statements
  reconciliation with bank accounts   113, *116-17*
  reconciliation with cash book   110-12, *115*
Banks, use of accounting statements   *333, 345*
Book value per share   244-5, *251*
Branch accounts   312-13, *318-20*
Buildings accounts, with depreciation and disposal   47, *70-1*
'Business entity' concept   329, *340, 346*

Capital accounts, of partnerships   282-7, *301, 302, 305*
Capital expenditure, on existing assets   44-5, *65*
Capital reserves   326, *335*
Cash, ratio to current liabilities   246-7, *253-4*
Cash accounts, from incomplete records   147, *164*
Cash books   21, *34*, 85, *88*, 110-12, *115-16*
  calculation of misappropriations   151-3, *170*
Clubs, *see* Receipts and payments accounts
Collection period   244-6, *251, 253*
Company accounts   204-12, *213-22*
Competitors, use off accounting information   *345*
Concepts, fundamental   326, 327, *332*
'Consistency' concept   *332, 338, 341, 346*
Control accounts   328, *341-2*
  correcting mistakes   97-8, *103-4*
  importance   98, *104*
  purchases ledger   93, *97-9, 101, 103, 106-7*, 206, *214*
  sales ledger   93-8, *101, 102, 103, 104*
Credit, distinguished from debit   326, *334*
Currency conversion   *332*
Current accounts, of partners   278-81, 282-6, *296-7, 298, 303, 306, 315-16, 324*
Current ratios   245-7, *252, 253-4*
  calculation   244-5, *251*
Customers, use of accounting information   *345*
Customers' accounts   22-3, *37-8*, 206, *214*

Day books   85, *88-9*
Debentures   208, *215*
Debit, distinguished from credit   326, *334*
Debt equity ratio   244-5, *251*

349

Debtors   49, 75, 97-9, *105-6*
  branch accounts   313, *319*
  ratio to sales   248, *256*
  total   48-9, *72-3*
  see also Collection period
Debts, *see* Bad debts; Doubtful debts
Decision-making, from accounting data   327, *339*
Defalcation, assessment from incomplete records   142-3, *155*
Departmental accounts   310-16, *317-24*
Depreciation   52-3, *82, 332*
  impact of inflation   329, *343-4*
Depreciation accounts   206-7, *214-15*
  reducing balance schedules   42-5, *58-9, 61-3, 66-7*
  set against profit   327, *337*
  straight line schedules   42-5, *58-9, 59-61, 65,* 248, *255*
  useful life underestimated   327, *337-8*
  usefulness   328-9, *342-3*
  see also Motor vehicles
Disposal accounts   206-7, *214-15*
Double entry book-keeping   326, *335, 347-8*
Doubtful debts   47-50, *71-6,* 97-100, *105-7* 206, *214*

Earnings per share   244-5, *251*
Employees, use of accounting statements   *333, 345*
Expenditure
  capital distinguished from revenue   326, *334*
  revenue and capital   327, *336-7*

FIFO, closing stock and trading account   51, *78*
Funds, *see* Source and application of funds statements
Funds flow statement   264-6, *271-2*

'Going concern' concept   332, *340*
Goodwill   329, *344*
Goodwill accounts   283-4, *302*
Government, use of accounting information   345

Income and expenditure accounts   177-80, *187-91, 192-4*
Incomplete records   141-53, *154-74*
  see also Receipts and payments accounts
Inland Revenue, use of accounting statements   *333, 345*
Insurance   52-3, *82*
  claims calculation from incomplete records   142, 153, *154-5, 172-6*
Insurance accounts   40, *54*
Interest earnings   244-5, *251*
Interpretation of accounts   243-50, *251-60*
Investors, use of accounting statements   *333, 345*

Journal entries   85, *87*
  for adjustments   120-3, *130-2,* 209-11   *217*

Ledger accounts   18-19, 21, *24-30, 34-6, 336*
  for assets and depreciation   42-3, *59*
  insurance   *54*
  partnerships   284-6, *304-7*
Lenders, use of accounting statements   *333, 345*
LIFO, closing stock and trading accounts   51, *79*
Limited liability companies, distinguished from partnerships   329, *345*
Liquidity
  and accounting profits   326, *335-6*
  ratio   245-6, *252*
Losses, *see* Profit and loss accounts; Trading and profit and loss accounts

Management, use of accounting statements   *333, 345*
Manufacturing accounts   223-31, *232-42*
  of partnership   286-7, *307-8*
Materiality   *341, 347*
  definition   326, *334*
Mechanised prime entry systems   *336*
Money measurement   *338-9, 340, 347*
Motor vehicles, disposal and depreciation accounts   42-3, 43-6, *58-61, 62-3, 68-9, 69-70*

Net assets   3, *10*

Objectivity   *341, 347*
  definition   326, *334-5*

Partnership
  conversion to limited companies   285-6, *305-7*
  distinguished from limited liability companies   329, *345*
Partnership accounts   274-87, *288-309*
  departmental   315-16, *323-4*
Payment period   244-5, *251*
Payroll control ledgers   206, *214*
Personal accounts   85, *88-9*
Petty cash accounts   86, *90-1*
  partnerships   275-6, *288*
Prepayment, distinguished from accrual   326, *334*
Prime entry books   84-6, *87-91,* 327, *336*
Profit and loss accounts   211-12, *219*
  departmental   311-12, *317, 318* , *320*
  insurance accounts   40, *54-5*
  see also Trading and profit and loss accounts
Profits
  adjustments   119-20, 123-5, *128-9, 133*
  and liquidity   326, *335-6*
  assumptions in computation   6, *15*
  calculation   2, *7, 8*

350

Profits — *continued*
  corrected   279-81, *297*
  definition   326, *334*
  gross, on sales and on cost of goods sold   245-6, *251*
  gross and net: adjusted   123, *132*
    computation   22-3, *37-8*
    on sales   51-2, *80-1*, 248, *256*
    on uncompleted contracts   332
    related to liquidity   262, *268*
Proprietor's interest   3, *10*
Provisions   326, *335*
  effect on profit calculation   328, *342*
'Prudence' concept   332, *341, 346*
Purchases accounts   50, 77
  nominal ledger   85, *89*
  partnerships   276, *289*
  see also Control accounts: purchases ledger
Purchases day books   85, *88*

Rates   52-3, *82*
  see also Rent and rates accounts
Ratio calculations   244-7, *251-5*
Realisation   *340*
  in partnerships   284-6, *304, 306*
Receipts, distinguished from revenue   326, *334*
Receipts and payments accounts   176-82, *187-203*
Reconciliation
  between cash book and bank statements   110-14, *115-17*
  of control accounts: with individual accounts   94-6, *102*
    with purchases ledger   93, 94, *102*
    with sales ledger balances   96, *103*
Rent   52-3, *82*
Rent and rates accounts   40, *55-6*, 207, *215*
Rent payable accounts   41, *57*
Rent receivable accounts   41, *57*
Research and development expenditure   332
Reserves   326, *335*
  in balance sheet   328, *342*
Retiring partner's account   283-4, *303*
Return on capital employed   245-6, *252*
Revaluation account, partnerships   283-4, *302*
Revenue
  distinguished from receipts   326, *334*
  rule for recognition   327, *339-40*
Revenue accounts   180-2, *194-5*
Revenue reserves   326, *335*

Sales accounts   50, 77
  nominal ledger   85, *89*
  partnership   275-6, *288*
  see also Control accounts: sales ledger
Sales day book   85, *88*
Share capital   207, *215*
Share premium   208, *215*
Shares
  earnings and book value   244-5, *251*
  earnings per share   247, *255*
  price/earnings ratio   247, *255*
Single entry book-keeping   326, *335*
Stationery accounts   42, *57*
Stock   52-3, *82*
  holdings   247, *255*
  on sale or return   248, *256*
  ratio to cost of sales   248, *256*
  turnover   244-6, *251, 252*
  valuation   51-2, *80-1*
Stock accounts   50, 77
  branch   312-13, *318, 319*
  LIFO and FIFO methods   51, *78-9*
Subscription income   178-9, *190, 200*
Suppliers' accounts   22-3, *37-8*
Suspense accounts   119-20, *129*

T accounts, see Ledger accounts
Taxation accounts   264-6, *271*
Telephone accounts   42, *57*
Trade creditors, use of accounting statements   333, *345*
Trading and profit and loss accounts   3-6, *10-11, 14-15,* 18-19, 20-2, *30, 32, 33*, 36, 50, 78, 125-7, *136, 139*
  departmental   314-15, *320*
  for partnerships, departmental   315-16, *323-4*
  from incomplete records   143-53, *156, 159, 161, 164, 166, 168, 171*
  in manufacturing accounts   224-31, *232-3, 236-7, 238-9, 241*
  in receipts and payments accounts system   177-80, *187-8, 192*
  partnerships   275-6, 277-81, 286-7, *289, 292-3, 294-5, 307-8*
  summarised   209-11, *217*
Trial balances   18-22, *27, 30-1, 33, 36*
  company accounts   205, *213*
  compared with balance sheet   326, *335*
  extended   125-7, *135, 138*

Working capital   246-7, *253*

351